Enigma Books

Also published by Enigma Books

Hitler's Table Talk: 1941–1944
In Stalin's Secret Service
Hitler and Mussolini: The Secret Meetings
The Jews in Fascist Italy: A History
The Man Behind the Rosenbergs
Roosevelt and Hopkins: An Intimate History
Diary 1937–1943 (Galeazzo Ciano)
Secret Affairs: FDR, Cordell Hull, and Sumner Welles
Hitler and His Generals: Military Conferences 1942–1945
Stalin and the Jews: The Red Book
The Secret Front: Nazi Political Espionage
Fighting the Nazis: French Intelligence and Counterintelligence
A Death in Washington: Walter G. Krivitsky and the Stalin Terror
The Battle of the Casbah: Terrorism and Counterterrorism in Algeria 1955–1957
Hitler's Second Book: The Unpublished Sequel to *Mein Kampf*
At Napoleon's Side in Russia: The Classic Eyewitness Account
The Atlantic Wall: Hitler's Defenses for D-Day
Double Lives: Stalin, Willi Münzenberg and the Seduction of the Intellectuals
France and the Nazi Threat: The Collapse of French Diplomacy 1932–1939
Mussolini: The Secrets of His Death
Mortal Crimes: Soviet Penetration of the Manhattan Project
Top Nazi: Karl Wolff—The Man Between Hitler and Himmler
Empire on the Adriatic: Mussolini's Conquest of Yugoslavia
The Origins of the War of 1914 (3-volume set)
Hitler's Foreign Policy: 1933–1939—The Road to World War II
The Origins of Fascist Ideology 1918–1925
Max Corvo: OSS Italy 1942–1945
Hitler's Contract: The Secret History of the Italian Edition of *Mein Kampf*
Secret Intelligence and the Holocaust
Israel at High Noon
Balkan Inferno: Betrayal, War, and Intervention, 1990–2005
Calculated Risk: World War II Memoirs of General Mark Clark
The Murder of Maxim Gorky
The Kravchenko Case: One Man's War On Stalin
Operation Neptune
Paris Weekend
Shattered Sky
Hitler's Gift to France
The Mafia and the Allies
The Nazi Party, 1919-1945: A Complete History
Encyclopedia of Cold War Espionage, Spies, and Secret Operations
The Cicero Spy Affair
A Crate of Vodka
NOC
The First Iraq War: Britain's Mesopotamian Campaign, 1914-1918
Becoming Winston Churchill

Hitler's Intelligence Chief: Walter Schellenberg
Salazar: A Political Biography
The Italian Brothers
Nazi Palestine
Code Name: Kalistrat
Pax Romana
The De Valera Deception
Lenin and His Comrades
Working with Napoleon
The Decision to Drop the Atomic Bomb
Target Hitler
Truman, MacArthur and the Korean War
Working with Napoleon
The Parsifal Pursuit
The Eichmann Trial Diary
Cold Angel

Thomas A. Reppetto

American Police:
A History

Volume II

The Blue Parade
1945–2012

Enigma Books

Published by Enigma Books, New York

Copyright © 2012 by Thomas A. Reppetto

First Edition

Printed in the United States of America

ISBN: 978-1-936274-43-7
e-ISBN: 978-1-936274-44-4

Publisher's Cataloging-In-Publication Data

Reppetto, Thomas A.
  American police : a history : the blue parade, 1945-2012 / Thomas A. Reppetto. --
1st ed.

   p. : ill. ; cm.

  Issued also as an ebook.
  Includes bibliographical references and index.
  ISBN: 978-1-936274-43-7

  1. Police--United States--History. 2. Law enforcement--United States--History. I.
Title. II. Title: Blue parade, 1945-2012

HV8138 .R462 2012
363.2/0973

Dedicated to the memory of America's
greatest expert on policing,

Professor James Q. Wilson
1931–2012

Contents

American Police: A History

Volume II

The Blue Parade
1945–2012

Introduction:

A Lifetime of Crime

Throughout history people have looked back on certain periods as ones that changed both their own lives and the course of the world. For many Americans, particularly Southerners, it was the Civil War. Other generations chose the stock market crash of 1929 or World War II. For me it was the 1960s. When I joined the Chicago Police Department in the 1950s, I had very little to learn about the world I was entering. I had known it, literally, since I was born. My neighborhood was home to many cops. My mother, a spirited Irish girl, had grown up in a nearby neighborhood were even more cops lived and in later years many of the friends of her youth became high-ranking commanders. For a time she was a police clerk. I was not yet ten, when one day I went to visit her at the police station where she worked and landed in the middle of a manhunt for a multiple murderer who had just killed an officer that she had spoken to at roll call that morning.

My father too was well acquainted with the police. I will leave out the details, except to mention that one of his friends was the first man to be put on the FBI's "10 Most Wanted" list. That fellow ended up in Alcatraz, whereas my father never went to jail, though there were efforts made to put him there. I attended my first mob funerals when I was eleven. One was that of a big-shot gangster, the other was a man who worked for my father and made the mistake of socializing with the big shot, despite being warned the fellow was hot. When the assassin opened up, both men were killed. Trouble came frequently in my parents' lives. I attribute this to the fact that they were both products of the

Roaring Twenties who loved the excitement. Not surprisingly they got divorced when I was very young.

When the '60s began, I was a patrolman rank detective chasing youth gangs around the streets. I had every expectation that I would spend the next thirty plus years as an active cop. If fortune smiled, I hoped to retire as a lieutenant and then go to work as a private investigator until Gabriel blew his horn. I did not envision what the '60s would bring or that for me the world would spin so rapidly. By the end of it, I had been promoted in succession to sergeant, lieutenant, captain then commander of detectives, earned a Harvard doctorate was present at civil disorders in a half a dozen American cities, marched alongside Dr. Martin Luther King (as head of a police security detail) while missiles and fireworks filled the air, and had been caught up in the 1968 Democratic Convention. Topping that, I was offered an important administrative job in the United States Department of Justice.

In succeeding decades, I was allowed to prowl the corridors of power of the nation's capital, state houses and city halls. One incredible day, I stood on the balcony of the Department of Justice alongside the attorney general of the United States watching a protest going on below us. We were both inundated by the tear gas the police were firing at the demonstrators. In New York, I was around for the World Trade Center attacks in both 1993 and 2001. In '93 I lived across the street from the South Tower. I wrote books and articles and lectured at professional societies and universities. I was a dean and later a vice president of a college in a major university. In 1960, I knew nothing of the American business world, by the '80s I was a regular visitor to the executive suites of Fortune 500 corporations and the great Wall Street houses. Through many newspaper interviews and TV appearances, I became acquainted with the operations of the leading papers and the famous networks. While one would like to think all this came about because of my own qualities, the truth is that I just happened to be in the right place at the right time. In the final analysis, I am what I have always been—a big-city detective wandering through various worlds observing and storing away what he sees and hears.

From a scholarly viewpoint, some of my most important experiences were that I am the only person who had an inside view of three of the great police reorganizations in American history. The first was Superintendent O. W. Wilson's 1960s attempt to professionalize the Chicago Police Department. In the 1990s I occupied a ringside seat when Commissioner Bill Bratton turned around the NYPD from a reactive to a proactive organization, employing a now widely copied system known as COMPSTAT. In the first years of the twenty-first century, I was privileged to study up close NYPD Commissioner

Ray Kelly's creation of, what history will surely regard as, the first police counterterrorism system in America.

The present work is the second volume of my history of American policing. Volume 1 originally appeared in 1978 under the title *The Blue Parade*. In 2011 I re-issued it in a much revised version. Volume 2 is an entirely original work which picks up the story where volume 1 ended in 1945 and continues it until 2012. As in the previous volume, while I deal with historical persons and events, I do not approach the subject as a historian. My own discipline is public/criminal justice administration and my inquiries are aimed at how organizations work and power is distributed and utilized.

Because volume 1 ended at a time when I was still in elementary school, I could not contribute my own observations to the work. This time, where it is appropriate, I will include my personal experiences as a street cop, commander, watchdog and advocate from the 1950s to the present. Since then, in addition to the activities I have noted, I have participated in the criminal justice system in five states and conducted research in many more. I also interacted with various federal agencies, committees and task forces. For over 26 years I headed the Citizens Crime Commission of New York City, a watchdog organization which looked over the shoulders of public officials. On occasion this upset many of them. They often praised me in extravagant terms, and then turned around and denounced me just as vigorously. I did not let that bother me too much. The fellow who headed the Crime Commission a generation ahead of my time was jailed, fired, made a pariah, and finally burned to death in a barbecuing accident. The commission then folded. When it was being revived, in the late 1970s, I was warned not to take the job. As they say, fools rush in. To date, I have not been jailed or barbecued.

Presenting one's personal experiences may strengthen the authenticity of a narrative. However, it also risks losing scholarly detachment. In the course of studying the work of many past writers, I have become aware not only of the insertion of their personal beliefs into their research findings, but that they often tend to exaggerate their own importance. Over the years I have been shocked to note how many writers, including those with good reputations, have placed themselves at the center of events that they had little or nothing to do with, or altered facts to fit the present. Even Winston Churchill, who was probably involved in more great happenings than anyone in the twentieth century, frequently claimed credit or absolved himself of responsibility when the truth was otherwise.

Some knowledgeable readers may want to apply to this book the comment Rudyard Kipling made about Lord Roberts' account of his forty-one years in the British Indian Army, "notable for what was left out." In my case it means I did not include what is sometimes referred to as "the low down on the higher-ups." That is, such things as what pillar of virtue had an insatiable roving eye. Despite knowing where the bodies are buried, unless the information affected the job performance of the individual, I see no need to embarrass him or his family.

In the present work, in addition to covering the main topics, I have sought to bring to light events in postwar policing that have been lost, or suppressed, often to protect powerful interests. For example, readers will be shocked to hear about one of the most vicious riots in American history—including the widespread rape of women—which occurred in the heart of one of America's most sophisticated cities. We will go behind the scenes to analyze command failures at events such as the 1968 Democratic convention in Chicago or the 9/11 attack in New York City. While the facts in the Watergate affair are well known, we will recall an attempted power grab in federal law enforcement by the Nixon White House that, had it succeeded, may have had an even more profound effect on America.

In volume 1 there was virtually no mention of policing in the South. I felt why write about something that is obvious. A cop's principal job there was to keep blacks in line, a fact that was already well documented. In the postwar period some of the greatest progress in American policing has been made in the South.

Policing, more than most occupations, is still a place where individuals make a real difference. Therefore I will profile the major figures in the field during the postwar period. In this respect, sorting fact from fiction about FBI Director J. Edgar Hoover almost requires a separate book. Though there have been many written, too often the authors chose to focus on gossip rather than analysis. Chief Parker of Los Angeles and his fellow Californian O. W. Wilson, who served as superintendent of police of Chicago, were once men of high standing. Now Parker is regarded as something of an ogre and Wilson is long forgotten. The two giants in the field today are Bill Bratton of Boston, where he served as police commissioner before assuming the same job in New York and later became chief in Los Angeles, and Ray Kelly, the current New York City police commissioner who also has held important federal law enforcement positions.

In 2008, I was surprised that incoming President Obama did not choose either Bratton or Kelly as secretary of homeland security. Four years earlier, I was shocked when President Bush did name former New York City Police Commissioner Bernard Kerik to the post. As I expected, Kerik's candidacy quickly collapsed and, despite the acclaim he received for his supposed work at the time of the 9/11 attack, the federal post he now holds is that of an inmate in one of Uncle Sam's prisons. As all cops learn, one can go from being a hero to a bum virtually overnight.

Besides its colorful characters and innate fascination, policing exerts a great deal of influence on American politics, economics, and society. Many a mayor has been ruined because he appointed the wrong person to head the police force. The virtual collapse in safety and order which took place in New York City, circa 1990, prompted national and international stories about the end of the Big Apple, the economic center of the world. While American racial problems have stemmed from a number of factors, one of the most important has been the nature of policing.

Let us proceed then to the retracing of the Blue Parade over the past sixty-seven years. In the 1978 book I said of it, "At the end, one feels that he has witnessed a colorful, even exciting spectacle yet is puzzled by its meaning." It is my hope that the present work will help solve some of the puzzles.

Chapter 1

Policing at the Crossroads

For 22-year-old Eddie McKern,[1] the meeting he was brought to on a March night in 1946 carried the same significance as his confirmation in the Catholic Church a decade earlier. In the Chicago stockyards district, where he had been born and raised, the Church, with its strict rules, was an all-encompassing influence in the life of the people.

At seventeen, Eddie had joined another rigidly hierarchal, highly disciplined organization, the United States Army, then gearing up for the war that would soon come. In the service, he developed from a skinny teenage private into a burly sergeant who, in 1944–45, would lead his infantry platoon across France and Germany. Now he was seeking to join another military-type organization, which considered its members to belong to it twenty-four hours a day: the Chicago Police Department.

In 1945, the City of Chicago announced that it would hire one thousand temporary police officers from the ranks of returned war veterans. Like so many decisions made by the municipal government—a term that in practice meant the Cook County Democratic machine—the reasons for it were mixed. During the war years, in addition to the normal deaths, retirement, etc., a number of officers had enlisted or been drafted. The city had been able to recruit replacements from the existing civil service eligible list. However, many of

---

1. A pseudonym for a former partner of the writer.

those on it had entered the service themselves or had obtained higher-paying jobs in war plants. By the beginning of 1945, the strength of the six thousand officer force was several hundred below what it had been four years earlier.

Crime had not been especially troublesome during the war, at least not more so than it normally was. Many young men who might have been committing offenses were away in the service or working overtime in industry. The crime numbers had remained steady during the war years, although, given the slipshod methods of reporting, one could never be sure whether the official figures were correct.[2] However, the public was uneasy. Chicago journalism was geared towards sensationalism. The papers regularly ran front-page stories about murders or big-time heists.

In 1946, a serial killer used one of his female victims' lipstick to write above the mirror on her bathroom sink, "Stop me before I kill more." Another of his victims was Suzanne Degnan, a six-year-old girl who was abducted from her bedroom, dismembered in a nearby basement and her body parts scattered around the neighborhood. In that case, the police had initially declared two separate innocent men guilty of the crime. Not for some time was the actual killer, a brilliant student at the University of Chicago named William Hierens, captured. The affair did not enhance public confidence in the police department.

Another reason for hiring a lot of cops quickly had to do with racial tensions. During the war, many blacks had left the South to come to Chicago because they had heard that high-paying jobs were available there. Once in the city, they learned that prices were also very high. Although Chicago was officially integrated, de facto much of it was segregated. Certain parks, beaches and other public facilities were off limits to African Americans. Blacks who stepped across invisible, but well-known, boundaries risked being assaulted. If they bought a house in a heretofore all-white neighborhood, it might be torched or bombed.

In 1943, both New York and Detroit experienced major race riots. In New York, the spark was an incident in a Harlem hotel where a white police officer wounded a black soldier. Mayor La Guardia and Commissioner Lewis J. Valentine moved five thousand (of the department's sixteen thousand) cops into the area and supplemented them with one thousand five hundred black civil defense auxiliary police, who were issued helmets and clubs and deployed to the streets. The police managed to stop the riot, although six people, all of them blacks, were killed, four of them by the police. In Detroit, the initial

---

2. The annual number of murders, the most accurately recorded crime, had remained at a little above two hundred.

incident started with a clash between whites and blacks relaxing in a city park on a summer evening. The Detroit police, with only thirty-five hundred cops to cover the entire city, were unable to control the situation, and not until the U.S. Army was sent in was order restored. By then, thirty-four people had been killed, including twenty-five blacks (twenty-three of them shot by police). Of the nine whites killed, three of them were police officers.

Chicago had experienced racial conflict throughout the twentieth century. During World War I, there had been a similar influx of Southern blacks and a series of bombings of black homes. In 1919, the races clashed and thirty-eight people were killed—seven, all of them black, by the police—while sixteen whites and fifteen blacks were killed by members of the opposing group. Not until the state militia was deployed did the rioting cease.

Despite its penchant for sensationalism, during World War II the Chicago press followed a policy of suppressing stories of racial conflict to avoid inflaming racial tensions. While well meant, this was a mistake. When an incident occurred, rumor would multiply it tenfold. A simple fight between a white and black man would soon make the rounds, where it was transformed into a story of a woman (and in some cases her child, too) who had been murdered by members of the other race. Given the city's history, what was happening elsewhere and the rumors going around, both white and black citizens worried about the possibility of a major racial clash.

There were also benefits for the political machine in recruiting temporary officers. During the Depression, police jobs were much sought after. In 1937, fifty thousand men had signed up for the police test in full knowledge that less than five percent of them could hope to obtain appointment to the force before the eligible list expired. It was also widely believed that individuals who scored high on the exam had an influential sponsor or had paid off a politician—five hundred dollars being the price usually mentioned. The same rules were thought to apply to serving officers who sought promotion to sergeant, lieutenant or captain (with appropriate adjustments to the going rate at each rank level). Putting one thousand cops on the job without requiring a test (and later blanketing them into the regular service) was a way to make a number of individuals and their families grateful to the party bosses.

The city administration parceled out the jobs among the city's fifty Democratic ward committeemen, the formal title for the local boss who ruled over a district of 70,000 or so people. Ward bosses themselves invariably held important political positions such as county sheriff, city alderman, state senator or U.S. congressman, even a judgeship. Mayor Edward J. Kelly himself was a ward committeeman.

While the appointment process might have been expected to fill the police department with incompetents, it produced many high-caliber recruits who became the backbone of the force over the next generation. In some respects, the ward bosses produced better candidates than civic reformers could have done.

Good government types—or "Goo Goos," as they were known—were never popular in Chicago. In 1931, the country's leading police expert, Bruce Smith, a wealthy, ivy-educated New Yorker, who operated out of that city's Institute of Public Administration, was brought in to study the Chicago police force. His recommendation was that the entire force of sixty-seven hundred cops be fired.* With the Depression on, replacements could easily have been found, but since the environment would have remained the same, after a while they would have been operating in the same fashion as their predecessors. No one paid much attention to Smith's recommendations in Chicago or any other city he studied.

While many ward bosses were men who grew wealthy in politics and filled the government payrolls with their relatives, they also possessed other qualities that enabled them to hold power. Like the Catholic Church, urban political machines functioned as philosopher, guide and friend to blue-collar white immigrants and their offspring, then the dominant voting bloc in Chicago and many other American cities.

Eddie McKern was brought to ward headquarters by a member of the state legislature who was a neighbor. There he joined other young men and their sponsors waiting to meet the local boss. The mighty man personally scanned each applicant's discharge papers and asked a few questions about his military experience. Ultimately he gave the nod to those who had been officers or noncommissioned officers in combat units. Others, whose service was less distinguished, such as a sailor who never left California or a soldier who dispensed drinks at an officer's club in Paris, were fobbed off regardless of their political standing. Probably the boss reasoned that a former infantry sergeant like McKern would fit well in a hierarchal organization and was capable of exerting authority over other men. He could also be sure that McKern was a man who could keep his head in a stressful situation and not swoon if a gun were fired in his vicinity. All of the foregoing qualities made for a good cop. In addition, the fact that he was a boy from "Back of the Yards," whose family was well thought of, suggested he would be understanding of blue-collar urban life. That is, he would not be too severe on hardworking fellows who gambled on horses, cards and dice, or partook of a little too much liquor on Saturday night. Within days, McKern was in the police recruit training school, and after a few weeks there, he began pounding a beat in a district adjoining his home neighborhood. The police department had a policy of not assigning officers to the district in which they resided, though a man who possessed a big "clout" (Chicagoese for very powerful political connection) could obtain an exemption.

Based on the later recollections of individuals from other wards who made the cut, the procedure followed in the Stockyards district was the same as that in neighborhoods such as Bucktown, Smoky Hollow, Austin, and other locales where cops were traditionally recruited.

When a recruit class assembled, the room was full of men who had won Silver Stars and other decorations. There were no Medal of Honor winners in the police. (There was one, a marine captain, in the fire department, though he had been on the job before the war.) There was a sprinkling of ex-commissioned officers, but not many. In 1946, men who had been lieutenants and captains usually took advantage of the GI Bill to enroll in college and went on to professional or managerial positions. Among those from "Back of the Yards" who joined the police force—though he did so a bit later via civil service exam rather than the ward process—was twenty-six-year-old Jim Schaffer, who had risen from private to major, ultimately commanding an infantry battalion in some of the fiercest fighting of the Pacific War. Former officers who joined the force were never quite "one of the boys."[3] Many continued their military service in the reserve and National Guard, often rising to high rank.

Prewar cops who returned as military officers faced a dilemma. Should they remain on the job or try civilian life? Some were college graduates who had joined the force during the Depression. In 1946, they would have been snapped up in the private sector, but they worried about what would happen five years down the line when a Depression hit. In the end, most opted to stay put; in later years, they regretted it. Police headquarters had the reverse dilemma: what to do with returned patrolmen who had been captains or majors. (Colonels were usually men who had been ranking officers in the department before the war.) Some brass argued that they could not be put back on a beat. Others said "why not?" The fire department created a battalion chief

3. Schaffer, though modest and friendly, was not especially popular with his peers. Nor did the police department call upon his skills. It was not uncommon in the postwar era for five hundred or even a thousand cops to be assigned to a civil disorder situation. Yet in no instance did the department hierarchy utilize the experience of Schaffer or other former officers within its ranks. The major also had outstanding community relations skills, but they too were not sought by the department. Instead he was assigned as liaison with a well-known community activist group which was disliked by city hall. In that capacity, he impressed many important people, including U.S. House Speaker John McCormick of Massachusetts. In the 1960s, when a drastic shakeup, following a police scandal, caused a lot of changes in the top echelon, some officers (such as this writer) were permitted to advance four or five grades in just a few years, Schaffer, by then a full colonel in the Reserves, was only promoted to sergeant.

level job specifically for their Medal of Honor winner. The police department compromise was to make some ex-officers detectives, though their military rank better fitted them to be patrol supervisors and commanders rather than investigators. However, a detective appointment was within the gift of the police commissioner, while promotion to sergeant and beyond required passing a civil service test.[4]

The story was much the same in other traditional cities, although most simply scheduled an entrance exam and called up candidates off the resultant list. Then a sergeant or detective would conduct a background investigation to determine whether the applicant was up to department standards. If approved, he would be provided by the instructors in the police academy with a few weeks of rudimentary training. Then, in his first duty station, the veteran cops would tell him to forget what he had been told and proceed to socialize him into the "real job." If the rookie did not conform to the norms of his colleagues, he would find life difficult.

The Chicago police force that McKern and the other thousand rookies entered was the same in kind as city police departments from the Atlantic to the Pacific, though it differed in degree. The typical department was shaped by its organizational culture more than by statutes, regulations or the lofty pronouncements of the mayor or the police commissioner. If officer A saw officer B struggling with someone on the street, he was expected to jump in and help his colleague without question. Anyone who failed to do so would thereafter be scorned by his peers. Informers too were despised, particularly in Irish-dominated forces with a folk memory of British spies in the old country. A cop who was labeled a coward or a stool pigeon would become an outcast.

Police work was a career service, where most recruits remained until retirement. Cops regarded themselves as "professionals," although the word did not have the same meaning as in law or medicine. Police officers acquired their core skills from practical experience, not formal education. In only two respects was policing a true profession. Its mission was not to make a profit but to perform a service to society, and its certified members were the only ones who could practice it. Just as only a licensed attorney could represent a criminal defendant or a doctor write a prescription, for practical purposes only a cop could arrest somebody for a crime not committed in his presence.

The duties of a police officer were generally the same everywhere: investigate crimes, enforce laws over which he had jurisdiction, maintain public order and render certain non-law enforcement services. In practice, uniformed

---

4. Because political considerations favored retaining the list from the 1937 sergeants exam, a man appointed to the force after that time had no chance for promotion until a new list was posted in 1952.

cops only conducted cursory criminal investigations and made few arrests for felonies or graver misdemeanors. Instead, a cop was expected to keep his beat "clean" by suppressing public-order violations such as young men loitering on corners or drunks breaching the peace. To do so, he relied more on verbal commands than arrests. Contrary to legend, the police were not free with their clubs on young men hanging out. Bar fights, particularly in towns with honky-tonk nightlife areas, were a different story, and participants in bottle-throwing, chair-swinging brawls were well advised to depart the scene before the cops arrived.

The most common type of police call, then as now, was for disturbances. In the domestic kind, a rookie, who was barely twenty-one and unmarried, might have to assume the role of family counselor. Also, police frequently encountered mentally disturbed persons or, in the slang phrases, "psychos" and "nut cases." Since they had virtually no training in dealing with such people, they tried to calm them down. If that failed, arrest or transportation to a hospital was the only recourse. Rookies soon realized that their basic police training, which had largely stressed firearms, self-defense and drill—all subjects that Uncle Sam had already taught them—were of little value in their actual street duties. Of course, the rookie would also note that gentlemen with "Dr." before their name and a string of letters after it did not seem to have much success in dealing with family disputes or the emotionally disturbed.

In some localities, police did little non-police work. They did not rescue cats from trees or take sick people to the hospital. In others they did both, and also conducted building inspections or processed license applications. In Boston, they took an annual census.

* * * *

In 1945, American policing entered the postwar period with its major problems unresolved. In the hundred years since the first modern force was formed in New York City, charges of corruption and excessive use of force had been common. Even in the NYPD, from 1934 to 1945, under the incorruptible Mayor Fiorello La Guardia and the equally honest police commissioner, Lewis J. Valentine, payoffs took place, although more discreetly. In "sin cities" like Chicago, New Orleans and San Francisco, graft was a fact of life.

In 1937, a former FBI agent hired to investigate the San Francisco Police Department charged that one hundred thirty-five houses of prostitution were operating and that the payoff to police from gambling and prostitution was one million dollars annually. The attorney for the police association countered that the houses of prostitution numbered at least three hundred and the payoffs were over four million dollars annually. One vice detective admitted to banking over eight hundred thousand dollars.**

It was an old story. Puritan morality clashed with political reality. Laws written by state legislatures, dominated by rural Protestants of English stock, were not in tune with the beliefs of city dwellers, who were increasingly non-Protestants from Ireland or the European continent. Descendants of the Puritans believed that the Sabbath should be a day of rest. Newer immigrants were used to the continental Sunday of sport, drinking and dancing. Urban police were required to placate both groups. In the nineteenth century, German beer gardens and Irish saloons in New York, Chicago and many other cities were officially closed on Sunday. But in actuality they went full blast, providing they paid off to cops and politicians. So astute a man as Theodore Roosevelt foundered as president of the New York City Board of Police Commissioners because he attempted to enforce Sunday closing laws.

In 1920, the old order, spearheaded by members of the Protestant clergy and women's groups, imposed national Prohibition.[5] It proved to be disastrous. It not only led to massive police and political corruption, it changed the balance of power between politicians and gangsters. Before Prohibition, the gang bosses had to seek the permission of the political machines to operate. By the end of Prohibition, the gangsters, enriched by millions from illegal liquor trafficking, became as powerful as the political bosses, sometimes more so. In Chicago, the once mighty First Ward organization, fountainhead of municipal corruption, became an adjunct of what locals called the Capone Gang or the "syndicate." By the 1940s, Tammany Hall was subservient to the "Prime Minister" of New York City organized crime, mobster Frank Costello.

In the Depression era, violent clashes between management and labor were regular occurrences. Police were usually mobilized on the side of the former, and sometimes shot the latter. In Chicago, on Memorial Day 1937, striking workers marched on the Republic Steel plant with the intention of seizing and holding it, a new tactic called a "sit-down strike." Police, seeking to halt them, opened fire, killing ten people and wounding scores. In the South, police continued to enforce "Jim Crow" laws designed to keep blacks down. In some places, membership in the Klan was a prerequisite for obtaining a police badge.[6] Not infrequently, even Northern white servicemen were manhandled by Southern cops. By 1945, though, the New Deal's empowerment of

---

5. Americans have forgotten that in the early years of the twentieth century many progressives, like William Jennings Bryan, pushed hard for dry laws. Because excessive drinking by the men folk blighted the lives of their wives and children, Prohibition was always an important "women's issue."

6. Recollect that such well-known liberals as Senator (later Supreme Court Justice) Hugo Black and Senate Majority Leader Robert Byrd were Klansmen early in their careers.

organized labor made union bosses into important political figures with significant influence over mayors who controlled local police. Blacks, on the other hand, were no better off politically in 1946 than they had been before the war.

In 1945, the predominant element in American policing was, as it had always been, the forces maintained by medium-size and large cities. The 1920s had witnessed the emergence of state police, but most, including those of major states such as California and Ohio, were just highway patrols. In a few that did confer general authority on its officers, the troopers, as they were often called (because the early state police forces were mounted), confined their activities to rural areas rather than cities. In the 1930s, J. Edgar Hoover and his FBI assumed great prominence. But not it, the Secret Service or other federal agencies were police departments. They did not patrol the streets or exercise general law enforcement authority. Instead they investigated a narrow range of federal crimes.

After World War II, municipal police were organized and operated much as they had in the nineteenth century. In cities of sufficient size, the force was distributed across districts (precincts or divisions). Within them, individual cops were assigned to patrol, on foot or by vehicle, smaller areas known as beats (posts or sectors). Each district was commanded by a captain (or equivalent in rank), who functioned as a de-facto local police chief. Administrative services and certain large field operations, such as the detective bureau and the traffic division, operated out of headquarters or their own substations.

There was no uniform pattern of higher police management. In New York, mayors selected their police commissioner from among prominent civilians (mostly lawyers) and NYPD career cops. Detroit mayors followed a similar practice, although they sometimes named a career officer from outside their city. In Chicago, the mayor invariably appointed a local officer as commissioner. In Philadelphia and Cleveland, civilian safety directors, chosen by the mayor, supervised the police department. In Boston and Baltimore, civilian commissioners responsible to the governor were in overall charge of the city force. In San Francisco, Los Angeles and St. Louis, a board of part-time police commissioners, appointed by the mayor or governor, oversaw the career chief.

Of course, the people who really named the head of a police department were usually business or religious leaders, a powerful newspaper publisher, a political or mob boss. Others might not select the chief but could exercise veto power over anyone proposed. In postwar Chicago, a man who was unacceptable to the publisher of the *Chicago Tribune* had no chance of getting the job. In Los Angeles, certain Protestant ministers swung great weight. In one major American city (not Chicago) there was a legend that in the 1960s, when an outside reformer took over as police commissioner, he visited the Catholic cardinal archbishop. Finally, after much stumbling and fumbling, he informed his eminence he would like to make the department's personnel decisions himself. The commissioner was relieved when the archbishop replied, "Oh, thank you, lad, it's been a burden to me all these years."[7]

In Washington DC, where until the 1960s there was no mayor, executive control was vested in a board of three district commissioners. However, the police superintendent's real master was the congressional committee that oversaw the district government. In some cities where the police head was a civilian, operational management of the force was left in the hands of a career cop, titled chief inspector in New York and superintendent or chief of police in other cities.

Whatever the system, police superior officers were always attuned to the power realities of a community. They knew to be polite to local politicians, businessmen and members of the clergy (including some who were African Americans). Others had close connections with a newspaper or journalist. The *New York Daily News* and the *Chicago Tribune* always had the inside track on police stories in their cities. *New York Mirror* columnist Walter Winchell had a huge "in" with the NYPD. When Los Angeles writer Florabell Muir gave advice to the chief of detectives, he listened.

One benefit that emerged from the Depression was an influx of high-quality recruits. Men who, before the 1929 crash, would never have considered joining the force did so in the 1930s out of economic necessity. The NYPD recruit class of 1940 contained many college graduates, including lawyers and CPAs. Some later earned doctorates and, in at least one case, an MD. The LAPD recruits of 1940 included future mayor Tom Bradley and two men who would rise to chief, Tom Reddin and Ed Davis. Beginning in 1945, a number of war veterans with memories of the Depression chose to join the police force, regarding it as a one-time opportunity to secure a steady job.

The elite of urban policing, at least in the public's mind, were the detectives. Glorified in print and film, some were better known than the local chief of police. Despite the press fascination with them, American police investiga-

---

7. The notion of the archdiocese screening candidates for promotion was not irrational. In many forces the police hierarchy was overwhelmingly Catholic. The Church had files on its members dating from their boyhood. Thus they might know if a married man with five children also had a teenage mistress. In instances where a candidate could not "pass the personal," it might spare the police department from a future scandal. As recent events in America have demonstrated, who knows what impulses lurk in the hearts of even the highest officials? A couple of generations ago, among Catholics, the parish priest or the local bishop might know. The downside was that a rising officer who got divorced usually ceased to rise.

tors were years behind their counterparts in Europe. There, many detectives were university graduates who had studied academic theories of criminal behavior and regularly employed scientific methods of investigation. In the United States, detective work was carried on in a hit-and-miss fashion. In the early 1930s, despite the efforts of the FBI, the NYPD, and the New Jersey State Police—three of the top departments in the country—it took two years to capture the killer of the Lindbergh baby.

* * * *

Three cities illustrate the state of American policing in urban areas at the beginning of the postwar period.

New York City

New York, the most populous and cosmopolitan of America's cities, was the de-facto capital of the United States (though the smaller and less important Washington, DC was the actual seat of government). In 1945, Mayor La Guardia was finishing his twelfth year in office. During his tenure, he had managed to restore integrity to the city government, including the police department. But the voters had tired of the caustic and combative "Little Flower." Polls indicated that he could not be re-elected. After sixteen years of Depression and war, New Yorkers wanted a return to the fun days of the 1920s. The polls found that the most popular choice for mayor was Jimmy Walker, the charming rogue who had presided over the city from 1926 to 1932. As mayor, the married Walker had spent more time in night spots than he did in city hall, and he preferred meetings with his girlfriends to sessions with his commissioners. However, until the Depression set in, he was very popular. Then, under pressure from both Governor Franklin Roosevelt and the Catholic archdiocese, he resigned and, accompanied by his girlfriend, moved to England. During Walker's tenure, he had gone through four police commissioners in less than seven years, and his police department was shot through with corruption.

In 1934, nine months into his first term, La Guardia chose Chief Inspector Lewis J. Valentine to run the department. Valentine had made his name as a shoofly (a cop who policed other cops). He immediately began shaking up the force, firing officers of all ranks. In late 1945, with La Guardia a lame duck, Valentine accepted an offer to assist in reorganizing the Japanese police, then under the direction of General MacArthur's military occupation government.

La Guardia wished to appoint as commissioner Arthur Wallander, another clean cop, though not a shoofly. Wallander had made his own reputation directing special squads such as the aviation and emergency service units. The latter dealt with everything from barricaded criminals to individuals threatening to jump off a bridge. During World War II, Wallander had served as deputy mayor in charge of civil defense—a vital task at a time when it was expected that New York City would be subjected to air raids or sabotage. However, the lame duck La Guardia hesitated to make the appointment because incoming mayors traditionally chose their own commissioner. So he approached the man who would be his successor, William O'Dwyer. "Bill O," as he was called, was as personable as Walker, whose health had not permitted him to run for mayor—he died the following year—but he was a more serious person. He had risen from beat cop to judge and district attorney in Brooklyn, where he received much favorable publicity for directing the investigation of a group of mob hit men, dubbed by the press "Murder Incorporated." In 1941, O'Dwyer had been the Democratic nominee for mayor and would probably have won if Franklin Roosevelt had not crossed party lines to endorse the Republican La Guardia. After Pearl Harbor, O'Dwyer went into the service and rose to the rank of brigadier general, carrying out special missions.

Despite his sterling résumé, O'Dwyer possessed significant baggage. In the Murder Incorporated case, a key witness had somehow fallen out of a sixth-floor window despite the fact that he was being guarded by five cops who reported to Capt. Frank Bals, head of District Attorney O'Dwyer's detective squad. According to O'Dwyer, the death of the witness, Abe "Kid Twist" Reles (who became known as the "canary who could sing but not fly"), made it impossible to prosecute Albert Anastasia, a mob boss whose role in Murder Incorporated earned him the nickname "the Lord High Executioner." It was widely suspected that "Kid Twist" had been pushed, not jumped, out of the window. In addition, O'Dwyer was never able to give a satisfactory explanation of why, in 1943, he had taken time out from his military duties to make a secret visit to the Manhattan apartment of mob chief Frank Costello.

To La Guardia's delight, O'Dwyer agreed that "Wally," who as a sergeant had been one of O'Dwyer's instructors in the police academy, was a fine choice. Under O'Dwyer, the NYPD went back to what it had been in Walker's time. The police commissioner would be a figurehead to cover the machinations of the police, politics and organized crime alliance. Frank Bals was appointed to a new post of seventh deputy commissioner in charge of a squad enforcing laws against gambling and vice. Some reporters speculated that Bals's unit was a means to funnel graft to city hall. However, organized crime figures did not like the new setup. As one of them said, "the ice" (payoffs) would be up to the ceiling. Sixty days after the squad was formed, bowing to pressure from organized crime, elements of the police department and the press, O'Dwyer abolished Bals's unit. Early in 1949, Commissioner Wallander voluntarily retired. By 1950, the La Guardia/Valentine era was largely forgotten (both men had died in 1947).

In the late '40s, members of what was called "New York's Finest" were envied by other blue-collar workers and respected by most New Yorkers. Crime was relatively low; however, gambling and vice flourished. A young cop named Jimmy Reardon, assigned to a headquarters' confidential (vice) squad, quit the force to run a gambling empire in partnership with a Brooklyn bookie named Harry Gross. Reardon was not discreet. He moved to an exclusive section of Connecticut, where he maintained the lifestyle of a country squire. Soon a New York reporter began writing about "Mr. G and the squire." The Brooklyn district attorney, Miles McDonald, started a probe, and Judge Samuel Leibowitz, assigned to supervise a grand-jury investigation, usurped the mantle of a special prosecutor. Commissioner Bill O'Brien and the mayor fought back, blasting the DA and the judge. Finally, after the judge summoned O'Brien to his chambers to listen to wiretaps detailing the graft payoffs, the commissioner resigned. Mayor O'Dwyer also resigned, secured an appointment as ambassador to Mexico and remained there for several years, safe from any criminal charges in New York City.[8] Back in New York, eighteen police officers, including some of high rank, were indicted. Others were named unindicted co-conspirators. Three cops committed suicide. Scores of officers quit or were fired.***

The voters of New York had gotten their wish. They had elected a charming mayor who presided over a revival of the 1920s, complete with his own sudden departure to foreign climes. O'Dwyer's successor, City Council President Vincent "Impy" Impelletieri, was an obscure functionary when he had been picked to run with O'Dwyer in order to give the ticket geographic and ethnic balance—i.e., a Manhattan Italian with a Brooklyn Irishman; it was completed by Lazarus Joseph, a Bronx Jew who was elected city controller. When Impelletieri ran in the special election to fill out O'Dwyer's unexpired term, Frank Costello put gunmen to work in support of a rival mayoral candidate, Tammany-endorsed Ferdinand Pecora, while another mob boss, Tommy Lucchese backed "Impy."

The victory of the Lucchese faction over the Costello group created a dangerous situation in the world of organized crime because it was likely to

---

8. It is generally believed that President Truman made the appointment at the behest of powerful Massachusetts Congressman (and later Speaker of the House) John McCormick. With a safe seat in Massachusetts, McCormick was free to do favors for important people as a means of boosting his own career.

lead to a mob war. It was also the time that Sen. Kefauver's investigating committee set up shop in New York City. Soon, guns began barking and Costello was wounded and deposed as boss, while Albert Anastasia, the key figure in the principal Brooklyn mob, was murdered and the family boss Vince Mangano disappeared. Vito Genovese took over Costello's group, which henceforth became known as the Genovese family, and Carlo Gambino assumed leadership of the principal Brooklyn group, which became the Gambino family. The Brooklyn and Manhattan waterfronts continued under mob control. When Idlewild Airport (later called JFK) became a major cargo terminal, several families grabbed a piece of the action. At the same time, the postwar building boom filled the coffers of mob-controlled construction unions.

"Impy," as the press called him, appointed as police commissioner Tom Murphy, who had just finished successfully prosecuting accused Communist Alger Hiss for perjury. Later at a Senate hearing, when Murphy was being considered for a federal judgeship, he had to admit that he and the mayor had a mutual friend named Tommy Lucchese. When Murphy left, Manhattan assistant district attorney George Monaghan was appointed as his successor.

In 1952, Bruce Smith was called in to conduct a survey of the police department. His report proposed some of the same administrative remedies that he had offered in other cities. However, when he declared that New York cops were not "the finest," he provoked a storm. Arthur Godfrey, the most popular TV entertainer of the time, was among many celebrities who defended the police. A patrolman lying wounded on a Times Square sidewalk was said to have muttered over and over, "To hell with the Bruce Smith report."[9+] As usual, Smith's recommendations had little impact. It was his last major study. He died three years later at the age of sixty-three.

Chicago

The New York police, whether under reformers like La Guardia or machine-backed mayors like O'Dwyer, retained a certain autonomy. This was never the case in Chicago. There, most of the captains of districts were subject to direction from the local ward bosses. A captain who defied him might be transferred overnight to a Siberia post.[10]

---

9. Many years ago, I was informed by individuals who were in a position to know that the cop actually used a stronger term related to the reproductive function.

10. Of course, a particular captain might possess significant clout of his own. One was a brother of the heroic leader of the 1916 Irish rebellion. Another was related to the cardinal archbishop of Chicago. A phone call to the mayor from a VIP might save a captain from being transferred.

Two important subdivisions of the force were more autonomous. The central detective bureau, with about one-third of the city's investigators—the other two-thirds worked under the district captains—was divided into specialized units: homicide, robbery, burglary, cartage, auto theft, confidence (fraud). Each concentrated on professional criminals and investigated major cases. An assignment to the detective bureau carried no extra pay but great prestige. It also was rumored to provide other emoluments. Detective commanders were not so beholden to ward bosses. Their support often came from newspapers and business groups, or they were friends with a top figure in the department. The chief of detectives was generally regarded as the second most important individual in the force, and in many respects had more power than the commissioner. It was the chief who had the key to the golden treasure newspapers sought: inside information on the latest front-page crime. In an era when there were both morning and afternoon papers, the chief could time the announcement of a confession or arrest to favor either the a.m. or p.m. paper. In some instances, he might give an exclusive to a reporter. However, unless the chief rotated such favors among the various papers, the others would seek to destroy him. For a time, the most important police official was a captain who worked as chief investigator for the state attorney's office. Long suspected of being a member of the Chicago mob's ruling group, Capt. Dan "Tubbo" Gilbert would become known as "America's richest cop."

The central detective bureau also constituted a mobile anti-crime force independent of the uniformed division, whose district stations were controlled by ward bosses. One of its key tasks was to pick up known criminals or suspects and hold them on an "open" charge until they were processed through the "show-up" (or "line-up," as it was called in some cities), where they were viewed by detectives and crime victims. Those who possessed illegal weapons or stolen goods, or were fingered by crime victims, were booked. Those who cleared the show-up were charged with disorderly conduct and released on bail.

Such tactics led to few convictions. In 1914, the U.S. Supreme Court ruled that items unlawfully seized had to be excluded as evidence in a federal trial. A minority of states adopted their own "exclusionary rules." Not until 1961 did the Supreme Court impose the rule on all states.[++] The only industrial state that voluntarily adopted the practice was Illinois. As a result, suspects caught with loaded guns were routinely discharged. Not all pickups were illegal. In some instances they could have been carried out lawfully. However, both cops and defense lawyers were satisfied with the system. For the cops, the pickups kept criminals off balance, thereby preventing them from taking over the streets, and it discouraged gunmen from carrying their pieces.[11] The defense bar recognized that if cops were forbidden to do these things, the legislature might be forced to enact less restrictive laws or even adopt a state constitutional amendment to remove the exclusionary rule.

The traffic division was run by forces outside the police department. A former suburban police lieutenant, Franklin Kreml, was director of the Northwestern University Traffic Institute, which was sponsored by insurance companies to promote highway safety. Gen. (his reserve military rank) Kreml introduced the traffic division to modern management methods of the type advocated by Bruce Smith. While the patrol districts continued to operate on a traditional basis, distributing personnel relatively equally across shifts regardless of workload, and its patrol officers followed no particular system or method, one thousand traffic cops were deployed on foot, motorcycle or car according to managerial analyses of service demands and its officers followed standard operating procedures prescribed by the Traffic Institute. In the 1950s, the Chicago Police Department presented an organizational pattern that bridged three different eras. Its traffic division was managed as cops would be in the 1960s, while its patrol force was stuck in the 1930s and the detective bureau operated as though it was still the Prohibition era of the 1920s.

In 1947, the Democratic machine leaders determined that Mayor Ed Kelly, who had been in office for fourteen years, was so unpopular that he could not be re-elected. So they replaced him with an honest businessman named Martin Kennelly. With the ascension of Kennelly, it might have been an opportune time for someone like Kreml to revamp the entire police department. However, the machine had no intention of doing that. Kennelly was a figurehead mayor, and while the politicians did not object to improved traffic policing, particularly since the powerful insurance industry was behind it, they were very much interested in how law enforcement was carried out in the districts where their constituents lived and the machine earned its graft.

In 1950, the Cook County Democratic chairman—the boss of the party—decided to run Capt. Gilbert for county sheriff. What prompted this decision is uncertain. The negatives about Gilbert were well known. When Senator Kefauver's investigation committee came to Chicago, he was allowed to testify in executive (secret) session. However, an enterprising reporter for the *Sun Times* procured (stole) a transcript, and it was splashed across the front page, leading not only to Gilbert's defeat but also to that of Senate Majority Leader Scott W. Lucas. The fall of Lucas, a Downstater with no ties to Chicago's

---

11. See also Chapter 8, pages 138–39.

organized crime, paved the way for the rise to majority leader of Lyndon Johnson of Texas.

Around the same time, an off-duty Chicago detective, assigned to the squad that worked out of the office of the state's attorney, became embroiled in a bar fight with two men. He finished third and, in the process, was relieved of his firearm. He procured a replacement gun and began scouring the area, looking for his assailants. During the course of the search, he encountered three men in a parked car. None of them had been in the tavern or had any knowledge of the brawl. But the detective opened fire, killing two of them and wounding the third. The officer came from a well-connected political family, and a grand jury, controlled by the state's attorney's office, exonerated him on the grounds of self-defense. The state's attorney himself was on summer vacation. He was not acquainted with the detective, but he was assured by subordinates that everything was above board in the case. Then the roof fell in. Eventually, the detective was given a life sentence for murder. The state's attorney, who was being groomed for the governorship, was defeated for re-election and sent into the wilderness. The party elders had stumbled badly with Gilbert as a candidate and the mess in the state's attorney's office. In 1952, after another resounding defeat, this time in a gubernatorial election, Richard J. Daley was chosen to head the county committee. In 1955 he was elected mayor, remaining in office until his death in 1976. It was Daley and his successors, especially his son Richard M. (mayor from 1989 to 2011), who would shape Chicago over the next six decades.

Los Angeles

In 1945, Los Angeles was on its way to becoming the great metropolis it would be in the second half of the century. Before World War I, it had not even been the most important city in California. That honor belonged to San Francisco, with its magnificent harbor that made it the principal port for American commerce with Asia. Between 1920 and 1950, the population of Los Angeles would grow from five hundred ninety-seven thousand to nearly two million, making it the fourth-largest city in the United States. Unlike the older cities, Los Angeles was populated by migrants from other areas of the country who did not have allegiance to any local neighborhood or political organization.

Before World War II, the key to political success in the City of Angels was to win the support of both the hellfire Protestant preachers, who had large followings, and the business community, led by the *Los Angeles Times*, which wanted to hold labor costs down by keeping the city a non-union town. Once in office, a politician could take payoffs from gamblers and madams. In a political environment that was no more honest than that in most Eastern cities, the police department operated in a heavy-handed, corrupt and loose manner. The "Red squad" satisfied the business community by suppressing labor organizations, and the vice squad took its orders from the gamblers. Within the department, many politically connected cops held "brevet" or acting ranks higher than their civil service ones.[12] The "brevet" captain of the "Red squad" was only a one-hundred-eighty-dollar-a-month patrolman. However, his earnings as a "business consultant" enabled him to lose more than that in one day at the racetrack.

In 1938, the system was dealt a fatal blow. Civic leaders hired a shady former LA detective named Harry Raymond to investigate the police department. One day, as he was starting his car, a bomb went off, giving him seventy-two shrapnel wounds. He somehow survived. An investigation disclosed that the bomb had been planted by the LAPD intelligence squad, which was under the direct control of the mayor. The squad commander, another "brevet" captain, was sent to prison and the mayor was recalled in a special election. The man who took his place, Judge Fletcher Bowron, undertook a cleanup of the police department, abolishing the "brevet" ranks and the "Red" and intelligence squads.

During the World War II period, the department was still a second-class operation. When many regular police officers went into the service, the city hired emergency cops from among men who previously could not pass the exams for the force. Many were unsuited for police work. In 1943, servicemen clashed with young Mexicans, whose flamboyant dress caused them to be known as "Zoot Suiters." For several days, bands of soldiers and sailors hunted down and beat the "Zoots."

In 1949, a young detective, Sgt. Elmer Jackson, who had been a member of the elite class of 1940, was sitting in a parked car with his girlfriend when a bandit attempted to hold them up. Jackson managed to draw a concealed weapon and kill the robber. Later, it was discovered that the girlfriend he had been with that night was the city's top madam, Brenda Allen. Jackson had become acquainted with her while he assisted the FBI on a vice raid. Supposedly Allen was paying Jackson nine hundred dollars a week to allow her girls to operate. One rumor was that the assailant in lovers' lane was trying to hold up Jackson for the money. The resultant scandal led to the dismissal of the chief of police. His temporary replacement was a marine general who,

---

12. On the police ranks, see Appendix C.

under the law, could not become the permanent chief. That job could only be filled by a career officer who passed a civil service examination.

When the examination was held, the top two names on the list were deputy chiefs William Parker and Thaddeus Brown. Bill Parker was an administrative type with an arrogant and abrasive manner. Thad Brown, head of the detective bureau, was an old-time sleuth, popular with his men, reporters and the public. Although there was considerable reluctance to give Parker the job, the city administration recognized that he was the best man to lead a cleanup of the force. It was Bill Parker who would create the modern LAPD. After his death, successors, who imitated his style, would maintain the Los Angeles police as a virtual fourth branch of local government.

* * * *

Postwar America was the first time average people had the leisure or money to spend on pleasures since the 1920s and, after Depression and war, they were eager to spend it. The good times rolled and cops got their share. In 1950-51, the Kefauver Committee held hearings in various cities where it revealed, among other things, a good deal about the state of American policing. In New York, the committee exposed former Mayor O'Dwyer's cozy relationship with mobster Frank Costello. In Chicago, they heard the testimony of Capt. Gilbert, "America's richest cop." In Los Angeles, the committee received the cooperation of Chief Parker, but uncovered a number of problems within the Los Angeles sheriff's office. In one instance, a mob lawyer, recently murdered, was revealed to have had secret dealings with a top sheriff's commander. In Philadelphia, when the head of the vice squad was summoned to testify, he killed himself. The commission's final report noted that some Philadelphia police captains were paid a thousand dollars a week by local gamblers.

While corruption was endemic, violence was not especially troublesome in the immediate postwar era. During the fighting, psychiatrists had expressed alarm that psychotic GIs would engage in murderous rampages. In September 1949, in Camden, New Jersey, a spectacular incident of that nature occurred. A mentally disturbed twenty-eight-year-old World War II combat veteran named Howard Unruh went on a shooting spree. In twenty minutes he killed thirteen persons, three of them children, and wounded others. Unruh was captured at the scene and remained in state custody until his death in 2009. He never gave a coherent explanation for his actions. When arrested, he carried a list of people who he believed had offended him, but some of those he shot were not on it, including children aged six and two.[+++] The press whipped up concern about "walking time bombs," but very few similar incidents occurred.

In general, the early postwar years are looked back on as a happy time. But beneath the surface there were sinister elements that sometimes were deliberately ignored. The VJ Day celebrations that initiated the postwar era are recalled today by pictures of joyous crowds dancing in the streets and servicemen kissing smiling girls. What occurred in San Francisco, though, was so shocking that it has been virtually erased from history.

San Francisco, with its gaudy night life, beautiful scenery and air of Old World charm and sophistication, was a favorite spot for visitors. It was such a mannerly town that respectable women would not think of going downtown without wearing white gloves. Of course, the country knew, or thought they knew, what went on in vice districts like the Barbary Coast and the Tenderloin, but that was part of the fun.

The San Francisco Police Department retained some of the flavor of big-city departments from earlier in the century. A large portion of its officers were Irish, many of them born on the "auld sod." Its chief, Charles Dullea, was one of the best-known cops in America. After service in the Marines, he had joined the force at the time of the 1914 Panama and Pacific Exposition and had spent most of his career in detective work. In 1945 he was president of the International Association of Chiefs of Police.

On the first night of VJ Day, the crowds were mostly well behaved. On the second night, though, they suddenly began smashing windows and overturning cars in the downtown area. These were not thugs or ghetto people—for practical purposes, there were no ghettos in San Francisco—but young servicemen undergoing military training at the many bases in the area. Most resembled the boy next door from Anytown, U.S.A., the lads who were fighting "for mom's apple pie and the girl next door." Deputy Police Chief Mike Riordan's thick brogue could be heard shouting on his bullhorn for the crowds to disperse. City and military police attempted to move the rioters back, but there were too many. As one group was driven off, more would take their place. Finally the violence overrode all bounds of decency. The rioters began attacking respectable young women who had been celebrating VJ Day, throwing them down on the street, removing their clothes and raping them. According to a San Francisco deputy chief of a later era, the 1945 commanders had no coherent plan for dealing with any problems that might arise and largely reacted to events.[^]

The first decisive response came from the commander of the Pacific Fleet. Admiral John McCain (grandfather of the present-day U.S. Senator) sent word that the sailors at sea were disgusted and ashamed with what was happening in

San Francisco, and he issued orders that all necessary reinforcements be sent to the area to restore order. Finally, with the aid of a huge military police contingent, the police stopped the rioting.

Initially there were numerous investigations into what had happened, but soon the matter was dropped. For years there appeared to be an unspoken taboo on mentioning it. It was reported that eleven people were killed, but other than identifying one municipal worker, there seemed to be no details about the victims. Supposedly no rape reports were filed, but there were plenty of reliable witnesses, including reporters who saw what happened. Perhaps the events were covered up so as not to cause national embarrassment. Had the facts become publicized, it might have made for interesting conversations in the future when young people asked their fathers or grandfathers, "You were in San Francisco on VJ Day; what did you do then ?"[13]

Looking back, the event seems a harbinger of the youth rebellion that became a feature of American life in the 1950s and the student riots of the 1960s—although these never approached the ferocity of VJ celebrations in San Francisco in 1945. For veteran cops the affair simply confirmed what they had always known—that the bonds of civilization were easily broken.

By 1950, American policing was at a crossroads. It could go on as it had for a hundred years, inefficient and often corrupt, or it could adopt the kind of professional management style advocated by reformers. At least, those appeared to be the choices at the time. As it turned out, postwar policing would be dominated by discussions far beyond how to make cops more honest, polite and efficient. Instead it would be caught up in large social questions involving race relations and what constituted the fair administration of justice.

---

13. A year later, the riots still affected the city. Military personnel were forbidden to congregate in certain downtown areas. As a boy visitor, I used to enjoy watching the nightly scenes that played out on Market Street. If a group of sailors, fresh off a ship, stopped to look in a store window, a detachment of the shore patrol would pull up and arrest the lot of them. The fun was listening to the stunned sailors trying to comprehend what they had done wrong. Apparently, their ship's captain had not warned them how to behave on the streets of San Francisco, or they had not listened when he did.

Chapter 2

Professional Policing Emerges:
Parker in Los Angeles,
Schrotel in Cincinnati

The vice scandal of 1949 shook the Los Angeles police hierarchy, but it did not have much effect on the public. Spectacular scandals were an old story in Los Angeles. Hollywood was always good for a couple every year. Measured against the intelligence squad blowing up private investigator Harry Raymond back in 1938, Elmer Jackson's dealings with Brenda Allen were small potatoes. The postwar case that really shook the city began in 1947, when cops responded to a call about a body in a vacant lot. Upon arrival, they found 22-year-old Elizabeth Short with her mouth slashed from ear to ear, her body mutilated, burned and cut in half at the waist. The press dubbed the tall, slim, black-haired, light-skinned woman with a rose tattoo on her upper thigh "the Black Dahlia."[1] Despite intensive investigation, the murder would remain a mystery into the twenty-first century.[2]

Lured by the glamour of Hollywood, at seventeen Short had run away from her home in Massachusetts. During the war, many people had come to Los Angeles to work or pass through on their way to the Pacific war. Some fell

---

1. Shortly before the murder, Hollywood released a film entitled *The Blue Dahlia*. It starred Alan Ladd as a former Navy pilot suspected of murdering his wife and Veronica Lake as a woman who tries to help him clear his name.
2. On the Dahlia murder, see Appendix A.

in love with the climate and lifestyle and decided to live there permanently. On the surface, the city appeared relatively safe. It did not contain vast areas of high-density slums like those in the East. It sprawled across 450 square miles (twice the size of Chicago and ten times that of Boston). People of modest means could live in bungalows on small lots. The Dahlia case, however, suggested there was menace behind the palm trees. The community wanted the murder solved. When the police failed to do so, it was taken as an indication there was something wrong with the LAPD.

When Marine Gen. William Worton was appointed acting chief of police, following the scandal of '49, he immediately shook up the force military style. He ordered that cadets be required to attend a basic training program at the academy for 90 days.[3] He transferred ordinary cops and superior officers left and right. An experienced naval intelligence officer, he restored the old police intelligence squad. He promoted the martinet Bill Parker to deputy chief in charge of an internal-affairs unit investigating police misconduct. Had the law not required that a permanent chief be selected via a civil service exam that was open only to ranking LAPD officers, Worton might have been chosen to fill the post. Instead, as noted earlier, the choice was between Parker, who had finished first on the test, and Detective Chief Thad Brown.

Born in the Black Hills of South Dakota in 1902, William Parker had come to Los Angeles at age twenty-one. Intensely ambitious, he drove a cab to support himself while he attended a downtown law school. It was the kind where young men learned enough to "beat the bar" exams and upon graduation hung out a shingle and hoped to get some clients. It was not one whose graduates went into established law firms, and it was light years away from such ivory-tower schools as Harvard and Yale. In 1927, Parker joined the LAPD. By the mid-1930s, he was a lieutenant. Despite later attempts to portray him as a hard-charging street cop, much of his time was spent as an office aide to chief of police Jim Davis. Best known as a champion pistol shot rather than a police administrator, Davis was widely believed to be on the take. However, there was never any suggestion that Parker had accepted graft. During World War II, he served as a military police captain and was awarded a Purple Heart at Normandy.[4]

While Parker was considered highly competent, his cold manner made him unpopular. Thad Brown was much better liked. Had the choice been a popularity contest, Brown would have won. Born in Missouri, he had joined

---

3. At the time, some recruits in major cities received virtually no training. The chief of police in a city of half a million people once told me that, circa 1950, he had been sworn in as a full-fledged officer in the afternoon, issued a gun, badge and uniform and sent out alone to patrol the streets on the midnight shift.
4. On Parker, see Appendix B.

the department in 1924. He was not a Hollywood-style, granite-jawed detective like Charlie Dullea, who had run the San Francisco Inspectors (detective) Bureau in the 1930s, then served as chief of police until 1947. Brown was a folksy, friendly sort who schmoozed witnesses and suspects, often persuading the latter that confessing was the best thing they could do. In this, Brown was actually following the teachings of the great Hans Gross, an Austrian magistrate cum law professor whose writings were the Bible of European detectives. Gross taught that a criminal, if given the opportunity, would generally confess his crime. Of course, Brown probably never heard of Gross. Like most American detectives, he operated from instinct and learned from experience. In his early days as a detective, his mentor was his illiterate partner, a man from the Missouri hill country.

The board of commissioners was divided three to two in Brown's favor. However, his easygoing style and lack of interest in administrative work suggested he was not the man to conduct a major overhaul of the department. The most influential groups in Los Angeles, such as the Chamber of Commerce, the Downtown Businessmen's Association, the Merchants and Manufacturers Association and, most powerful of all, the *Los Angeles Times*, realized that if their town was to be a world-class city, it had to substantially improve its police force. There could be no more scandals, no Black Dahlia killers walking around free.

Parker was smart enough and tough enough to accomplish an overhaul of the department, but another factor against him was that he was a Catholic in a Protestant town. When one pro-Brown commissioner suddenly died, the board was divided. It was Brown himself who broke the deadlock by withdrawing. As he explained to his friends, he did not relish the prospect of being chief with Parker behind him holding a knife.

Los Angeles reflected the problems of American police leadership. There was no core of administrators from which to select a chief because there was no institution to train them or mechanism to move them into the right jobs. In the U.S. Army, an officer seeking to rise to general would have to pass high at the staff college, where his performance and the confidential report submitted on him would greatly influence the rest of his career.

After World War II, Britain established a police staff college in Bramshill, Hampshire. As in the military, some of those who did well later rose to be chief constables. In Britain, the national government had a great deal of say about police administration. Headed by a powerful cabinet minister, the Home Office provided financial support and oversight to local police forces. For practical purposes, no one could become a chief constable without the approval of the Home Secretary.

The United States had no true staff college and no government agency with the power to designate who could become a police chief. The FBI provided a few weeks of management training for police executives, as did the Southern Police Institute at the University of Louisville. Frank Kreml's Northwestern University Traffic Institute offered more extensive training. Neither the Southern Police Institute nor the Traffic Institute had much influence in the selection of major city police chiefs. In some instances, a recommendation from Hoover at the FBI would have been a kiss of death. After the 1950 Brinks robbery in Boston, the local cops and the Bureau battled for years over control of the case. About the same time, in New York City, one of the perennial struggles between the FBI and the local police erupted over civil-rights investigations and the alleged downgrading of local crime figures.[5] Hoover hated certain police chiefs like Parker so much that he refused to allow officers from their departments to attend the FBI Academy even though it was a government facility, not his private property.

Professional policing advocates were a small and scattered fraternity. The most prominent was Bruce Smith of New York's Institute of Public Administration. Early in the twentieth century, the IPA (then known as the Bureau of Municipal Research) had been founded by upper-class Easterners who sought to take control of municipal government from bosses and put it in the hands of an educated elite. Their mantra was to proclaim that public administration was not a matter of whose values should prevail, but about applying neutral management principles. Of course, urban immigrants did not buy that line. For them, governing was about the granting of favors and benefits—a break in the police court for young Tony charged with stealing, or a scrub woman's job at city hall for widow Murphy. And they knew these were more likely to come from a boss who was one of their own kind, rather than a silk-hatted reformer. In the 1930s, America's leading scholar of government, Professor Harold Lasswell of Yale, in his classic *Politics: Who Gets What, When, How*, had rejected the notion that governing was a form of scientific management.

Only when the political bosses got caught in a major scandal was the public willing to "throw the rascals out" and put in reformers. Most did not last long in office. Mayor La Guardia in New York, himself a man of the people, was able to fend off the bosses for twelve years. But he had the support of Franklin Roosevelt.

Bruce Smith's idea of police reform was that cops should be efficient and incorruptible public servants. He did not go so far as to approve of his sister

---

5. In that era, the busiest NYPD cop was "Det. McCann," so named because of the practice of tossing many crime reports into the garbage can. When a report could not be located, an officer might whisper to his superior that it was a case that had been assigned to McCann.

marrying one of them. The Western school of reform, headed by Berkeley police chief August Vollmer, was more ambitious. It advocated turning cops into professionals like doctors and lawyers. The former notion was sufficient for the "Goo Goo" reformers. The latter appealed to career cops. Vollmer's ideas were never implemented beyond a few small cities. In 1923, he was named chief of police of Los Angeles. Vollmer lasted only a year, because he was unable establish a mutual understanding with the gamblers and vice operators, along the lines of "You stay in your backyard and I'll stay in mine."

Among the national police leaders in 1950 were two outstanding figures. Donald Leonard, commissioner of the Michigan State Police, and O. W. Wilson, August Vollmer's protégé and former chief in Wichita, Kansas. Leonard, born in 1903, had joined the state police at the age of twenty. In 1947 he was named commissioner. The force had a reputation within law enforcement as a crack outfit, much praised by people like Bruce Smith. During his service, Leonard earned bachelor's and law degrees and, while still only a captain, served as president of the International Association of Chiefs of Police. In 1952 the city of Detroit tapped him to be its police commissioner.[6] There he succumbed to the siren song of politics, running three times for governor of Michigan. Although he came close to victory, he did not make it and ended his career as a lower-court judge in Detroit.

O. W. Wilson was born in South Dakota two years before Parker and came to California with his family as a boy. In 1920 he entered Vollmer's police program at the University of California, Berkeley. Vollmer's college cops were an elite group. Patrolling Wilson's adjoining beats were William Dean, later a major general in the United States Army who was captured in Korea, and African American Walter Gordon, a star on the college football team who went on to become governor of the Virgin Islands and judge of the United States Court of Appeals.

In 1928, Wilson was named chief of police of Wichita, where he remained until 1939. Later he lectured at Harvard and during the war served as a colonel of U.S. occupation forces in Germany. In 1950 he was appointed dean of the School of Criminology at Berkeley. In that same year he authored a text on police administration that invariably appeared on the list of books that civil service examiners recommended cops seeking promotion should read. Like Smith, he also worked as a consultant for management improvement groups like the International City Managers Association (ICMA). Though well respected among professional policing advocates, like Vollmer he was dismissed

---

6. At the time, Detroit, the automobile capital of the world and fifth-largest city in America, was a far more livable and vibrant community than it would be at the end of the century.

by big-city cops as a small-town chief with no experience in the big leagues of law enforcement. Had the Los Angeles city charter permitted the appointment of chiefs from outside, either Leonard or Wilson would have probably been a better choice than Parker.

The fact that Parker was a civil service chief was crucial. It made it hard to fire him. The five-man board of commissioners were all civilians who could spend only a few hours a week on police business. They had no staff other than what the department furnished them, and the personal prestige and expertise of most were modest. Only a major scandal would have enabled them to oust Parker.

Organized crime was also less of a problem than it had been. In the 1940s, local gamblers began transferring their operations to Las Vegas. However, one Los Angeles mobster, Mickey Cohen, still operated as if he were back in the old days. He constantly popped off to reporters, was a frequent target of assassination by other gangsters and engaged in various public disputes with Parker. In 1957, Parker filed suit after Cohen told ABC network reporter Mike Wallace that Parker was "sadistic and alcoholic." The network settled for sixty-seven thousand dollars.

For a time, the Los Angeles Sheriff's Office was a thorn in Parker's side. Sheriff Eugene Biscailuz was a local celebrity, whose department was frequently accused of having ties to gamblers. In 1957 he retired, and a former FBI agent named Peter Pitchess replaced him. Pitchess ran a clean organization and steered clear of controversy with Parker.

With Hollywood in his backyard, Parker immediately began to raise his profile. While most police departments had a press spokesman, Parker had twenty officers, headed by a captain, working full time to polish the image of the LAPD and its chief. The staff included Sgt. Gene Roddenberry, creator of *Star Trek*.[7] The public information office turned out puff pieces and distributed them throughout Southern California. It also put out an LAPD magazine. The department had a motion-picture unit and a police band that made promotional appearances all over the region. Parker himself was always willing to speak to civic and professional groups. Finally, the cops provided oversight for the country's second-highest-rated TV show, *Dragnet* (*I Love Lucy* was first), which broadcast a virtual infomercial for the LAPD every week in prime time. Many viewers came to believe that Sgt. Friday, played by actor Jack Webb, was typical of Los Angeles detectives.

Parker also moved to beef up the intelligence squad. Part of the reason was to keep organized crime out of Los Angeles. But it also compiled dossiers on

---

7. Who supposedly based the character of Spock on the chilling and rigid Parker.

persons of importance or anyone critical of the police. Parker secured a court ruling that the intelligence files were not public records but his personal property. In Tinseltown, spreading gossip and engaging in blackmail were well-established practices. Anyone who knew what was in Parker's dossiers could silence a critic or extract a favor from someone in power.

Parker imposed strict standards of discipline and appearance on LA officers. His force became the highest paid in the country and, with a twenty-year retirement, attracted many recruits. There was also prestige. Cadets in the academy were constantly reminded that they were the one-in-twenty-five applicants accepted by the department. Cops were checked periodically for fitness. Unlike some cities, where recruits were known to gain thirty pounds within a few years of graduation from the academy, Parker's officers were required to keep in shape.

To outsiders who visited the city, LA cops had a different aura than the ones they were used to back home. Parker's young, physically fit, spit-shined cops resembled military police more than the older and stouter rumpled men who patrolled most American towns. In the typical city, police responding to a call would take the time to sort through the versions of the various parties involved and would often hesitate in deciding whether or not to make an arrest. Parker's cops were taught to assume control of the situation immediately and take decisive action. A patrolling police car crew in another city might drive past a drunk staggering down the street. Parker's cops would stop, arrest the man and haul him to the drunk tank. The policy of requiring quick, decisive action was a two-edged sword. Sometimes hesitancy was a bad idea. A petty dispute might escalate into a full-scale brawl, or a citizen might think he could back the cop down from an arrest. But in some instances, swift action led to mistakes.

One problem was that Los Angeles had too few cops. At the beginning of Parker's administration, there were about two per thousand of population. The ICMA recommended three per thousand as the standard. By the end of the decade, the ratio of cops had declined to about 1.8 per thousand, or four thousand five hundred officers to police two and half million people. Chicago and New York had three per thousand. Had Parker asked for a significant increase in the police force, the fiscally conservative city administration would not have liked it. Instead, he relied on the aggressiveness and productivity of his cops to make up for the shortage of numbers.

Parker also knew better than to interfere with Thad Brown's detectives. Brown had many friends in city government, the business world and the newspapers. Besides, Parker, like many professional-style police chiefs, had little interest in detective work. His worst fault, known to insiders, was that, though a strict disciplinarian, he was not always disciplined himself. He drank frequently and to excess. On some occasions he became unable to care for himself. His chauffeur, future police chief Daryl Gates, later recounted how many a night he carried Parker into his house and put him to bed. Finally it got so bad that the chief was called on the carpet by Mayor Norris Poulson. He was the business community and the *Times*'s handpicked mayor. So Parker could not defy him or use another favorite weapon of that era—quiet whispers that someone was a Red. Poulson, who was to the right of Richard Nixon, had defeated Mayor Fletcher Bowron by branding him a Socialist for proposing that the city build public housing. If the mayor had told the business community that Parker was an unreliable drunk, likely to embarrass the city, it would have ended the chief's career. So Parker took the pledge. For a while, that made him more difficult to deal with than when he was drinking.

Attorney General Robert Kennedy was a great admirer of Parker. Some accounts suggest that he wanted to fire Hoover and put Parker in as FBI head. In 1963, when Frank Sinatra, Jr., was kidnapped, Hoover's FBI agents swarmed through Los Angeles, ignoring the locals completely.

By the end of the 1950s, the LAPD was generally rated the best police department in the country; thus, Parker could ignore criticism. African American Tom Bradley, LAPD class of 1940, had managed to rise to the rank of lieutenant, but he never hit it off with Parker. Eventually he resigned and in 1963 was elected to the city council. There he became a frequent critic of the police department. However, the council was no more powerful than the weak board of commissioners. Parker could always brush off Bradley's criticisms. Many of the city's blacks, who had come from the segregated South or Northern ghetto neighborhoods, regarded Los Angeles as a much better place to live. In his Pulitzer Prize-winning *The Making of the President 1960*, author Teddy White declared:

> Los Angeles is that city of the United States where the Negro probably receives the most decent treatment and has the best opportunity for decent housing. In Los Angeles, in 1955, Negroes constituted 11.3 percent of the population—yet only 14 percent of the jail population, 18 percent of those in public housing, 18 percent of those on relief. It is possible, if the Los Angeles figures are valid, that when Americans of any color are given full equality in jobs and in housing, they behave with full and equal responsibility too.[*]

In 1961, when Sam Yorty was elected mayor, Parker and the LAPD worried. In the '30s, Yorty had been known as an extremely radical leftist lawyer, and there were voluminous files on him in the intelligence squad. Yorty in the '60s was a much more conservative man and, as mayor, was a stronger supporter of Parker than Poulson had been.

The only major battles Parker lost were with the courts. In 1955, LAPD detectives planted secret microphones in the homes of a number of gamblers. In a case that arose from the arrest of one of them, Charles Cahan, the California Supreme Court ruled that the department had gotten its evidence through illegal trespass, thereby violating the Fourth Amendment guarantee against unreasonable searches and seizures. As a result of the Cahan decision, California became the only major state other than Illinois to have the exclusionary rule imposed upon police by its courts. A number of other judicial decisions in California limiting police power also rankled the chief.

* * * *

Coincident with the rise of Parker and the professional model of policing in Los Angeles, a similar scenario was being played out in Cincinnati, Ohio. Since the 1920s, local politics had been dominated by the Charter Party, a faction that had forced a change in the city charter to permit nonpartisan local elections and the direction of municipal government by a professional city manager. Often touted as a panacea, Charter was actually an alliance between civic-minded people of various political leanings, who had been shut out of local government by Democratic and Republican party bosses. By combining, the Charterites were able to outvote the other two parties. The movement did not extend beyond the local level, so Charterites remained Democrats or Republicans in state and federal elections.[8] Given their status as municipal reformers, the Charterites were committed to honest and efficient policing. However, until the middle of the century, the force tended to be a bit stodgy. In 1950, thirty-six-year-old Stanley Schrotel topped the civil service exam for chief (ranked as a colonel) as he had done in all other promotional tests he had taken. Like Parker, Schrotel had earned a law degree and distinguished himself in a number of departmental posts. While a strict and serious administrator, unlike Parker, he was not considered arrogant or abrasive. In a city with deep ties to its German heritage, Schrotel, a native Cincinnatian, fit in well. He also benefited from the fact that he had strong support from both the powerful conservative business community and many Democratic liberals who were Charterites. While the charter form of government called for a director of

---

8. One of the most notable figures in the Charter Party was President William Howard Taft's son Charles. Charles was much more liberal than his brother Robert, and when he ran for offices like governor on the Republican ticket, he was unsuccessful. Robert, who remained a Republican locally, was a U.S. Senator. In 1952, he narrowly lost the Republican presidential nomination to Dwight Eisenhower.

public safety to supervise police and fire divisions and the city jail, the director rarely interfered with Schrotel's operations.[9]

Cincinnati cops, like their Los Angeles brethren, were drawn from above-average young people who, in addition to passing the usual exams, had to appear in front of a selection board. At such sessions, Schrotel would often inquire of the other members whether they thought the candidate looked like a junior executive. If the answer was negative, he was unlikely to be appointed to the police division. In some instances, individuals were washed out on vague criteria such as "unsuitable appearance," which in a later era would have led to litigation.

Like the LAPD, the Cincinnati Police Department was relatively small, with the same ratio of about two officers per thousand population. Field interrogations were a staple of the vigorous, proactive patrolling characteristic of professional police departments. However, carrying them out was more difficult in Cincinnati because cops cruised in one-man cars. This made it harder for the officer to physically control the suspect.

A white businessman driving home late at night might be stopped after running a red light and asked for his driver's license. When the motorist fumbled through his coat pockets for his wallet, the cop might furtively grasp the handle of his revolver, though not withdraw it from his holster. Then he might require the motorist to step outside and place his hands on the car while the cop frisked him. A black citizen walking down a side street carrying a large shopping bag might be suspected of having the proceeds of a burglary. He, too, would be stopped and searched even though he protested that he was a half a block from his house. Friday evening was a traditional shopping time in the inner city, and as one black officer told the writer, "You were really busy [stopping people] then."

Both the white businessman and the black citizen were likely to vent to friends about their experience. However, the degree of sympathy they got would differ. When a businessman related his story to his fellow country-club members, some had probably heard Schrotel speak or read articles praising the Cincinnati police and few had experienced any bad encounters with cops. So they would tell the man that what happened was simply the small inconvenience one is subjected to in order to maintain a high level of public safety. When black citizens, who often had similar encounters with cops, heard the story, they might attribute the incident to racism.

Cincinnati also had an anti-loitering ordinance designed to assist police in maintaining public order. An Ohio state law required that

---

9. On Schrotel, see Appendix B.

within twenty-four hours of arriving in a new town, ex-convicts had to register with the police. Both were vigorously enforced.

Cincinnati police operations were essentially based on commonsense reality. Individuals carrying packages at night might well be hauling stolen goods. Cops were sometimes attacked by individuals they had stopped to question. Groups of street loiterers frequently engaged in disorderly conduct and harassed or frightened neighborhood residents. Ex-cons had high recidivism rates, and those who were rousted in Cincinnati might, in the future, avoid the city entirely.

For blacks, though, there was also another reality. In the 1950s, racism was pervasive. Cincinnati, often described as "a Northern town with a Southern exposure," was a five-minute drive across the bridge to Kentucky, where segregation was still the law. Some locals reflected the racial attitudes of their Southern origins. Even native Cincinnatians were not always as enlightened as Charles Taft.

By the end of the 1950s, Schrotel's police force was hailed as one of the best in the United States, and the Cincinnati police were written up in national publications such as *Life*, with Schrotel's picture on the cover. Like Parker, he was often spoken of as a possible replacement for J. Edgar Hoover as head of the FBI.

* * * *

In the '50s, policing as practiced in most of the country was far different from that in Los Angeles and Cincinnati.[10] A professional management style of policing could only exist in a community where political reform had been institutionalized and businessmen and professionals ran the local government.

Most police departments were traditional-style organizations. Professors James Q. Wilson of Harvard and Jerome Skolnick of the University of California, Berkeley, in their influential books *Varieties of Police Behavior* and *Justice Without Trial*, contrasted the different styles.[11] They described a professional police department as being governed by general rules that operate independently of circumstances, whereas the traditional department was more likely to rely on the highly personalized judgments of individual officers. According to them, the personnel of the professional departments were normally highly cen-

---

10. According to Bruce Smith, the two were among the top five in the country, the others being Detroit (under Donald Leonard), St. Louis and Milwaukee.**
11. Wilson referred to the traditional style as "watchman" and Skolnick as "old line." The terms did not catch on. Both men used the term "professional" for the alternative style.

tralized and tightly controlled, whereas a traditional department was decentralized and loosely controlled, with informal relationships more important than formal structure. Professional officers tended to be recruited on the basis of open competition without regard to residence. Their department posited crime control as their primary mission and used quantitative measures to gauge an officer's productivity in effecting arrests and clearing crimes. Traditional officers were generally recruited from among local residents, and maintenance of order was regarded as a policeman's principal task.

Boston was a prime example of a traditional force. In 1950, the ratio of police officers to population was 3.2 per thousand—one of the highest in the nation—and there were as many local police stations (sixteen) as in Los Angeles, which had three times the population and ten times the area. The police department was controlled by the Massachusetts state government, but the costs were assessed to the city government. Police worked shifts that hearkened back to the days of the night watch. Day cops worked from 8 a.m. to 6 p.m. and night cops from 6 p.m. to 12:30 a.m. and 12:30 a.m. to 8 a.m. on alternate nights. Despite the fact that a day man averaged a fifty-hour week and a night man thirty-five, cops with sufficient seniority usually opted for day duty, since the workload was lighter and their evenings could be spent with their families. Lieutenants in charge of each shift worked on the station desk rather than supervising patrolmen in the field.

The recruitment of police officers in Boston was also somewhat unusual. Whereas most cities relied on an intelligence/aptitude test to select cops, Boston applicants were required to memorize a one-hundred-nineteen-page state manual known as "the Blue Book," which contained information on laws, procedures and first-aid techniques. Since these were taught in the police academy, it was a waste of time to require pre-service applicants to master them. So the Boston police exam was essentially a memory test.

The police commissioner was Col. Tom Sullivan (whose military rank came from his militia service and whose last period of active duty was during the Spanish-American War). An engineer by profession, he had been appointed commissioner in 1943 in the aftermath of a major scandal.[12] Seventy-two years old in 1950, he would remain in office until 1957. The commissioner was virtually autonomous. He was appointed to a seven-year term by a governor who himself was elected for only two. As long as there were no major scandals,

---

12. In December 1942, the Coconut Grove nightclub caught fire, killing nearly five hundred people, many of them trampled trying to escape. An investigation determined that more patrons had been allowed to enter the premises than the club license allowed. A broader investigation of Boston nightlife disclosed alleged payments to the police from gamblers and nightclub operators. A number of officers, including the commissioner, were indicted (though not convicted) in the affair. The police commissioner was not reappointed.

governors were content to let "Colonel Tom," noted for his integrity, run the force without interference.

Second in command of the force, and the one relied on to supervise actual police operations, was Superintendent William Fallon, a career cop who had held the job since 1936. Indicted in the 1943 scandal, he had beaten the rap and remained superintendent until his retirement in 1959.

The chief problem in the 1950s was not corruption but a law-enforcement feud. In January 1950, local criminals held up the Brinks garage in the North End section of the city and made off with over a million dollars in cash and one and a half million dollars in checks and securities. During the investigation, the city police and the FBI repeatedly clashed and worked at cross purposes. Six years later, as the statute of limitations was about to run out, the FBI arrested eleven men for the crime. All were ultimately convicted at a state court trial. Most received life sentences and served on the order of fourteen years.[13]

After Col. Sullivan retired, another civilian commissioner was appointed. In 1961, CBS television aired a documentary entitled *Biography of a Bookie Joint.* The network set up its cameras to observe a Boston key shop which served as a front for a gambling center, and identified a number of people who came and went as Boston police officers. There were no arrests until U.S. Treasury agents and Massachusetts State Police conducted raids as the TV cameras rolled. The fallout led to the police department's being returned to municipal control and FBI Agent Ed McNamara (one of those involved in the Brinks investigation) being named police commissioner. While he was able to curtail corruption, he did not change the basic pattern of operations.

It might have been expected that Washington, DC, the national capital, would have maintained a professional police force of the type that reformers sought and which was functioning in places like Cincinnati and Los Angeles. However, the Washington Police Department in the '50s was no different from the other traditional forces. Since there was no mayor, the police superintendent (ranked as a major) was responsible to a three-member appointed board of municipal commissioners.

In practice, the superintendent took his orders from the congressional committee that controlled the district. In the 1940s, the chairman of the committee was Mississippi senator Theodore "The Man" Bilbo, arch symbol of Southern racism. When Bilbo was named to the chairmanship, he immediately warned all gangsters to get out of town within twenty-four hours. That prompted a good laugh from reporters and a yawn from gangsters.

---

13. On the Brinks robbery, see Appendix A.

Because Washington was a national city, its exam was open to residents of other states. Still, the department had trouble attracting recruits.[14] One thing that Washington did not have was a major organized crime problem. The mob realized that firing machine guns in the backyard of Congress and the president could lead to a federal drive against organized crime nationally. Despite the findings of the Kefauver committee, FBI director J. Edgar Hoover still maintained there was no such thing as a national crime syndicate. Had a body been found on the steps of the Capitol, Hoover might have been forced to take action.

With access to the federal treasury, the Washington police had nearly as high a ratio of cops to population as Boston. In addition, there was a separate U.S. Park Police and a capitol police force, which not only guarded Congress but also patrolled the adjoining streets.[15] Despite the brevity of their training, all Washington cops—Metropolitan, Park or Capitol—knew the cardinal rule of police work in the district: never offend a member of Congress.

In Washington, blacks, who by the end of the 1950s constituted thirty-five percent of the local population, had little influence. Certain facilities in the city, such as swimming pools, were still segregated. Within the police department, when a detail would be required at some presidential event, department orders would contain a paragraph directing commanders to "send white officers only."

Across the Northern states, in a belt of factory (mine and mill) towns running from New Jersey to Illinois, conditions were even worse. At least in the large metropolitan cities, there were elite social reform groups to put pressure on city government and powerful local newspapers who exposed scandals. In the mill towns, reform elements were scarce and most newspapers feared retaliation if they were too critical. Political bosses often had ties to organized crime or corrupt unions, and it was not unknown for violence to be used against critics. In many towns there were large sections of rough dives where a hardworking factory hand could find betting, booze, babes and brawls.

---

14. In the 1950s, the Washington police exam held in Chicago was conducted at the U.S. Customs House. Exactly two applicants (one of them the author) showed up to take the test. While four U.S. civil service officials patrolled the cavernous exam room, I busily answered multiple-choice questions geared to about eighth-grade level. A few days later, I was notified to report for duty in Washington. Had I not been about to enter the Chicago Police Department, I would have accepted the job. I was later informed that the recruit class I would have been joining received two days' instruction and then was sent out on patrol. In Chicago, I spent eleven weeks in training.

15. Most cities at the time had more than one police department. In Chicago the Park District Police, about a tenth the size of the city department, patrolled parks, beaches and boulevards. In Boston the Metropolitan District Commission Police, about a quarter the size of the city force, had similar responsibilities. In Los Angeles the Sheriff's Office and several separate municipalities had jurisdiction over certain enclaves within the city. New York City had a transit police force of several hundred officers and a bi-state agency, the New York/New Jersey Port Authority, which deployed about half of its thousand officers in the city.

In such communities the cops were drawn from townies, who exchanged their coveralls for blue uniforms. No one had to explain to them the political nature of their job or tell them that, in a city where a Saturday night carouse was not complete without a fight, the best defense was a good offense. It was no coincidence that such places produced a disproportionate share of professional football players.

In the late 1940s, William Westley, a graduate student in sociology at the University of Chicago, studied the police department in the steel manufacturing town of Gary, Indiana. Gary was an exceptionally rough place with a long history of political corruption. In 1953 a reform county district attorney and sheriff had been elected, but within a few years they, too, were sent to prison for graft. In the aftermath, a union leader explained that when politicians came to him for support, he would ask them, "After you are through stealing everything for yourself, what will you do for my boys?"***

At first the cops hesitated to speak to Westley, but eventually they began to open up about use of force, graft and political interference in criminal justice administration. Westley faithfully recorded the information and sought to explain, not condemn, the police activity.

Finally there was a non-municipal model of policing that had once been the hope of reformers like Bruce Smith—the state police. While most states only had highway patrols, which concentrated on traffic control, some maintained state police forces that provided full law enforcement service to the rural areas. The oldest and largest force was the one in Pennsylvania, formed in 1905 as a militarized constabulary to police labor and other disturbances in the mining districts. In essence, the Pennsylvania State Police were much more like the Royal Canadian Mounted Police, the Royal Irish Constabulary, the French Gendarmerie and the Italian Carabinieri than American police forces. The Pennsylvania troopers' critics often referred to them as Cossacks.

Cars and motorcycles came to replace horses, but the troopers did not take over traffic patrol duties. Instead, in 1923, a separate Pennsylvania Motor (traffic) Police was formed. Not until 1937 did the two forces merge, and the dominant image of the organization remained that of police rather than traffic cops.

In 1945 the troopers were headed by a sixty-four-year-old commissioner, Col. Cecil Wilhelm, who was one of the original 1905 appointees. Despite his age, he would remain in office until 1955. His department contained a relatively small complement of detectives and other specialists. Instead, the troopers spent most of their time on patrol and lending assistance to other police forces.

In a mill town area, the existence of a state police force (or even a large well-managed highway patrol like the one in Ohio) provided an alternative for those who sought a police career but did not wish to join a force mired in corruption. In Pennsylvania, the typical state police recruit was a high-school graduate, possessed superior athletic skill, and had a good military record. For some the state police was a virtual continuation of being in the Army, except that they spent their careers in their home states.

While professional policing was much praised by reformers and certain journalists, sometimes the practices of the traditional style were preferable. In the '50s a highly regarded management consulting group was contracted to provide advice to the Chicago Police Department. Its lack of knowledge of how the CPD functioned led them to a disastrous error which neither they nor the public realized. Most Chicago police districts had a detective car on duty twenty-four hours a day. Though manned by officers in plain clothes, the vehicle was a regular marked car with a red light on top. At first glance, it seemed incongruous to have detectives in a marked car. However, it meant that trained investigators arrived at the scene of a serious crime shortly after it occurred, whereas in many instances, hours could pass between the commission of a crime and the assignment of a detective from headquarters or the local district to investigate it. In addition, during busy periods they could be assigned to ordinary calls like disturbances if a regular radio car was not available. All in all, it provided a great resource for the police department—i.e., detectives who could do double duty as patrol car officers. The men who worked in them were among the most energetic officers on the force. The consultants recommended that the district detective cars be abolished and their vehicles be manned by run-of-the-mill uniformed cops, restricted to a particular sector of the precinct. It was the same kind of thinking that lay behind proposals to abolish the United States Marine Corps.

The whole affair was an example of how so-called experts did not understand police work, and knowledgeable cops lacked the ability to present their views in a coherent form. Unlike the U.S. Marines, who had a number of general staff officers, the American police did not have educated professionals to make their case.

Chapter 3

Detectives, Hoover, the Mob, and Youth Gangs

In 1953, most Americans did not feel threatened by conventional crime. Sometimes a gruesome murder, like the Black Dahlia case in Los Angeles or the mutilation of little Suzanne Degnan in Chicago, sent a wave of fear through a community. However, the national public was not so shocked by a murder in decadent Hollywood or notorious Chicago. At the time, there were no 24-hour TV cable networks with the capacity to assemble platoons of reporters, commentators and attention seekers to make a case two thousand miles away seem as immediate as a body dumped on the viewers' front lawn.

So, on a September morning in 1953, when a middle-aged woman came into an exclusive Catholic school in Middle America, Kansas City, Missouri, and announced that she was there to pick up her six-year-old nephew, the nun she spoke to was not suspicious of her story. The woman explained that the boy's mother had suffered a heart attack that morning and she was going to take him home. The school allowed her to leave with Bobby Greenlease, the son of a multimillionaire owner of a chain of auto dealerships. Not until afternoon, when a solicitous nun called the Greenlease home to offer sympathy and Mrs. Greenlease answered, did anyone suspect that Bobby had been kidnapped.

Mr. Greenlease immediately notified the Kansas City police chief, who alerted the FBI. When a demand was made for a six-hundred-thousand-dollar ransom, law enforcement officials urged Mr. Greenlease not to pay. However, he gathered the money, put it in a duffel bag and dropped it off at a specified location. It was the largest ransom paid in America up to that time.

The kidnapper, Bonnie Brown Heady, and her accomplice, Carl Austin Hall, then residing in St. Joseph's, Missouri, were a couple of losers who spent most of their time consuming drugs and alcohol. The plain-looking Heady, a former horsewoman and dog trainer, had no criminal record. The good-looking Hall came from an upper-middle-class private-school background and had served in the Marines during World War II. After running through a small inheritance, he began sticking up cab drivers in Kansas City. In 1951 he was arrested and sentenced to five years in the Missouri State Penitentiary. He was released after fifteen months.

Even before the ransom was paid, Hall killed little Bobby and disposed of his body in quicklime. After picking up the money, the kidnappers headed for St. Louis. There, Hall abandoned Heady, leaving her with just two thousand dollars, and moved to a motel, where he began paying a taxi driver to procure prostitutes for him. By then the kidnapping story was all over the news and the driver, suspicious of Hall's free spending, notified the boss of the cab company, who was also mixed up in local mob activity. Investigators later concluded that the owner called his friend, a St. Louis police lieutenant, Louis Shoulders, and between them they cooked up a scheme to obtain the ransom money. Shoulders, accompanied by Cpl. Elmer Dolan, a uniformed officer he had commandeered, went to the hotel where Hall was staying, arrested him, confiscated the ransom and later picked up Heady.

In Washington, FBI Director J. Edgar Hoover announced that the case had been solved by his bureau and identified Heady as a notorious criminal. Hoover's information was not correct. The FBI played no part in the capture, and the kidnapper, Bonnie Brown Heady, was not the hardened criminal with the same name. When Hall attempted to blame the crime on a derelict named Thomas Martin, the FBI did not find his story credible. Then, in a 360-degree turnaround, it ordered a nationwide manhunt for Martin on a charge of illegal flight to escape prosecution for murder. Eventually, it was determined that Hall's account was false. Hoover's efforts to claim unwarranted credit for breaking the case, his Bureau's misidentification of Heady and the wild goose chase it launched for Martin made the FBI look like Keystone cops.

The St. Louis Police Department—lauded a year earlier by Bruce Smith as one of the best in the country—suffered an even heavier blow to its reputation. When questioned by the FBI, Hall claimed that when he had been arrested, most of the six-hundred-thousand-dollar ransom had been with him in the motel. However, the St. Louis officers only vouchered half that amount. They were brought before a federal grand jury and questioned about the discrepancy. Shoulders and Dolan were charged with perjury, convicted and sentenced to three and two years' imprisonment, respectively.[1] In December 1953, just three

---

1. Dolan would later receive a presidential pardon.

months after kidnapping Bobby Greenlease, Hall and Heady were executed in the Missouri gas chamber.

The Greenlease case revealed many flaws in American detective work even when carried out by the vaunted FBI and a well-regarded big-city police department. Neither agency had broken the case. Rather, it was a cab driver, acting as a pimp, and his shady boss, in alliance with an equally shady police lieutenant, who fingered the kidnapper. In the larger sense, the case confirmed the truth behind the image of American detectives. They were not men of superior intelligence who solved crimes through a series of brilliant deductions or clever ploys. For practical purposes, such individuals were only found between the covers of a novel.[2] Nor were they professionals who had mastered a rigorous scientific discipline. American detectives were craftsmen who learned their trade from veterans by the apprentice system. Their traditional method of operation was to rely on informers, who sought rewards, revenge or absolution for their own crimes. In the 1920s, a famous New York detective, Mike Fiaschetti, declared: "It makes me tired to read how those bulls in books solve mysteries with their deductions. In the honest-to-God story of how the detective gets his man, it's stool pigeons." An even more famous New York detective of the time, John Cordes, said: "The most important pinches I have made came because some stool I knew phoned me and said, 'You'll find the hood who pulled the west side killing up in room 514 at the Bedford Hotel.'"[*] It took the FBI six years to make the arrest in the Brinks holdup, and then it came about because one of the gang fell out with the others and talked. The problem with informants, though, was that sometimes the detectives became too close to them. Many police scandals arose because an informer blew the whistle on a cop (or cops) he had worked with. The worst situation was when the officer knew the pigeon was committing serious crimes but turned a blind eye because he was too valuable to lose or too close to hurt.

In the 1950s, detectives had no interest in social scientists' theories of criminal behavior. It is doubtful that most chiefs of detectives in major cities had even heard of the work of top American criminologists like Edwin Sutherland or Thorsten Sellin, much less the European master Hans Gross. Continental detectives conducted their interrogations according to psychological principles, whereas in America it was catch as catch can. European police files contained much more information on criminals than was found in Ameri-

---

2. Usually it was an English one, in which an upper-class amateur sleuth solves a crime that professional "coppers," with a propensity for dropping their H's, cannot. Not only did such works provide a view of upper-class life—most murders seemed to take place at country-house parties—but they confirmed the essential superiority of the class system, where it was believed that a gentleman could always outdo a professional. Today we are presented with TV shows in which a British police detective, with a smattering of polish, is the hero and Oxford University, a hotbed of homicide.

can departments. In France and other countries, individuals checking into hotels were required to show their passport, and a list of the guests was furnished daily to the police.[3]

After the 1932 kidnapping and murder of the infant son of aviation hero Charles Lindbergh, a psychiatrist suggested to police that the kidnapper-killer had committed the crime to prove his own superiority to the man who had become the world's greatest hero by flying solo across the Atlantic. He believed the killer had so great an ego that if taken to a clinical setting instead of a police station and questioned by trained interrogators, he would likely boast of his exploits. Police brass, fearful that all that would do was build an insanity case for the defense, refused to follow the advice. Bruno Richard Hauptmann, the man eventually arrested, convicted and executed for the crime, fit the psychiatrist's profile to a tee, but the fact that he never confessed led to endless speculation that he may have been innocent.

Such forensic laboratories as existed played an auxiliary role in homicide investigations and usually a minor one in property crimes. However, because the public had seen movies and TV shows in which cops dusted for fingerprints, some officers carried talcum powder so that, when taking a burglary report, they could spread a little bit of it around and say they had checked for prints. The greatest shortcoming of all was that the priority in detective work was geared to solving crimes, which provided fodder for the media—the murder of a beautiful blonde who kept a little black book containing the names of her rich and famous gentlemen friends, or million-dollar jewelry heists. Less attention was paid to garden-variety crimes, which constituted the vast bulk of offenses.

Despite the shortcomings of American detectives, they became a major component of policing. In some cities, such as New York, Chicago, Los Angeles and San Francisco, the detective bureau often operated as an autonomous entity. Its strength came from the very fact that Hollywood and the news media constantly glamorized detectives, causing people to believe that cops in plainclothes possessed a higher rank and had greater skill than their brethren in blue. In the movies, patrol commanders, who obtained their ranks via a civil service examination, deferred to detectives (most of them civil service patrolmen) who were chosen by selection, which in practice often meant they were picked because of their political influence.[4]

---

3. In 1899, an Italian general was imprisoned for registering in a Nice hotel under a false name. Police suspected that he was engaged in espionage. However, a month later the president of France pardoned him when it was determined that his deception was prompted by the fact that his traveling companion was a Milanese ballerina.

4. A detective in Chicago became a local legend for his brilliant interviewing. Once, after a man was shot, the investigating officers could not get information from him because he spoke only Spanish. So our hero

Within the detective forces of major cities, its members were usually divided between headquarters specialists and district (precinct) generalists. In some, only the headquarters squads worked for the chief of detectives, while the precinct officers were under the command of the local patrol captain. The headquarters special squads usually handled big cases, such as high-profile murders, large-loss robberies, burglaries, hijackings and fraud. Many of these were perpetrated by professional criminals, so that a headquarters robbery detective had to know who the leading stickup men in the city were; and a burglary squad officer could sometimes tell by the way a lock was attacked which gang was responsible for the crime. An exception was the homicide/sex unit, which handled crimes not generally committed by professional criminals. The district generalists were expected to know the crime patterns and criminals in the few square miles of the district to which they were assigned.

The specialization of detectives sometimes led to ludicrous results. A police department with both burglary and narcotics squads might find its burglary detectives giving a pass to drug offenders in return for information on break-ins, while the narcotics detectives were showing similar leniency to burglars in return for information regarding drugs.

Most crimes were not solved by detective investigations. Indeed, most property crimes were not solved at all. Because thieves, burglars and robbers worked frequently, however, the law of averages kicked in and they were eventually caught. The ultimate value of detectives was not so much the cases they solved as that in a basically patrol organization they constituted the one element exclusively focused on crime. The good detectives were out and about picking up information that often proved helpful in future investigations. Some veteran detectives were walking encyclopedias on crime. The problem was that they preferred to convey their knowledge orally to colleagues rather than by writing up reports that could be read by a larger group.

Certain detective bureaus also ran a "charm school," where they made the city's elite feel that they were being given inside information on the cases that dominated the headlines. It was amusing to listen to the CEO of a Fortune 500 company telling his fellow executives, "Jim [the chief of detectives] told me they know who killed the chorus girl, and it's not the one that the papers think

---

pushed himself forward, saying: "Let me talk to him; I worked among these people and I understand their lingo." Thereupon he proceeded to ask the victim, "Señor, who shoota you." So strong was his clout that he could not be returned to uniformed duty. At the opposite end of the spectrum, an international con man once told a Chicago officer that he was an American secret agent. The basis of a con man's success is his ability to convince people that he is telling the truth. The detective, utilizing non-directive interrogation techniques, allowed the man to go on and on with his story. The suspect spun a long tail of his adventures in China during World War II. In the course of this, he said that he had worked under the direction of the U.S. provost marshal in Kunming, China. When the detective (truthfully) informed him that he had been the U.S. provost marshal in Kunming, the air went out of the suspect and he confessed.

did it." At the time, I thought it was silly. But many organizations, including Hoover's FBI, survived and thrived because they took care to cultivate the elite. A detective commander who had powerful friends in the business world could not easily be removed by his superiors. In addition, police brass were usually of an age close to retirement eligibility, and the prospect of a well-paid corporate post was attractive to them.

Some crimes were not solved because of inherent problems in investigating them. A criminal had a better chance of avoiding arrest if he left town, because there was no nationwide criminal intelligence network. In the 1930s, a so-called "Mad Butcher" cut off two dozen heads in the Cleveland area, but local police, directed by Elliot Ness, never caught him. Some investigators believed that the killer had previously cut off a dozen heads in a particular area of Pennsylvania and that he may have gone on for years, killing over a hundred people in other states.** Not until the 1970s did the problem of interstate serial killers receive major attention.

My own experience with serial killers began on July 14, 1966, when an intruder stabbed to death eight student nurses in their town house dormitory a few blocks from the Chicago hospital where they worked. A ninth nurse, who managed to hide, escaped the slaughter. Detectives from the homicide section initially took charge of the investigation. In addition, detectives from the burglary section (whose 350 members I commanded at the time) were assigned to the case on the possibility that the killer may have been a professional thief. While examining the crime scene one of my detectives, a former merchant seaman, noticed that the nurses had been tied with sailors knots. Across the street from the murder site was a Maritime Union hiring hall. The detective and his partners went to the hall and came up with the name of one Richard Speck who had recently sought to find a berth on a departing ship. When one was not immediately available he behaved in a truculent manner.

A man of the same description as Speck had been seen around the neighborhood on the day before the murders. Later it would be learned that Speck had a criminal record with over 40 arrests in different states and at the time was a wanted on a burglary charge in Texas. Detectives began combing the cheap hotels and bars in the Port Calumet district looking for him. They came close to catching Speck but they were always a few minutes behind him. A detective sergeant had a hiring official call Speck to tell him that he had found a ship for him, but the suspect would not bite. When fingerprints found at the scene were determined to match those of Speck, the public was alerted to be on the lookout for him. With his picture in the papers and on television Speck fled to the near North Side skid row district along Clark Street with my detectives following right behind. Again, they just missed him at several locations. Realizing he was trapped and arrest was imminent, the fugitive cut his wrist and elbow and was taken to a hospital where an alert doctor identified him from his newspaper picture.

The burglary detectives who had developed the case became the arresting officers. During the chase they had invited me to join them in making the arrest. I declined because I had not personally contributed much to the investigation and for me to be photographed with the prisoner would have been deeply resented by the homicide section and the top brass of the police department. Later, when newspapers inquired why burglary had to do homicide's job, I stated that on orders of a deputy chief my officers had been detailed to work for the homicide commander, so, in effect, homicide had broken the case. It's the kind of answer that doesn't win you much glory but convinces your colleagues and superiors that you are a team player. It also was essentially the truth.

A notable feature of the case was the quick identification of the killer and the way that the detectives were able to elicit information about his whereabouts and keep on his trail until he was caught. It was an illustration of how well savvy streetwise detectives could operate in cases of this nature. I was interested in what other crimes Speck may have committed since it was learned that several women he had known across the country had either turned up dead or disappeared. I suspected that he was a serial killer before that term was in general use. There were few details about his other liaisons with women, so I thought it might be sensible for the prosecution to offer a life sentence in lieu of the death penalty if Speck would confess to all of his crimes. But the idea was impractical. There would be severe public criticism of such a deal, and from a defense standpoint, it would leave Speck open to the death penalty for murder if another jurisdiction demanded his extradition.

Speck was sentenced to death, though when the U.S. Supreme Court outlawed capital punishment, he was commuted to life imprisonment. Two decades later he received national publicity when hidden cameras caught him and other convicts in state prison living the life of Riley. In 1991, a day short of his 50th birthday, he died of a heart attack. Usually even the worst murderer can elicit sympathy in some quarters. However, to my knowledge, there was never any for Richard Speck.

Solving other cases could prove embarrassing to important people. In 1955, international financier and criminal Serge Rubinstein, forty-six, was found strangled to death in his five-story Manhattan mansion. Police quickly concluded that the killer, or killers, had not forced their way into the home but had been admitted. Rubinstein's wealth was in excess of ten million dollars (equivalent of nearly one hundred million dollars today). A business associate volunteered that Rubinstein had not been murdered by robbers but that it was "a mob job." Police questioned a number of the victim's enemies, including three men who had been arrested on charges of attempting to extort five hundred thirty-five thousand dollars from him.

Among the financiers and politicians Rubinstein had relations with was a prominent U.S. senator. An intensive investigation might have embarrassed a number of powerful people, even if they were not involved in the murder. The NYPD caught some of the fallout. It was learned that Rubinstein had employed private detectives to tap phones of rivals and his mistresses. So the police raided a wiretapping center on East 55th Street and seized equipment. For some reason they did not charge anybody criminally, and the raid was kept secret. When the operating head of the Citizens Crime Commission of New York City, William Keating, revealed the affair, he became the one that law enforcement targeted. District Attorney Frank Hogan summoned him before a grand jury and demanded that he identify his informants. When Keating refused, he was immunized and ordered to talk. When he still declined, he was jailed (for one week) for contempt of court. Ironically, it was Hogan who had recommended Keating, one of his assistant district attorneys, for the Crime Commission job. While working for the DA, Keating had solved a mob murder on the waterfront and sent the killers to the electric chair. So impressive was his work that Hollywood made a movie entitled, *Slaughter on 10th Avenue*, with Richard Egan as Keating.

The Keating affair might have been meant to serve as warning to investigators not to interfere in the Rubinstein case. Given the many leads and the knowledge that some investigative agencies possessed about Rubenstein, it does not appear to have been an exceptionally hard case to solve.[5]

There was also the problem of competition within police ranks. In the late 1950s, a series of child murders in Chicago was investigated by city detectives from the homicide, sex and youth squads, as well as from districts where other children had been killed. When the corpses of two murdered sisters, named Grimes, were discovered in an unincorporated area of the county, the Sheriff's Office became involved. Sheriff Joe Lohman was a sociologist-politician who lectured at the University of Chicago. In 1954, because of the disasters the Democratic machine had sustained in the 1950 and 1952 elections, not the least being running America's richest cop, "Tubbo" Gilbert, for sheriff, the

---

5. The Rubinstein murder was the subject of a Hollywood movie, *Death of a Scoundrel*, but the crime has remained a mystery into the twenty-first century. Keating was fired from the commission, and became a pariah. In 1957 he was burned to death in a barbecuing accident. By that time the commission itself had folded. Over twenty years later, when a new crime commission was being formed, individuals approached about heading it recalled Keating's fate and declined to be considered. As noted in the Introduction, I took the job and remained in it for nearly twenty-seven years.

new county chairman, Richard J. Daley, selected a "blue ribbon" ticket of candidates, who had not previously sought elective office. Lohman the scholar seemed like a good choice for sheriff. However, he harbored the modest ambition of becoming governor. In 1957, when his county detectives arrested a skid-row drifter named Benny Bedwell for the murder of the Grimes sisters, it was obvious to the city police investigators on the case (like this writer) that Bedwell was totally innocent. Yet Lohman warned Chicago detectives not to interfere. The case was so weak that within twenty-four hours the state's attorney dismissed the charges and the press had a field day attacking Lohman. The affair did nothing to persuade Chicago cops that academic training was of any value in criminal investigations, or that elite scholars were of higher moral character than street cops.[6]

The country's most famous and powerful detective chief was FBI Director J. Edgar Hoover, even though he had never worked a case in the field. Holder of a law degree from a Washington night school, he had become a government bureaucrat during World War I, although as a former captain of his high school's ROTC unit he might have been expected to don a uniform. In 1919, at age twenty-four, he was named head of intelligence for the U.S. Department of Justice. There he was the architect of the crackdown on radicals which culminated in the famed "Red Raids." Despite his role in the raids, in 1921, when his bosses, Attorney General A. Mitchell Palmer and Bureau of Investigation Director William Flynn, were dismissed, Hoover was appointed assistant director of the Bureau. In 1924, after his new bosses, Attorney General Harry Daugherty and Director William Burns, were ousted for using federal agents to spy on U.S. Senators investigating the Teapot Dome scandal, Hoover again avoided blame and was made director of the Bureau. He quickly fastened his grip on the agency and retained it for the next forty-eight years.

In an agency with offices scattered from Hawaii to Puerto Rico, there was bound to be a powerful drive for local autonomy. Not so in Hoover's FBI. Every agent, supervisor or special agent in charge molded his conduct to the rules, both formal and informal, that "Mr. Hoover" laid down. Because the Bureau did not operate under civil service, an employee could be dismissed at will. No women and very few minorities were hired as agents. In an age when some federal doors were closed to Catholics, Hoover hired them because the Church's conservative views, particularly its attitude towards Communism, appealed to him. Fame and accolades came to Hoover and the FBI for carrying

---

6. Lohman had to settle for election to the state treasurer's office, but his stock had fallen so low that he resigned and took O. W. Wilson's old job as dean of the School of Criminology at the University of California, Berkeley. He died in 1968 at the age of fifty-eight.

out the 1930s war on "Public Enemies" and the World War II era roundup of Axis agents.

The favorable publicity that Hoover generated made him and his bureau very popular with the public and gave him great political influence. Still, he never felt secure in the Washington jungle. He strove constantly to protect and expand his turf. During World War II, U.S. Army Chief of Staff General George C. Marshall described Hoover as "more like a spoiled child than a responsible officer."**** Within law enforcement Hoover had few supporters and many enemies, though most of the latter kept quiet because of fear of retaliation by the Bureau.

Hoover's greatest failure was his unwillingness to take on organized crime groups. In many cities the mob not only ran gambling and vice operations but also were a significant presence in labor unions, legitimate businesses and politics. In the 1960s, an eminent attorney, appointed to look into the mob's influence in New Jersey, found that organized crime had infiltrated virtually every facet of life in the Garden State, with the exception of the Church. He noted that "too many local governments are responsive more to the mob than to the electorate that put them in office."+ In New York City, the five mob families had a stranglehold on the garment industry, the waterfront and construction. In Chicago, legislators and other elected officials controlled by the mob were so well known that newspapers simply referred to them as "the West Side bloc," though the "bloc" was not confined to that part of town. The New Orleans Mafia family had immense power in the city and state. The mob's inroads in the Teamsters Union gave them a voice in national transportation policy and also provided them with funds to build their Las Vegas casinos.

Despite the national scope of organized crime, as documented by the Kefauver committee, Hoover continued to maintain that the mobs were local gangs whose activities did not violate federal statutes which the FBI was authorized to enforce. In the aftermath of the Kefauver investigation, Hoover made a slight concession. He instituted a "Top Hoodlum Program" (THP), in which agents compiled reports on major organized-crime figures. In 1954 a report from the San Francisco FBI office, which was circulated to offices across the country, identified "presumed heads of the Mafia" in sixteen American cities. The problem was not that Hoover was unaware of the Mafia but that he did not want to do battle with it. While some writers have attributed this to his being bribed or blackmailed, forty years after his death there has yet to be any evidence uncovered to support either allegation.[7]

---

7. While there is no evidence that Hoover was ever entrapped in some blackmail scheme, such tactics were standard in the world of organized crime. When Senator Kefauver came to Chicago to hold hearings, he allegedly wound up in a bedroom at the Drake Hotel with a young beauty. As a souvenir of the occasion, the

Hoover's real reasons were most likely political. He had witnessed the disastrous attempts of the Prohibition Bureau to enforce the dry laws, an undertaking that came to be characterized by widespread bribery of its agents, disgrace for the administrators and a general lessening of respect for law enforcement. His own agency had come into existence in 1908 when the U.S. Secret Service had been stripped of some of its authority in retaliation for bringing a case that led to the conviction of a U.S. senator. Unable to use Secret Service men to conduct its investigations, the Department of Justice obtained authorization from President Theodore Roosevelt to create its own bureau of investigation. (In 1935 it was given the prefix "Federal.") Attacking organized crime could expose Hoover's agency to similar problems, and himself to retaliation from the Mafia's political friends.

At the local level, many police departments were controlled by politicians who were on mob payrolls. In some neighborhoods, gambling was a popular recreation and the men who ran it contributed to neighborhood charities and churches. Even the business community, normally in favor of reform, did not want to see vice shut down. Cities like Chicago and San Francisco were popular convention and tourist towns. In Kansas City, hard by the Bible Belt, local business leaders reminded the police that visitors "did not come to town to sleep."

Some cities had special police anti-mob units, like Parker's LAPD intelligence squad. Chicago had "Scotland Yard" (the popular name of a special squad working directly for the police commissioner until it was abolished in 1955) and New York had a central intelligence bureau. Mostly such units harassed local organized crime figures, tapping their phones and occasionally rousting them. But their efforts were essentially designed to keep the mobs off balance so that they did not become too bold. In 1946, Genovese gangsters caused a furor in New York City by murdering a political worker on Election Day. Later a Lucchese capo, Johnny Dioguardi, had journalist Victor Riesel blinded by acid for writing stories exposing the rackets. In 1952, the Chicago mob killed a political candidate, Charlie Gross, causing a huge outcry. In situations like this, the local police anti-gangster squads went into action for brief periods. Some journalists and civic organizations forecast that if not stopped, organized crime, *aka* "the Mafia," would become so powerful that it would run many states and cities and would exert significant power at the

---

Chicago mob presented him with a film of the event. This is thought to explain why Kefauver allowed Capt. Gilbert to testify in executive (secret) session.

In 1961, the former Notre Dame and Buffalo Bills star quarterback, George Ratterman, ran for sheriff in mob-dominated Campbell County, Kentucky. After he met somebody for a drink in nearby Cincinnati, he ended up in a Kentucky bedroom with stripper April Flowers lying alongside him. In this instance, Attorney General Robert Kennedy rode to the rescue, exonerated Ratterman and jailed the men behind the frame-up.

national level. By the 1950s the mobs were already so strong that only the national government was capable of stopping them.

On November 14, 1957, the FBI would experience a Pearl Harbor-type event that would force them into a war against the American Mafia which continues into the twenty-first century. Near the southern New York village of Appalachian (pronounced locally "Apple-aykin"), state troopers arrested sixty-three mob figures, from all over the country, who were meeting at the rural estate of a local boss, Joe Barbara. Among those seized were Vito Genovese, head of New York's premier mob family, and an individual usually thought of as the top Mafioso in the United States. Other notables arrested included the bosses of three more of New York's five families and the head of the Philadelphia family. Later it was established that among the estimated thirty or forty men who escaped the scene, arrived in the area after the raid or were clever enough to remain in Barbara's house (which the police had no authority to search) were New York City's fifth family boss, Tommy Lucchese, and the mob bosses of Detroit and Buffalo. Of the men who could be proven to have attended, more than two-thirds were from the East, eight were from the Midwest, three from beyond the Rockies and four more from the South or Cuba, plus a visitor from Italy. They ranged in age from forty-three to sixty-six. The raid itself has often been presented as hick cops stumbling on the meeting. However, it later came out at the federal trial which arose from it that state police sergeant Edgar Croswell, who had been keeping an eye on Barbara for years, got wind of the meeting, if not its purpose, via wiretapping.

The news of the raid produced both joy and embarrassment. The law enforcers and journalists who had been warning about the Mafia in the wake of the Kefauver committee were delighted. Skeptics—FBI Director J. Edgar Hoover among them—who had denied that there was a national syndicate, were hard pressed to explain what all those gentlemen were doing in a remote corner of New York State. It was never determined exactly why the meeting took place. Most likely it was a combination of reasons. Longtime mob boss Frank Costello, the "Prime Minister" of New York City organized crime, had been shot and wounded six months earlier, and his top ally, the "Lord High Executioner" Albert Anastasia, was assassinated a few weeks before the Appalachian meeting. There were also decisions that had to be made about the narcotics trade. In any event, the stunning fact for the FBI was that a virtual congress of the leading elements of American organized crime was convened, and the only police agency on the case was a rural patrol force assisted by a couple of federal alcohol tax agents. As Robert Kennedy, then counsel to a Senate rackets committee, told associates, "The FBI didn't know anything, really, about these people, who were the major gangsters in the United

States…. That was rather a shock to me."[8] After Appalachian, the FBI went after the mobs, but not at the same pace with which they had pursued public enemies in the 1930s. Then, in 1961, the appointment of Bobby Kennedy as attorney general by his brother, the president, lit a fire under Hoover.

The Kefauver investigation, which alerted the public to the workings of organized crime and its relationship to police and political corruption, spilled over into American policing generally. In 1952, a new city administration in Philadelphia scrapped the safety director post and named a tough career cop, Tom Gibbons, as commissioner to lead a cleanup of the department. In 1954, a new administration in New York appointed Frank Adams, a prominent lawyer, as police commissioner; when he stepped down, he was succeeded by Chief Inspector Steve Kennedy, a no-nonsense career cop. In 1956 the newly elected mayor in San Francisco chose Detective Inspectors Frank Ahern and Tom Cahill, who had worked with the Kefauver committee, to be, respectively, chief and deputy chief of police.

* * * *

The 1950s was the final era of the local police detective celebrities, men like Los Angeles' John St. John, Texas Ranger John Klevenhagen and his frequent side partner Houston detective Buster Kern, and Chicago's Frank Pape.

John St. John just missed becoming as famous as the mythical Sgt. Joe Friday of *Dragnet*. He joined the force in 1941 and eight years later was transferred to the homicide division. One of his first assignments was working on the Black Dahlia case. Shortly afterward he was more successful in solving a murder in which the victim's body had been dismembered in Griffith Park. Because it had been so mutilated, it took some time for St. John to reassemble the parts. His work on the case earned him the nickname "Jigsaw John." Among other well-known cases he handled was the murder of a police officer that was made famous in Los Angeles detective Joe Wambaugh's *The Onion Field*.

After a book about him entitled *Jigsaw John* appeared, NBC-TV producers believed so fascinating a figure would make for an interesting TV series. In 1976, *Jigsaw John* went on the air. But by that time the public no longer favored businesslike cops such as Joe Friday of *Dragnet*. They preferred characters like Kojak, Baretta, Columbo, and Dirty Harry. Where Friday used to listen respectfully to his captain, Harry Callahan dressed down mayors and police

---

8. In fact, as the report from the FBI's San Francisco office indicated, the Bureau knew more than it let on. However, Hoover, who did not like Robert Kennedy, did not provide him with as much information as he possessed.

chiefs. St. John served over fifty years in the LAPD, retiring in 1993 when he was seventy-five. In honor of his long service, he was allowed to wear detective badge number one.

Texas Ranger John Klevenhagen operated in a milieu not entirely removed from the Wild West. In 1929, impatient to be a cop, though only seventeen, he used false ID and makeup to appear older and became an officer in Bexar County, which included San Antonio, Texas. Soon he progressed from riding a motorcycle to being a detective. In 1941, he won appointment to the Texas Rangers, an elite force of state police investigators, and was assigned to a detachment based in Houston. The nature of his work is exemplified by his remark that he never shot anyone who did not shoot at him first. In Houston, he frequently worked with a local detective, C. V. "Buster" Kern. In 1952, the pair charged one Diego Carlino for murder. Mr. Carlino was defended by nationally known attorney Percy Foreman. Foreman argued that Kern and "Texas Johnny" had beaten Carlino into confessing. Both denied it on the stand, however, when the jury returned a not-guilty verdict, the two lawmen vaulted over the railing separating the defendants and their attorneys from the witnesses and began pistol-whipping Foreman with their .45s. At the time, Percy was on crutches. Both officers were brought before the judge and fined twenty-five dollars, which they refused to pay. In the end, an admirer paid it for them.

Texas Johnny remained a legend and was promoted to captain of Rangers. He died of a heart attack in 1958 at age forty-five. Buster Kern went on to become the longtime sheriff of Harris County (Houston). A later successor as sheriff was John Klevenhagen, Jr., son of Texas Johnny.

In 1963, during his time as sheriff, Kern experienced echoes of the Foreman incident. He jailed one William Whirl for burglary, but the district attorney dismissed the charges for insufficient evidence and ordered the prisoner released. Somehow Whirl got lost in the shuffle and remained in jail for nine more months. He then sued the sheriff for detaining him and also for not returning his artificial leg. A judgment of twenty-five thousand dollars was levied against Kern, who claimed that he could not pay it. So several thousand local citizens each put up five dollars to pay the debt.

One day a crowd of civil-rights protesters was marching in a picket line outside Chicago police headquarters. They were demanding that the deputy chief of detectives, Frank Pape, be fired as a brutal racist. Among those marching in the group was an individual of medium size and boyish appearance who could have been taken for a Sunday school teacher. He began asking others in line about how Pape looked so he could boo the villain should he suddenly come out of police headquarters. One of the leaders of the demonstration described Pape as a huge, brutal-looking man. Of course, the questioner was Pape himself.

Frank Pape joined the Chicago Police Department in 1935 when he was only twenty-three. He quickly drew an assignment to the detective bureau, so obviously he had some well-placed friends. Still, he was not a political cop but a hardworking investigator. For ten years he labored in obscurity. Then, one day, he and his partner were assigned to arrest a fugitive wanted on a robbery warrant from Cleveland. When they spotted him, the man started to run. Pape's partner called out to the man to halt but instead the fugitive pulled out a gun and shot and killed the partner.

Over the next few years, Pape killed several criminals. He and his machine gun became a famous Chicago pair. Ethnically his targets ran the gamut from Irish (he was himself Irish and German) through Italian, Greek, etc. The only groups missing were blacks and other racial minorities. Pape rose to lieutenant in charge of the robbery squad and was eventually a deputy chief of detectives. During the time he headed the squad, it was the only investigative unit in the bureau, other than narcotics, that had black detectives. African-American cops who worked for him swore by Pape as a man who was totally fair and completely color-blind.

One night a woman reported that as she and her husband entered their home, a gunman attempted to hold them up and had shot and killed her husband. As was standard procedure, she looked through police photo books of known robbers and almost immediately picked out a black man who was suspected of other murders. Pape personally led the squad that went to arrest the fugitive. It turned out that the woman was lying. Her boyfriend had killed the husband and she had selected the suspect's picture almost at random. The affair led to an oft cited Supreme Court ruling on whether a plaintiff had to exhaust his state remedies before being allowed to bring a case in federal court.[++] Those in the department who never liked Pape took advantage of the opportunity to cut him down to size.[9]

Each of the aforementioned detectives reflected the values of his time and place. Klevenhagen and Kern were the personification of a heroic Old West lawman, a type long admired in Texas. St. John was more systematic and professional in his work, like the scientific management that lay at the heart of the LAPD. Pape was a big-town guy who knew the city intimately and whose personal courage (and the support of admirers) allowed him to step boldly into difficult situations and take charge.

---

9. Let the record show that while I respected Pape, I doubt that the feeling was mutual. I suspect this was because he was a man who acted on instinct, while I was more analytical. Both types have been successful in their investigations, and on occasion both have fallen on their faces.

* * * *

Major police attention in the 1950s also began to focus on a phenomenon different from handling big cases or combating organized crime. Every American generation has decried the shortcomings of youth. Young people are thought to be less industrious and more inclined to misbehave than their forebears. In the twentieth century, this feeling was accentuated by the transition from a small-town rural society to an urban one that occurred about the same time that ownership of automobiles became common. Both developments allowed youngsters the means to roam about far from their homes.

In 1955 there was a fight or "rumble" between two gangs in the southwest Chicago neighborhood known as Bridgeport. Youth gangs were an old story in Chicago, but their altercations generally did not result in homicide. In this instance, though, a fourteen-year-old kid nicknamed "Cookie," who had been in the paratroopers before they discovered his age, had brought a shotgun to the fight. During the heat of the battle he fired it, killing another youngster. Although I had nothing to do with the case, "Cookie's" shotgun blast helped shape my life.

The killing shocked the neighborhood, especially its political leader, Richard J. Daley, who had just been elected mayor of Chicago. Daley ordered the police to create a special squad to deal with youth gangs. To head the unit, the department selected Lt. "Iron Mike" Delaney. His nickname came from the athletic fields rather than his behavior on the police force. Once a star athlete in every sport, now in his forties, he was a devout Catholic, soft-spoken and a polished gentleman.

Each district was ordered to forward names of officers who might be assigned to the new unit. The usual procedure in such a situation was for districts to send the names of their drunks and disciplinary cases to get rid of them. However, with Mayor Daley personally involved, it didn't seem like a good time to play games. In addition, a deputy commissioner, one of two in the department, was conducting interviews for the unit which indicated the importance headquarters placed upon the matter. So the district captains sent for interview cops who were neat, sober and reliable, the kind who, in the Army, would have been detailed to an honor guard. The one thing that most lacked was a political sponsor. Now each was, in effect, being given a chance to become a detective on merit. The trouble was, virtually none of the interviewees wanted the job. For some it smacked too much of social work. Others thought it would be a temporary assignment, after which they would be returned to their districts.[10]

Building on the foundations of the old juvenile bureau, Delaney revamped the unit by picking active young cops of an athletic "all-American" appearance to engage in proactive policing against the city's violent youth gangs. While Delaney's outfit was a favorite of the mayor's, it was looked on with suspicion by the department hierarchy. Indeed, it was believed that if it were up to the police commissioner, it would not have existed. One problem was that Delaney was a decade ahead of his time. Influenced by the liberal wing of the Catholic Church, he was constantly decrying racial injustice and making public statements such as, "Welfare should not be cut, it should be increased." His unit was praised by social workers and human-rights advocates, who were not generally fond of police.[11]

Any other commander who voiced similar views would have found himself transferred to a Siberia post like the dog pound. But Delaney in person was not a shouting scold, and some brass still recalled him as their boyhood hero. Catholic leaders held him up as a model member of the laity; besides, the mayor liked the unit. Its roving squads were the primary police element in keeping gangs under control. Yet in doing so, it did not incur charges of brutality or civil-rights violations.

At a meeting in 1957, a group of social workers congratulated Daley on his fine youth bureau. Pleased, he announced extemporaneously that he was going to expand the unit into the largest such squad in the country. When the police department checked to determine what number of officers were required to achieve that goal, it was found that it would probably take another forty or fifty transfers into the unit. This made the police commissioner apoplectic, but he knew better than to make a liar out of the mayor. So into the unit came forty or fifty new all-American boys.[12]

Other cities were experiencing youth problems. New York had spawned a number of so-called "fighting gangs." From the time he took office as

---

10. I was one of those interviewed. My plan was to impress the deputy commissioner, then talk him into sending me to the cartage (hijacking) squad or some similar unit. A wily old veteran, he knew how to handle young whippersnappers. He asked me the trick question, "If you were sent to the new gang unit, would you do a good job?" No one was foolish enough to say no, so naturally I said I would do my best wherever I was sent. Thus I became one of Mike Delaney's boys.

11. He was also a close friend of the leftist writer James T. Farrell, who was persona non grata in his old Southside community for telling too much about his neighbors and friends in his books. Delaney, who appears in the Studs Lonigan series as Dan O'Donoghue, was one of the few people portrayed favorably by Farrell.

12. Delaney's unit was not composed entirely of ex-seminarians. However, it was not touched by corruption, and there were strict orders against using force except in self-defense. One problem was that occasionally one of his all-American boys got involved with an (adult) all-American girl, and the affair ended up in the tabloids under captions like "The Kissing Cop."

commissioner in 1955, Steve Kennedy constantly warned about the menace from violent youth, sparking a debate with social workers that continued until the end of Kennedy's tenure. In 1960, in typical New York fashion, a gang killing in a Manhattan park was turned into a hit musical, *West Side Story*. Its philosophy seemed to be summarized in one of its songs, which declared "We are depraved because we are deprived." Another classic movie summarized the youth crime situation by titling it *Rebel Without a Cause*.[13]

Mexican gangs had long been targets of the LAPD. At Christmastime 1951, a group of drunken officers at the Wilshire division started beating up seven young Mexicans whom they (wrongly) believed had maimed a police officer attempting to arrest them. Four officers were sent to jail over the affair, six were fired and a number of others received disciplinary action.

From my little corner of the police world I began to discern that detective operations like cartage investigations were the past, and gangs were the future. Because of the many contacts our unit had with the African-American community, I also took early notice of the emerging civil-rights movement. When civil-rights protests and youth rebellion became commonplace in the 1960s, I was not surprised, nor did I see it as J. Edgar Hoover did: part of some sinister plot.

---

13. At that time, the most feared gang in Chicago was a group of violent white youths from my neighborhood, the Stockyards district, who called themselves the Rebels. Eventually, law-enforcement pressure put the gang out of business.

Chapter 4

Reading the Riot Act:
Jenkins in Atlanta, the Bull in Birmingham

A merica was always a land of violence, although in some periods this was
more apparent than in others. In the 1930s, there were many clashes
between strikers and management. In the immediate postwar period, there was
less domestic turmoil. In the fateful year 1960, beginning the decade that
changed America, there was a riot in the same city that had witnessed the VJ
Day riots. Again, it was a harbinger of the future, but it was not seen as such at
the time.

On the morning of Friday, May 13, 1960, the House Committee on Un-
American Activities held hearings in San Francisco's city hall. Its inquiry was
directed at Communist influence in the shipping industry and the Bay Area
generally. For over thirty years, the waterfront had been the scene of strikes
and riots involving the International Longshoremen's Union, run by the alleged
Communist Harry Bridges. So the investigation that the committee pursued
was not a new one.

The format of the hearings was a familiar part of the postwar landscape.
After preliminary questions, the members and staff got down to the crux of the
matter by asking witnesses "Are you now or have you ever been a member of
the Communist Party?" Usually the witness tried to make a speech and was
refused permission. He then declined to answer, citing the Fifth Amendment
protection against self-incrimination.

This time the script was different. The hearing room was filled with
students from the University of California at Berkeley and San Francisco State
who had come to support the witnesses. Soon they began shouting and
disrupting the hearings. Police from the city hall detail were insufficient to clear

the room, so reinforcements were summoned. Fire hoses were turned on the demonstrators and the police began removing them.[1]

Later, J. Edgar Hoover declared that the Communists had pulled off their greatest coup in the Bay Area in twenty-five years.* The director had cried wolf too many times for his statements to have any impact. The House Committee made a film about the affair entitled *Operation Abolition,* which would later be shown to law enforcement audiences. By that time, it was tame stuff compared to what was happening in their own cities.

The first place where civil disorder became widespread was the Old South. In 1945, socially and politically, the South had changed little since the end of Reconstruction seventy years earlier. Compared to the Northeast, Midwest and Pacific Coast, the inhabitants were relatively poor, rural and uneducated. It also contained within its boundaries two-thirds of the black population of the United States, many of whom lived only half free.

Excluding Texas, which was a combination of Western and Southern culture, there were few major cities in the South. The largest was New Orleans, where the population of 570,000 was minuscule compared to that of New York, Chicago or Los Angeles. In the Deep South, most of the major business corporations were branches of Northern firms. Local executives were often only on temporary assignment, and while in the South they lived in wealthy enclaves and knew little about the community they operated in. In Birmingham, the chief executive of one major corporation did his banking in Atlanta.

Politically, the region was still the solid South, where whites overwhelmingly voted Democratic, rather than for the party of Lincoln. Under federal law, blacks could not be denied the right to vote in a general election, but primaries were considered the same as elections in a private organization, which could restrict its membership to whites only. Since victory in the Democratic primary was tantamount to election, African Americans were essentially disenfranchised. In some sections of the South, blacks dared not vote, even in general elections, lest they be subject to violence. White attitudes on race ranged from the paternalistic views of the upper classes, who deplored violence against blacks but regarded them as simple children, to many poor whites, who believed that their colored neighbors had to be kept in line by the threat of force. Generally, the legal system of police and courts was sufficient to uphold the social order, although on occasion organizations like the Ku Klux Klan played a role. The Southern communities vigorously enforced laws

---

1. I was nearby at the time but could not see what was happening. On local TV that night I watched cops dragging demonstrators down the marble steps of city hall and outside to the patrol wagons.

against blacks riding in white sections of public transportation, using "whites only" drinking fountains or neglecting to use separate doors to public facilities.

While segregation and the maintenance of racial codes were the norm, some Northerners and a few Southerners realized that such practices could not continue indefinitely. World War II had been fought in part to defeat Nazi ideas on racial supremacy; they could not be sustained in postwar America. In 1948, President Truman ordered the Army integrated. So while Southern universities, supposed bastions of democratic ideals, were segregated, Southern army posts were integrated.

In 1946, Southern policing reflected several contrasting styles. State police departments were mostly highway patrol forces with limited jurisdiction. Small-town police forces and rural sheriffs' offices usually displayed minimal professionalism, and the worst of them were sometimes indistinguishable from the Klan. Police in the larger cities, such as Atlanta or Birmingham, operated on the surface like forces in Northern cities. However, the "black problem" was always at the center of police concern. In addition, even in periods when the national crime rate was low, the level of violence was high in the South. In 1961, Atlanta had a murder rate of fifteen per one hundred thousand population, or about three times that of New York or Chicago. Blacks (then about thirty-five percent of the population) constituted two-thirds of the murder arrests in the city that year. Southern whites, too, had a higher rate of violence than their counterparts in the North. It was traditional in the South to react violently to perceived insults to personal honor by resorting to arms. Such attitudes had come from the seventeenth- and eighteenth-century English gentry, who had set the tone in the mother country. In the nineteenth century, violent crime declined significantly in England, but it remained high in the American South.[2]

In 1945, Atlanta was the jewel of Southern cities. The old families, living in their historic mansions, still played a major role in municipal affairs. Relatively enlightened, their influence extended nationally. Editorials by *The Atlanta Constitution*'s Ralph McGill were read approvingly by New York City intellectuals and Harvard professors. Atlanta's own Margaret Mitchell recycled the myth of the antebellum South as a land of gallant cavaliers and their ladies strolling beneath the magnolias, while happy "darkies" sang in the background and poor whites tipped their hats to the local squire. Where previously such works had largely been sentimental melodramas not worthy of consideration by serious critics, the movie version of *Gone With the Wind,* with its top professional cast

---

2. On trends in violence in seventeenth- to twentieth-century England, see discussion in *American Policing,* Vol. I, pages 8 and 23.

and crew, stamped the lost-cause version of the Civil War on Northern consciousness.

Atlanta had not always been enlightened. In 1915, a local Jewish factory manager was convicted of murdering a young girl in his employ. Though Leo Frank was sentenced to die, the governor of Georgia commuted the sentence because of irregularities at the trial. It did not stop a mob from breaking into a prison and lynching him. The case became a national sensation, and in Atlanta it led to both a revival of the KKK and the founding of the Anti-Defamation League. At midcentury, new leadership came to the fore in the city. In 1937, William Hartsfield was elected mayor. He eschewed the usual racism of the region in favor of a progressive face. After Hartsfield left in 1961, he was succeeded by Ivan Allen, a man of similar views who, unlike Hartsfield, was also a member of the old elite.

In 1947, Hartsfield chose a career officer, Herbert T. Jenkins, to be chief of police. Jenkins was the son of a veteran motorcycle cop who had been killed in an accident. His 1931 appointment as a patrolman had required the usual political sponsorship, and his training was brief. On the first day, he was issued a badge, pistol, blackjack, whistle and a 1905 rule book, and sent out with a veteran officer to patrol the streets. Within a year, he had been assigned as chauffeur to the mayor. There he obtained an inside view of how police departments really worked.

At that time, the force numbered four hundred officers to police two hundred seventy-five thousand residents. Although it was ostensibly run by a chief, the real power in the department was a grocer, C. Dan Bridges, who chaired the police committee of the city council. The best way for a cop to get ahead was to buy his groceries at Bridges's store. The next best was to be active in the KKK, which was influential in local government. According to Jenkins, Bridges formed an alliance with the Klan. When Jenkins himself received his badge he became a pro forma member of the KKK. Later in his career he severed the affiliation.

Jenkins rose through the ranks and in 1946 was selected to head the county police force. The following year, when he came back to the city force as chief, Mayor Hartsfield had gained control of the department from the grocer Bridges and begun to introduce changes that he knew were inevitable, based on the postwar climate.[3]

In 1948, after years of demand from the black community and resistance from white police officers, the first African Americans were appointed to the Atlanta force. The sticking point, there as elsewhere, had been that no white

---

3. On Jenkins, see Appendix B.

Southerner would submit to arrest by a black man. The way it was accomplished reflected the gradualism that characterized the racial reforms instituted by moderate white Southerners. Rather than adopt the change overnight, officials rewrote the law so that black officers did not possess the authority to arrest whites. Arguably this was unlawful, but no one challenged it at the time. In addition, the black cops were not allowed to work out of headquarters, where they would have had to share a locker room with whites, but were based in a substation at a local YMCA. When they were assigned to street duty, crowds of whites would follow individual black policemen down the street. The new cops ignored them. White officers, however, made it clear that they would not tolerate assaults on a policeman even if he were black. So there was no violence.[4]

In the black community, some local gamblers declared that they would not submit to any interference from a black officer. To deal with this, a white sergeant picked out the smallest black cop and sent him in to arrest a loudmouthed gambler and march him down to headquarters.

* * * *

In 1945, Atlanta's chief rival among Southern cities was Birmingham, Alabama. In 1940, its population was almost equal to Atlanta's, and its leaders boasted publicly that it would soon become more important than its Georgia counterpart. Unlike Atlanta, Birmingham could not claim a Civil War history or look for leadership to its old families. The city was not founded until 1871, and its growth was a product of industrialism. It became the steelmaking capital of the South. By the twentieth century, it was completely dominated by Northern interests, so that in many respects Birmingham was a Northern mill town with all the problems of a Southern city. In race matters, Birmingham was notoriously resistant to change. It had the distinction of being the last Southern city of over fifty thousand people to hire a black officer.

If the face of the Atlanta police was the affable and dignified Herb Jenkins, a career cop, Birmingham's was Eugene "Bull" Connor, a professional politician, who was first elected public safety commissioner in 1937 and served in the position until 1953. In 1957, he made a comeback and held the office until 1963. In his heyday, many journalists and others who went to visit the fearsome "Bull" expected to find a huge sheriff type out of some Hollywood

---

4. In 1911, when the NYPD appointed its first black recruit (a few black officers had come over from Brooklyn when that force was merged into the NYPD in 1898), large groups of citizens followed him down the street and a city tour bus used to make his beat a regular stop and point out the black cop to the passengers—though that was not the term used but rather a word that began with an "N."

"southern." Instead, they encountered a five-foot, eight-inch, stocky, non-descript man who had never served as a professional policeman. Born in 1897, he had worked as railroad telegrapher. Possessed of a very loud voice (hence, the nickname "Bull"), he was a natural speaker, and he soon abandoned telegraphy to become a sports announcer on a local radio station. His political success was made possible by the adoption of an early-twentieth-century panacea, the commission form of government. In 1911, Birmingham replaced its mayor/council system with a board of five elected commissioners who ruled the city collectively, with each having responsibility for several departments. Elected safety commissioner in 1937, Connor became boss over police, fire, public schools and the public library. At first, he was known as a reformer who cracked down on vice and gambling and extended civil service protection to members of the force. It was generally believed that he was not a member of the KKK (though there were always some people who had their doubts). As commissioner, "Bull" kept a tight rein on the force, ignoring the civil service chief. He made it clear that anyone who didn't go along with him could expect no promotions or desirable assignments.

In office, "Bull" suffered the usual trials and tribulations of a "good old boy" politician. In 1951, one of his detectives (a member of the anti-"Bull" faction in the department) arrested him for being in a hotel room with his secretary. At the time, it was illegal in Birmingham to occupy a hotel room with a member of the opposite sex who was not one's spouse. Connor was found guilty and sentenced to 180 days in jail for having extramarital relationships, although eventually the Alabama Supreme Court threw out the charges for vagueness. The next year, the police department was subjected to a corruption investigation. A report criticized Connor and recommended that he be indicted. Again the charge did not stick. In 1953, he declined to run for a fifth term.

The following year, Connor ran for sheriff but was badly beaten. In the next few years, he was unsuccessful in several attempts to win public office. By the late 1950s, it appeared that Connor's political days were over, but developments in the South revived his career. In 1954, a unanimous Supreme Court rendered the *Brown vs. Board of Education* decision outlawing school segregation. By then the future was clear. Segregation could no longer stand. In 1955, a 28-year-old minister named Martin Luther King, Jr., son of a leader of Atlanta's black church community, became involved in a bus boycott in Montgomery, the capital of Alabama. The strategy employed in Montgomery would set the pattern for King's future efforts. He did not urge violence; instead, he practiced the nonviolent tactics of his hero, the Indian leader Mohandas Gandhi. In 1947, Gandhi's supporters had been granted freedom from British rule. The Montgomery protesters were told to refuse to sit in the rear of the bus and, if arrested, to go along peaceably. Nationally, even Northerners who had never been south of the Mason-Dixon Line knew that blacks, both literally and figuratively, rode in the back of the bus. If the practice were ended, it might lead to changes in other forms of segregation. The boycott had a major impact on the revenues of the bus company and the Montgomery economy. So the local business community overrode the city government and entered into an agreement with the protesters to end bus segregation. In February 1956, at a meeting in New Orleans, King was named the head of a new organization, the Southern Christian Leadership Conference (SCLC).

At Christmastime 1956, the Birmingham home of a local black minister, who was promoting integration campaigns in the same manner as King, was bombed. The next year, five more homes were bombed. No arrests were made in any of the cases. In 1957, "Bull" Connor was again elected public safety commissioner. In the climate of the time, he quickly became a national symbol of diehard segregation.

In 1961, groups of white and black "freedom riders" attempted to desegregate Southern bus terminals. At several locations, including Birmingham, the riders were badly beaten. In May, Birmingham police allegedly agreed to stay away from the bus terminal until fifteen minutes after the arrival of the "freedom riders" so that the locals would have time to go to work on them. Connor denied it, but the fact was that no police were there, even though the arrival of the "freedom riders" was expected and TV cameras were present.

In 1962, Dr. King sustained his first serious defeat. The previous year, the SCLC had targeted Albany, Georgia, for an all-out effort to break down the walls of segregation. Again, it was modeled on the tactics of Gandhi against the British in India: fill the jails with nonviolent demonstrators so as to paralyze the criminal justice system. In that way, Albany's leaders would be compelled to make concessions to the protesters. However, the Albany chief of police, Laurie Pritchett, was not a "Bull" Connor type but a clever professional. He arranged to obtain adequate jail space in nearby cities and counties to ensure that the local facilities were never completely full. He ordered his cops, when arresting demonstrators, to treat them courteously so there would be no pictures of them being beaten. In 1961–62, the SCLC could neither paralyze Albany nor obtain TV photos of cops behaving badly. As one of Dr. King's lieutenants explained it, "The Albany campaign was a good idea, if the goal was to go to jail." Otherwise, it was a failure. After Albany, the SCLC and King lost momentum. Luckily, with Birmingham and "Bull" Connor, they had a perfect target available. "Bull" could be counted on to use force and make outrageous comments. In 1962, Alabama voters also elected one of Connor's friends,

George Wallace, as governor. Wallace, too, would become a symbol of racism, and his highway patrol chief, Al Lingo, evolved into a sort of second-string Connor. Although the SCLC plan worked beautifully, it almost didn't happen.

By 1962, the leaders of Birmingham had grown weary of Connor and his behavior. For example, he often repeated the remark, "Negroes and whites will not be segregated together in Birmingham," making him a laughing stock on television. The Birmingham city fathers scheduled an election to determine whether the commission form of government should be abolished and the city returned to the mayor and council form. The proposal carried, effectively removing Connor as public safety commissioner. Supporters went to court to argue that the change could not take place until his elected term as commissioner had expired. The courts disagreed and ordered the mayor and council form to be adopted in late May 1963. King began his campaign in April. Had Connor not been in office, it might have been a repeat of the situation in Albany.

The demonstrations began with marches and arrests. "Bull" was out every day, mugging for the cameras and personally directing his officers. On Good Friday, April 12, the marchers came on, singing "We Shall Overcome." Their intent was to descend on downtown Birmingham. Cops grabbed King and some of the other leaders by the back of the shirt and hustled them into a patrol wagon. Worried about what might happen in Birmingham jails, President Kennedy directed his brother, Atty. Gen. Robert Kennedy, through Mrs. King, to inform Dr. King that the federal government would help. However, in his conversation with her Bobby Kennedy noted that "Bull Connor is very hard to deal with." Kennedy ordered FBI agents to check on King's condition and was relieved to learn that he was not being mistreated in the jail.

A few days before the court-ordered imposition of the mayor and council form of government took place, demonstrators stepped up their activities. Children joined in, helping to fill up the jails. On May 2, one thousand individuals were arrested, about thirty percent of them school-aged children. On that day Connor had the fire department break out high-pressure hoses, and the police brought their six K-9 dogs to the scene. The next day, four thousand demonstrators marched through the streets heading for city hall. Again the hoses were turned on and the dogs entered the fray, while the whole country watched in shock.

Connor, in his usual short-brim straw hat, was a highly visible figure. After lunch, at which he usually consumed a few drinks, he often made provocative statements for the media. Finally, after Connor was removed from office, the white business community stepped in and negotiated with the SCLC to grant certain concessions. Some angry whites began exploding bombs, including one at a local hotel that King normally used as his headquarters. Luckily, he had gone home to Atlanta for the weekend. In September, a bomb placed in the 16th Street Baptist Church killed four young black children. Even Connor denounced it as "the worst thing that ever happened in Alabama."

In 1964, the United States Congress passed the first modern civil rights act. It was also the year of the Mississippi "Freedom Summer" when, following the disappearance of three civil rights workers, thousands of protesters flocked to the state. After the missing boys' bodies were found by the FBI, it was another nail in the coffin of the segregationists.

In 1965, civil rights organizers of a voting drive in Selma, Alabama, requested the support of Dr. King in organizing a march to Montgomery. Local authorities blocked it, and TV showed the famous pictures of a police charge injuring a number of demonstrators. A second march was also prevented, but a third one, designed to protest the killing of a young black man by a state trooper, made it to the capitol to confront Governor Wallace.

Under the leadership of Dr. King, the civil rights movement had been victorious. The South began its efforts to adjust to the changed situation. Southern police leaders who wished to learn the new ways flocked to Atlanta to study Herb Jenkins' operations. The Southern Police Institute at the University of Louisville had always been a force for professional policing, educating both Northern and Southern officers. Under its executive director, Col. David McCandless, the former public safety director of Louisville, many cops were trained in the new ways of policing. At the operating level, men like E. Wilson "Bud" Purdy, a graduate of the Michigan State University Criminal Justice Program, a former FBI agent and Pennsylvania State police commissioner, made the Dade County, Miami, metropolitan police force a model organization. In 1966, John "Jack" Ingersoll, a former Oakland, California, cop, turned the Charlotte (N.C.) police force into a first-class agency. In 1973, he went on to head the federal Bureau of Narcotics and Dangerous Drugs (BNDD).

In many ways, the South, which had been beset with racial problems since the Civil War, did a better job of adjusting to the changes of the 1960s than the allegedly nonsegregated North, which, for a long time, rested on Abraham Lincoln's laurels. When the protests finally came to the Northern cities, they were often handled as badly as in the South.

In the nineteenth century, city police spent a fair amount of time practicing military drill and tactics. Disorder was common in industrial cities, and the training could be done on the cheap. Police officers had to spend a certain portion of their time on reserve duty in their stations. So it cost nothing to take them out to a park and drill them. In the early twentieth century, when reserve duty was abolished, to give cops field training would take them away from their patrol duties.

Most mid-twentieth century police had little riot training. Few could have explained the use of the line, diagonal or wedge formations unless they were former MPs. Cops in general worked in small units, not large formations. Even superior officers were at a loss about how to proceed in a riot situation. Very few even knew the words of the riot act.[5]

In the early 1950s, the Chicago Housing Authority decided to integrate the Trumbull Park Project in the steel-mill district known as South Chicago. The affair developed into a long-running disaster. On occasion, it took a thousand policemen to protect the handful of black families who had been moved in. Some nights, the local sky was full of fireworks while gunmen, perched on distant railroad embankments, sent bullets flying overhead. The city had to purchase searchlights to scan the horizon looking for the shooters. Many cops who served at Trumbull Park said the scenes reminded them of beachheads they had fought on during World War II. After a few years of skirmishing, the city abandoned its plan.

The beaches in Chicago were another sore point for African Americans. Legally integrated, they were informally segregated. In 1961, the city leaders opted to end the practice starting with Rainbow Beach, a strip of land alongside Lake Michigan, just north of the steel-mill district. The plan, though well meant, was poorly conceived. The nearby area was the most likely neighborhood in the city to react badly.

The plan called for black and white volunteers (mostly college students) to sit quietly on the sand and, if insulted, not to react. The planners wanted the first steps to be low-key, not a show of force, which they reasoned would set the wrong tone. A small group of plainclothes cops sat some way off and were ordered to assume a low profile. The scheme was clearly inadequate. The police detachment was too small for the mission. Because nobody wanted a failure, they did not plan for that possibility. So no tactics had been rehearsed to meet various contingencies that might arise.

---

5. The British statute, which the Americans copied, was enacted in 1714. Its original words were, "Our sovereign Lord the King chargeth and commandeth all persons being assembled, immediately to disperse themselves and peaceably to depart to their habitations, or to their lawful business, upon the pains contained in the act made in the first year of King George, for preventing tumults and riotous assemblies. God save the King." In the American version, the sovereign was the people of the state. The act was read when a crowd of twelve or more was, in the judgment of a justice of the peace or magistrate, an unlawful assembly. After hearing it, if the mob failed to disperse, individual members could be arrested. In America, judicial officers did not like to face hostile mobs, so the law permitted police officials to invoke the act. I was one of the few people who could recite the words of the law extemporaneously. I learned them by watching British historical films.

Luckily the commander that day, "Jungle Jim" Hackett, was a man who was head and shoulders above the typical police brass hat. He had been a ranking military officer in World War II and Korea. He also held a law degree from a prestigious university and in appearance and manner was a vigorous swashbuckler. However, he had recently been demoted two grades from full chief to commander. No doubt in some clash with his superiors, he had been right and they were wrong, but he was the one who lost out.

On the Sunday afternoon scheduled for the experiment, the trouble came fast. The volunteer group was surrounded by scores of yelling whites. The chief and a few cops ran to the scene and conferred with a black minister acting as group leader.[6] The situation was serious. To allow the demonstrators to be driven off the beach would have major repercussions. On the other hand, it would have taken more cops than were available to hold off a full-fledged attack by the local crowd. Even if a general call for assistance had been broadcast, by the time the reinforcements arrived, a lot of people could have been hurt. The chief asked the black minister what he preferred to do. When the minister said he and his group would like to leave the beach, everyone breathed a sigh of relief.

The next day, the incident was on the front pages of all the Chicago newspapers. At an emergency meeting downtown, the decision was made that the integrationist group would return to the same beach the following Sunday with a much larger police escort. They did, and demonstrated that integration could be accomplished—if a few hundred cops were present.

Over the rest of the year, the drama was played out every weekend. In the meantime, a number of minority leaders were attracted to the scene along with network TV cameras. On a day in August, they were rewarded when cops clashed with the demonstrators to the sound of bugle calls and the sight of two-hundred-man companies of police officers charging through the sand. Had any other commander been in charge, there would have been a disaster, but Hackett was a great leader.

The beach eventually closed for the season. The following year, the trouble started again. By then there were new issues to deal with and other cities for the networks to cover. Gradually Rainbow Beach faded from public attention.

Across the country, it was the same pattern. The early disturbances were confined to small areas—a park, a beach, a particular block. In 1962, Los Angeles cops clashed with some Black Muslims near a local mosque. When the doings were over, one Muslim was dead and five were wounded.

---

6. The writer, then a lieutenant, was present as an observer. When the trouble started, I discarded the hot dogs I had just purchased, ran onto the beach and ended up in the midst of things.

In 1964, on a hot July afternoon, a major riot broke out in a most unlikely area—the ritzy Upper East Side of Manhattan. Black summer-school students, from outside the neighborhood, sometimes walked on the grass or threw litter, to the annoyance of a local building superintendent. One day, he turned his hose on them. Pretty soon the kids were bombarding him with bottles, and he retreated into a vestibule. One youngster followed the man in and supposedly threatened him with a knife. An off-duty police lieutenant, hearing the commotion, ran to the scene and confronted the knife-wielding boy. When the kid refused to drop the knife and ignored a warning, the lieutenant shot him, killing the youngster. A crowd of 300 students began tossing rocks and garbage can lids. They were eventually dispersed by the tactical patrol force (TPF), made up of young officers, many of them ex-marines or paratroopers.

On the following Saturday night, a demonstration at a Harlem precinct, far from the scene of the original incident, was called to protest the shooting. When objects began to be thrown from roofs of nearby buildings, the police moved in. As the disturbance swelled, a police commander ordered the TPF to charge. This spread the disturbances in all directions. A number of police and citizens were injured in the clashes as the disorders went on through the night.

The next night, after trouble broke out at the funeral of the dead boy, it jumped across the river into distant Brooklyn, where rioting took place. It took six days for the police to bring the outbreaks under control. An official investigation exonerated the police lieutenant in the shooting of the youngster. For the first time, the Harlem precinct received a black captain as commanding officer.

About a week after the Harlem affair, similar troubles occurred in the City of Brotherly Love. In a black ghetto area of North Philadelphia, late on an August night, a black officer attempted to get a black woman to move her car. She refused and got into a struggle with the cop. When additional police arrived and took the woman away, bricks and bottles were tossed at the officers.

The police commissioner was Howard Leary, a career cop with a law degree but not noted as a leader. When looting began in North Philadelphia, six hundred officers were sent into the area. But the commissioner would not allow them to break up the crowds, and the disturbances continued unabated. A newly appointed deputy commissioner, named Frank Rizzo, protested to Leary about the restraints on his men. Rizzo, known by his troops as the "Cisco Kid" for his swashbuckling demeanor, was the city's top field commander. (He was, in effect, the "Jungle Jim" of Philadelphia, though much less educated and polished.) However, Leary told him, "You have your orders." With the highway patrol as a spearhead, Rizzo continued to hold the line against the rioters.[7] The next day, four hundred ten square blocks of Philadelphia were declared a curfew area. After two more days, two deaths and three hundred injuries, the riot was brought under control. Leary was criticized and Rizzo became a hero. It was a sign to the Democratic city administration that they were losing their blue-collar white base.

In July 1965, there was a riot in what had been known as America's best-governed city with the country's most highly esteemed police department. Put to the test, the LAPD failed badly. The trouble began when California Highway Patrol officers pursued a black motorist into a section of South Los Angeles which was near, but not in, a neighborhood called Watts. At first, the mood of the motorist was jovial, but when his family arrived on the scene and began yelling at him, it changed. Some bystanders got into the act, and a backup force of LAPD cops were sent to the scene. The legendary William Parker was still chief fifteen years after his original appointment. However, Parker was not the man he had been. He had severe heart trouble, from which he would die the following year. Through the next six days, rioting and lootings occurred in forty-six square miles of Los Angeles—an area as large as San Francisco. Parker placed two deputy chiefs in charge of combating the riot, telling one that he himself did not know how to do so. (Apparently he had forgotten his MP training.) Within the police department, chiefs squabbled, and it became a case of order, counter-order, disorder, as cops received conflicting directions. In some instances, large detachments of police sat at various locations waiting for orders that never came, while Watts burned and people were being killed. On the third night, the National Guard was called out. Even then, there was a foul-up. Lt. Gov. Glenn M. Anderson, filling in for Gov. Pat Brown (who was in Europe), did not want to order guardsmen to the scene. Finally, after receiving a direct order from Brown, Anderson acted.

The basic problem in Los Angeles was that no one, from ordinary citizen to high official, believed that such an event could take place there. A National Guard unit racing to the scene was actually halted by a toll collector, still doing business as usual, who would not let them pass until they had paid their fare. A force of fourteen thousand police and National Guardsmen regained control of the streets. Thirty-four people died in the disorders.

If Los Angeles was supposed to be the best-run city in America, Newark, New Jersey, was a strong contender for the worst. City hall was dominated by whites, some of them with ties to organized crime. Low-income blacks, who constituted the majority of the population, had limited political influence.

---

7. Highway patrol is a title usually applied to state troopers. In Philadelphia, though, it was the name of an elite unit established originally to combat auto bandits and used as an emergency response force. Easily identified by their boots and military manner, they were the equivalent of the NYPD's tactical patrol force.

The riot scenario in Newark followed what was becoming the usual pattern. In July 1967, a forty-year-old black cabdriver was arrested for driving with a revoked license. Passersby gathered and the mood quickly turned hostile. Police reinforcements were called to the scene. After six days of looting, shooting and burning that left twenty-six people dead and fifteen hundred injured, police and National Guard forces suppressed the riot.

A month later, it was Detroit that blew up. With memories of 1943 still alive, nobody in the city doubted that there could be a serious outbreak. In August 1967, a police raid on an afterhours club sparked five days of rioting in which Gov. George Romney sent in the National Guard and asked for federal troops, which President Johnson initially refused to commit. Finally Johnson relented and dispatched the 82nd Airborne Division. By that time Detroit had recorded forty-three deaths—the highest in any city during the riot era. Since 1967, Detroit has gone steadily downhill and is no longer considered to be a major metropolis.

In March 1968, Dr. Martin Luther King, tired from years of protest marches, arrests and jailings, declined to go to Memphis, Tennessee, to support a sanitation workers' strike. However, the plight of these low-paid workers moved him and he ended up going. On April 3, King delivered a speech at a local church in which he declared:

> Well, I don't know what will happen now. We've got some difficult days ahead. But it doesn't matter with me now. Because I've been to the mountaintop. And I don't mind. Like anybody, I would like to live a long life. Longevity has its place. But I'm not concerned about that now. I just want to do God's will, and He's allowed me to go up to the mountain. And I've looked over. And I've seen the promised land. I may not get there with you. But I want you to know tonight that we as a people will get to the promised land!**

At 6:01 the next evening, while he was standing on the second-floor balcony of the motel he was using as a temporary residence, King was hit by a bullet fired from a rifle. An hour later, he was pronounced dead. At the time, he was only thirty-nine years old. A white man named James Earl Ray would be convicted of the murder and sentenced to life in prison.

King had burst on the scene in Montgomery just thirteen years earlier. In the 1950s, most Americans saw him as just another black agitator. J. Edgar Hoover believed that he was under the influence of subversive groups. After Birmingham, even those who didn't particularly like him recognized that he had elements of greatness.

King's assassination was followed by riots in over 100 American cities. In Washington, DC, black militant Stokely Carmichael of the Student Non-Violent Coordinating Committee whipped up mobs saying, "Black people know that they have to get guns." Crowds surged through the streets looting and burning. The city's three thousand police were unable to control the situation and had to be reinforced by fifteen thousand U.S. servicemen. Marines set up machine guns on the steps of the Capitol, and the White House was guarded by a full regiment of soldiers. Two blocks away, the rioting raged. The disturbance left twelve dead, over one thousand injured and six thousand arrested. In nearby Baltimore, police and National Guard, assisted by five thousand U.S. soldiers, quelled disturbances. There six people were killed, seven hundred injured and forty-five hundred arrested.

In Chicago an area of several square miles on the west side was devastated by arson and looting. Approximately two hundred buildings were severely damaged, eleven people killed, five hundred injured and thirty-five hundred arrested. Ten thousand people were left homeless by the fires. Mayor Daley directed the police superintendent to issue an order to shoot to kill anyone in the act of committing arson and to wound looters (although it was doubtful police marksmanship was that proficient). His statement drew widespread criticism.

The number and size of the riots that could arise out of petty disputes were shocking. The fact that in some places it took up to twenty thousand police and soldiers to maintain order suggested that U.S. security forces were ill prepared to deal with civil disorder. However, the police were improving. In the late 1960s, I spent a lot of time in the field with cops in Cincinnati and Boston. In both places, in little things and large, you could see that the police were operating differently than they had been. A small sign was the way they reacted when a potentially riotous mob formed. In the early and mid-'60s, many departments waited until the rocks and bottles were flying before invoking the riot act. Later, in places like Cincinnati, when trouble began to brew, the police radio would broadcast that police sergeant X was going to read the riot act, and all cars in the vicinity would hurry to the scene to back him up.[8] More important, the cops were learning how to deal with street disorder. In Boston, I was part of a local police detachment that spent the night following Dr. King's assassination chasing looters in the upscale Back Bay area. At no time, though, did the cops lose control of the streets, and no troops were called out.

---

8. The most stately reading of the riot act I ever heard was in Cambridge, Massachusetts, across the bridge from Boston. One night after Harvard exploded, I watched a Cambridge captain intoning, "In the name of the Commonwealth," etc. In that setting, it seemed like we were back in Victorian England.

By the end of the '60s, it appeared that America was likely to collapse into a state of anarchy or, more likely, that a harsh military-type regime would be imposed. Suddenly it was all over. After 1970, riots and protests virtually ceased. Many civil rights leaders believed they had made significant progress, and it was time to enter the political arena. In urban ghettos, most people felt that setting fires only damaged their own community. The end of the Vietnam War removed a reason for large groups of people to protest American involvement. Many of the relatively small number of individuals who sought violence and revolution were imprisoned or in hiding. Whether the '60s experience was good or bad for America continues to be debated.

Chapter 5

Far From the Ivory Tower:
O. W. Wilson in Chicago

A big-city police headquarters in the daytime is usually a bustling place, with cops and visitors moving to and fro. At night, it presents a different appearance. Thus it was with the Chicago police headquarters in the early morning hours of January 12, 1960. One civilian elevator operator was sufficient to handle the traffic in the building, making him the only one who knew what was happening on all its floors. When two detectives (one of them this writer) arrived to work the midnight shift, they were surprised when the elevator operator took them aside and, in a low, conspiratorial tone, told them something big was happening. All night long, top bosses, who were normally off duty, had been coming and going. Occasionally they were accompanied by younger men in civilian clothes who were obviously cops. According to him, State's Attorney Ben Adamowski, Mayor Daley's leading political foe, had initiated the arrests of some officers—for what was not known.

That morning, Chicago awoke to headlines reporting that eight cops from the North Side Summerdale District had been charged with being part of a ring, including a professional burglar, that broke into stores. In most previous scandals, the police had been accused of protecting gamblers and madams, and the officers involved were usually detectives. Now they were a cross-section of the uniformed patrol force—one of them a young college graduate whose recently deceased father had been a highly regarded captain.

For nearly thirty years without interruption, the Democratic political machine had run the city and its police force. Despite the opposition of reformers, the town Carl Sandburg described as a "stormy, husky, brawling city of the big shoulders" preferred the machine. State's Attorney Adamowski was not a reformer, but a politician who had left the Democratic Party because his route to the mayoralty was blocked by Irish bosses. Now, Adamowski might have found the path to the mayor's office.

Daley realized that if the machine were to stay in power, he had to clean up the police department. The first casualty was the police commissioner, Tim O'Connor, a thoroughly honest cop who had gotten the job ten years earlier at the time of the Kefauver investigation. Back then, there were captains and higher officers who held law degrees and/or had served as colonels in World War II. O'Connor was neither college educated nor an ex-military officer, but there were no files on him at the Chicago Crime Commission or the *Tribune* that, if publicized, could derail his appointment.

In thirty-three years' service, O'Connor had never taken a sick day. Now, he was summoned to the mayor's office and handed a statement in which he declared he was stepping down for reasons of health. No replacement was named. The mayor realized that picking some Chicago captain, who himself might be in trouble as Adamowski's investigation widened, would be a disaster. So Daley set up a selection board composed of both the usual and unusual suspects. One member was a powerful labor leader who was very close to the mayor. A second was the president of the Chamber of Commerce, and a third was Frank Kreml, who had played an advisory role to the police department for years. Of course, Kreml had always confined his recommendations to technical matters such as traffic enforcement, not corruption. Two of the members were nontraditional. Virgil Peterson, a former FBI SAC had been head of the business-supported Chicago Crime Commission for eighteen years. He gave the committee credibility with reformers. The chairman was O. W. Wilson, dean of the School of Criminology at the University of California, Berkeley. His presence encouraged top police leaders from other parts of the country to apply for the Chicago job.

The committee settled down and began to interview candidates from within and without the department. The former provided a picture of department problems and their own strengths and weaknesses. Most were narrow and conventional in their approach to policing. Some outsiders did not make as good an impression as expected. One head of a large Eastern department came across to the press as arrogant. A former FBI man who was chief in a Western city was also a member of the far-right John Birch Society. Some outsiders simply used the process to obtain a pay raise in their own cities.

As the deliberations went on, Wilson was asked to step aside so that the committee could consider him for commissioner. After brief deliberation, they recommended his appointment and the mayor concurred. Later, it was widely believed that Wilson had been guaranteed the job before he ever arrived. But there was no evidence of that, and Daley was too astute an executive to confer an important post on a man he had never met. Peterson may have decided in advance that Wilson should be chosen. If so, he was smart enough to realize that a candidate seen as the Crime Commission's man would never get the job. While no one knew it at the time, Wilson himself was anxious to be appointed because his career in California was about to come to an inglorious end.

Orlando Winfield Wilson, né Vralson, was born in South Dakota in 1900, and grew up in California. In 1919, he entered Cal Berkeley with the intention of becoming a mining engineer. The tall, handsome student married a vivacious, divorced co-ed with acting ambitions. The couple enjoyed a good time and, despite Prohibition, an occasional drink. Soon Wilson flunked out of college. He returned to the university as a student in August Vollmer's police program. Not until 1924 did he receive his degree. Then he became Vollmer's protégé and, with his mentor's help, was named chief of police in the small California town of Fullerton. His college ideas did not mesh well with the locals, and he soon left. In 1928, again with Vollmer's help, he became chief of police of the hundred-man Wichita, Kansas, police force. He stayed there for eleven years. During that time, he somehow offended J. Edgar Hoover, thereby earning a place on the director's enemies list for the rest of his life. In 1939 he resigned to return to Berkeley, where he taught in the law enforcement program. There he was divorced and later married one of his students, who became his lifelong research associate.

Wilson was a favorite of the university president, J. Franklin Sproul, who proposed to appoint him a professor and dean of a new school of criminology. It was quite an accomplishment, for a man with only a bachelor's degree and no scholarly record, to be offered a full professorship at one of the world's great research universities.

Before Wilson could take the job, World War II broke out and he served with the U.S. military government in Germany as a lieutenant colonel, attempting to de-Nazify the country. In 1946 he returned to Berkeley and in 1950 became the dean of the new school of criminology. There he produced a textbook on police administration that eventually sold over one hundred thousand copies. He was also frequently called upon to conduct surveys of police departments. After President Sproul left, his successor, University

Chancellor Clark Kerr, decided to eliminate Wilson's "vocational" school from the campus. Wilson always attributed Kerr's attitude to academic snobbery and a basic dislike of police because they sometimes resorted to force. Had Berkeley not been a state institution, Kerr would have had his way. But Wilson mobilized police chiefs, district attorneys, the attorney general and even the governor to defend his school and was given a reprieve. Nevertheless, the handwriting was on the wall. If the school was to survive, Wilson would have to step down as dean. At age 60, it would be hard to rebuild his career.[1]

In Chicago, Wilson agreed to accept the police commissioner's job with a three-year contract and a salary of thirty thousand dollars a year. This was almost twice as much as he was getting at Berkeley and seven thousand five hundred dollars more than O'Connor had been making as commissioner.

Under state law, the police commissioner was required to be an Illinois resident at the time of appointment. So the selection committee, minus Peterson and Wilson (who were replaced by Daley allies), was designated the police board and Wilson was given the title of superintendent, under the theory that he was operating in the board's name. In many cities, that would have been a formula for conflict, but it worked. Daley had informed the new board that he intended to give the superintendent authority to run the department to an extent never before seen in the city. To dramatize the situation, the commissioner-superintendent's office, which had always been next to the mayor's at city hall, was moved to police headquarters, nearly two miles away.

Many recollections of Wilson in Wichita or Berkeley describe him as being a "martinet." It was not the impression he gave in Chicago. He spoke politely to reporters and cops in the reserved but friendly manner of a college dean. He took on the persona of an English gentleman so much that, when a TV series about a model police department was being cast, they named the English actor Leo G. Carroll, a Wilson lookalike, to play the lead role. Wilson changed Chicago police hats to the checkerboard pattern worn by Scottish police. He did not know that in Chicago checkered caps were worn by cabdrivers, so the arrangement did little to boost police status. Perhaps Wilson's previous colleagues' definition of "martinet" was different from that of the Chicago Police Department, where some bosses were truly martinets. In one typical incident, a newly minted sergeant (a reformed drunk) was so hard on a detective under his command that the officer committed suicide. This made the man's colleagues angry enough to contemplate killing the sergeant. One day a lieutenant did not jump when a chief told him to move some patrol cars. Instead he tried to offer an explanation of why he could not do it. The chief

---

1. On Wilson, see Appendix B.

stormed out of the station. A few minutes later the headquarters personnel section called the lieutenant to inform him that he was transferred "forthwith" to the dog pound. Not until the chief left the job, two years later, was the lieutenant able to bid goodbye to his canine friends.

Wilson's appointment meant that the leader of the professional policing school was now head of a police force that was long considered to be one of the most corrupt and politically dominated in the country. The key to the professional model of policing was centralized control. The decentralized pattern that existed in Chicago at the time was one where the thirty-eight districts ran according to the values of the local community, as expressed by its elected officials. For example, ward aldermen were always ready to respond to complaints from small businessmen that the cops were too hard on them. Of course, the small businessmen involved were usually bookmakers and dive owners. In previous administrations, if a store was held up, the owner might use influence to get a policeman assigned permanently to protect his place. The result was a small army of cops on special detail all over the city.

Under Wilson, the police department would sometimes go too far in the other direction. He sought to reduce the number of district stations and to compel the remaining ones to operate in a uniform fashion. When it came to police administration, little consideration was given to entreaties from politicians or citizens even though, in some cases, they had merit.[2]

Among the other tenets of Wilson's system was an emphasis on intensive patrol and rapid response to calls. In theory, this was best accomplished by the use of one-man cars. Twice as many vehicles could be assigned to patrol and, with smaller areas to cover, their average travel time to an incident would be cut in half. Of course, some calls were potentially dangerous. Then it required the dispatch of two units where, in the past, one two-man car would have been sufficient. In some sections of the city, officers in one-man cars were reluctant to initiate certain actions because there was no one to back them up. In practice, two-man cars remained predominant in Chicago.

The internal-affairs unit was greatly increased in size, and it conducted a number of "innovative" investigations of police misconduct. It perpetrated stings such as hiring actors to pretend to be comatose drunks lying in the street. Then they would put in an emergency call to see if responding cops

---

2. As a captain in a district that encompassed the lakeport, I once tried to explain to a headquarters staffer about the need to assign an additional car to a certain area, even though the workload did not justify it. The problem was that when ships steamed down the river, the bridges across it were raised for long periods. At such times, there was no easy way for police from the rest of the district to get into the port enclave. If the lone patrol car officer already assigned to the area was tied up, for practical purposes there was no police protection available. If he needed help, it would have to come via a circuitous route. My request was curtly dismissed.

would try to steal from the supposed drunks. The tactic was revealed when police took an "unconscious man" to a busy hospital. After examining the patient, the doctor realized the man was faking and stormed out of the room. The stunt had taken him away from ministering to truly sick people. When the doctor's complaint reached the newspapers, that type of sting was discontinued.

O. W. Wilson had never worked in a big-city police department, and he did not really understand the subculture of the police department or the city. He chose as his first deputy James B. Conlisk, Jr., son of a former high police official who had been deposed with other top brass when Wilson was appointed. For many years, Conlisk, Sr., had been the liaison between police headquarters and the political machine. A politician who wanted to secure a cop's transfer to a station closer to home or to a better assignment would call Conlisk, Sr., who would then determine how much attention had to be paid to the request. If the person making it was a powerful figure, close to the mayor, it was handled immediately. If he was not powerful, the request might be put in the circular file.

Mrs. Wilson, who had worked on many police surveys with her husband, never liked Jim Conlisk, who had spent most of his career behind a desk in the traffic division. She believed him to be a weak man who avoided difficult judgments and who displayed few of the traits of leadership necessary to succeed as a police administrator.* Her view was shared by a number of Chicago police officials. The department saw his appointment as a signal that the machine still had enormous power in the police department.

If not Conlisk, though, whom should Wilson have named? There were abler men, but their names were in confidential files in newspaper offices and law-enforcement agencies. The reason so many names were there was that ranking officers in the 1960s had joined the force in the 1930s and '40s. Back then, most accepted the job as they found it and went along with the system. Conlisk was not on any lists; instead he had spent most of his career doing paperwork.

In 1961, when Wilson announced that he was going to close seventeen of the city's thirty-eight district stations (the equivalent of precincts), local politicians were appalled. Many would lose what they rightly called "their station" and with it a lot of influence. One of them, saloon keeper/ward boss Paddy Bauler, was loud, crude and corrupt. His tavern never closed, and once, when a cop tried to arrest him for being open after hours, Paddy shot him. Chicago would not tolerate that kind of behavior. The cop was fired. At the time of Wilson's announcement, there were riots in Japan, and Bauler promised that any attempt to close the Hudson Avenue station would make "those Tokyo riots look like a tea party." When the station was closed anyway, Paddy said or did nothing. Only one man could have silenced him. Paddy, like any powerful ward leader, controlled about four hundred patronage jobs, ranging from ladies who handed out towels in bathhouses and men who swept the streets to city commissioners and judges. However, the party chairman could strip Paddy of all that patronage and make him a nobody, which would then lead to his being defeated at the next election. The chairman was Mayor Daley.

Chicago was a city of neighborhoods. Some families lived in the same two-block area for three generations. Police stations were part of the fabric of community life. Although they had numbers, they were generally referred to by their names: Woodlawn, Stockyards, Lawndale. Shutting them was a blow to local pride and somewhat disorienting. Some people preferred to deal with, or even be arrested by, what they called "my own station." Wilson's organizational model was better suited to a California motor-age town than a historic industrial-age city. Daley ignored complaints from his political base and backed Wilson. Later, after Wilson's departure, closing so many stations was seen as a mistake and some were reopened.

Wilson won the right to appoint all twenty-one district commanders and the five detective commanders. Of those chosen, only two were captains who had already been commanding existing districts. Some of Wilson's choices were not even captains but still lieutenants. Commander was not a civil service rank, and all of them served at the pleasure of the superintendent. Every year, the department held a luncheon for commanders and chiefs. It became known as "the survivor's dinner" because a number of people who had been at the previous year's event were no longer in the hierarchy. Some of those dropped had made the mistake of questioning the new system. For example, in the old detective bureau, officers spent much time on the streets rousting thieves and not enough time investigating. In the new system they spent virtually all their time investigating, which mostly meant filling out reports. Soon the burglars, hijackers and other pros noticed there were no cops looking over their shoulders. On paper the patrol force was supposed to do that, but besides the fact that the cars were too busy answering calls, the young officers who manned them did not know the pros. The answer was for knowledgeable detectives to spend a portion of their time cruising the streets, but that was forbidden. If a detective commander uttered words like, "Chief, this new system doesn't work," he would be demoted to captain, put in uniform and sent out to supervise the midnight shift in a patrol district station. In my own case, I simply wrote up a report loaded with statistics and presented it as "innovative." Therefore I received permission to let some of our best detectives occasionally roam the streets and actually catch burglars, aided by computer printouts of high-crime spots.

Some top staff jobs were given to men whom Wilson had known throughout his career, such as army officers, former students, technical experts, etc. Their talents and personalities varied. Some were quite competent; others less so. Some were nice guys; some were not. None were ever accepted by the career force. One of the outsiders was a man who bore the same name as a foreign movie actor famous for playing the lead in steamy love stories. This made it easy to spread rumors in the department about the outsider's alleged degenerate behavior. The truth was that he was a straitlaced family man.

The Crime Commission's and the FBI's favorite mob-fighting cops, Joe Morris and Bill Duffy, had been ensconced, respectively, as deputy superintendent in charge of inspectional services (which included internal affairs, intelligence, organized crime, etc.) and director of the organized-crime division. Morris had been head of the old Scotland Yard confidential unit, which had existed until 1955. Duffy had been his star detective. Both were much disliked by the mob. Back then it was believed (falsely) that Scotland Yard had tapped the personal phone of party chairman Daley. Actually they had tapped the phone of a big-time gambler who operated out of the same downtown hotel in which Democratic Party headquarters was located. In the '60s, Daley could have blocked Morris and Duffy from being elevated to such high ranks, but as long as Wilson wanted them, he did not.

Among the public, Wilson had many supporters. He was liked by civic reformers, Republicans, liberal Democrats, the press and blacks. The last named were especially delighted with his orders to completely integrate the department and by his placing African Americans in jobs they had not held before.

Within the department, many cops were glad to be free of the machine. Gone were the days when the ward boss could burst into a district station and demand the release of a prisoner. A politician who did that in Wilson's time could end up in the newspapers, because the cops would make sure to notify their favorite reporter. The politician could no longer strike back by getting an officer transferred to a Siberia post. Wilson would not listen to such requests, and if Daley learned that a politician was meddling in the department, he might make a phone call that would leave the man shaken. Of course, many of the police brass had friends in politics for whom they might do a favor. Others reasoned that reform would not last, so they did not want to burn their bridges. Wilson's reformed department effectively negated any fallout from the Summerdale scandal and was the best advertisement for the Daley machine. In 1963, Adamowski ran against Daley for mayor but was defeated. When

Wilson's three-year contract expired, Daley announced that as long as he was mayor, Wilson would be superintendent.

When Wilson sought to bury the hatchet with J. Edgar Hoover, the director refused to consider it. In 1963, Atty. Gen. Bobby Kennedy asked the FBI for a report on police corruption in Chicago. Then he used it as the basis of a speech. Kennedy did this because he was angry that a certain Chicago congressman fronted openly for the mob in Washington. When Kennedy asked the Daley machine to remove him, they were slow to do so. The honorable member was just a windbag who nobody took seriously, though eventually he was pushed out. When the FBI report was leaked to the newspapers in Chicago, another branch of the federal government furnished Wilson with a copy. It named key officers, including commanders and chiefs, who were taking payoffs. One supposedly kept the mob fully informed on police plans. Another was said to own a house of prostitution. A ranking officer on Wilson's personal staff was identified as a former collector in one of the city's hottest districts.[3]**

Poor Mike Delaney was mentioned for refereeing football games in the Big Ten Conference. Being a crew chief in the most prestigious college football conference in America was considered an honor in the sporting world, but technically it was a violation of the rules because referees received a small honorarium. For Delaney, to be cited for such a minor thing on a list with men accused of owning houses of prostitution, or helping the mob carry out murders, was almost like receiving a Good Conduct Medal. Yet Wilson never promoted Delaney beyond the equivalent of a commander rank, probably because he believed that Iron Mike was too much of a social worker.[4]

The federal report contained some inaccuracies and in certain instances lacked the evidence to draw the conclusions it reached. Still, virtually everybody in the top ranks of the police department could identify the people cited, even though their names were not listed.

Wilson himself was somewhat indiscreet in public. He enjoyed a drink or two and occasionally appeared to be intoxicated.[5] Daley, on the other hand,

---

3. This man's past affiliations were well known. When they were called to Wilson's attention, he affirmed that he had confidence in him. Wilson apparently did not understand that a collector's ultimate loyalty was to the politicians and organized crime figures he had dealt with.

4. When a war between youth gangs broke out, Wilson ignored Delaney's unit and, on the advice of a district commander, had both gang leaders into his office and treated them like heads of state. Wilson managed to broker a truce, although those of us who knew the gangs could only shake our heads. The truce lasted a few hours, after which the war resumed and members of both groups were shot. Wilson ended up looking like a prize fool, and the newspapers raked him over the coals.

5. The foregoing paragraphs have been hard on O. W. Wilson. He was both a capable and decent man. After all, he promoted me five times, although as they say in Chicago, "What has he done for me lately?" His troubles arose because he was unfamiliar with what the city was really like. He should have employed people who understood the world he was entering. For example, he could have appointed a Chicago journalist as

would accept a drink upon entering a social gathering (lest he come over as an effete blue-nose), but observers noted that when he left the room, the discarded drink had barely been touched.

Eventually, the upheavals of the 1960s doomed professional policing in Chicago and elsewhere. In 1966, Dr. Martin Luther King targeted the city for an all-out drive to win concessions, realizing that if Daley, the most powerful mayor in the nation, were made to back down, officials in other cities would too. Daley was no "Bull" Connor. Many blacks had top jobs in his administration, including congressmen, judges, etc. But the pace of change was slow. A story, circulated years later, claimed that when a bright young man from North Carolina came to Chicago with a letter from the governor of his state addressed to Daley, the mayor sent him out to a local Democratic ward organization, which gave him a minor vote-hustling post. In the normal course of events, the young man, if he were lucky, could expect to rise to the lower house of the legislature after about twenty years of gopher work. The prospect did not appeal to Jesse Jackson, and he found other outlets for his ambition.

When King arrived, he was invited to have coffee with Wilson at police headquarters. Wilson promised him full cooperation and, as King remarked, his reception was a far cry from that in the South. Unfortunately, racial tensions had been a fact of Chicago life since before World War I. As noted earlier, in the 1950s, it had taken a thousand police to permit a few black families to move into the Trumbull Park Housing Project. In the '60s, it had sometimes required several hundred officers to permit blacks to use Rainbow Beach. A cup of coffee and friendly words were not going to bridge a great social divide.

King's followers were out almost daily. In one major march through the Marquette Park area, one thousand cops had to be assigned, and there were clashes with motorcycle gangs and white supremacists.[6] During a march in the Loop, some demonstrators sat down in the middle of the street, blocking traffic. The police were under orders not to be too harsh, and the protesters were not arrested. The next morning at a briefing, Wilson was in the process of congratulating police officials for showing restraint the day before, when suddenly he was called away from the podium to take an urgent phone call. When the superintendent returned, he appeared pale and he tensely announced that if the demonstrators sat down and blocked traffic again, they should be arrested. Obviously, Mayor Daley had given the order. Wilson did not understand the mayor's position. King had thrown down the gauntlet in a direct

---

public information officer. Instead, he gave the job to a former army colonel from outside the city.

6. One day, as part of my police escort, I marched alongside Dr. King. He said little, but his bearing made it clear that he was an American version of Gandhi.

challenge to Daley, and the mayor was not going to allow Wilson or anyone else to tell him how to respond. In the Stockyards District, there was no such thing as a co-winner. Somebody won; somebody lost.[7] In the end, King left town and Daley was re-elected to a fourth term.

In May 1967, on his sixty-seventh birthday, Wilson announced he would return to California. With his strong endorsement, First Deputy Conlisk was named as successor. The police board, which under the law was supposed to vet the candidates, had not even had time to consider a replacement. So it simply rubber-stamped the appointment. Immediately there were signs of what was to come. Wilson's outside experts were sent packing. Some high-ranking officers who had cooperated with the Wilson Administration were subtly punished. It was made clear that Wilson was no longer a presence in Chicago and his name should not be mentioned.

Until the spring of '68, Chicago had not had a riot comparable to that in Los Angeles, Newark or Detroit. Then King's assassination caused major disturbances in Chicago and resulted in several deaths. During the course of the rioting, much of the West Side was burned out. That was when Daley directed Superintendent Conlisk to issue a shoot-to-kill order.

In August the Democratic National Convention was scheduled to open in Chicago. Anyone familiar with the history of violence in the city would not have placed it there. When the nation was experiencing troubled times, Chicago was invariably one of the principal battlegrounds. In 1877, twenty people were killed there during a national railroad strike. In 1894, during another national railroad strike, thirteen people were killed in Chicago. In 1919, a time of great national unrest, a Chicago race riot produced thirty-eight fatalities. In 1937, with labor protests sweeping the country, the police shot and killed ten demonstrators marching on the Republic Steel plant in South Chicago. Shootouts between police and criminals were a regular affair in the Windy City. In the 1920s, the chief of detectives organized a special anti-gangster squad equipped with machine guns and told them, "Shoot first and shoot to kill.... If you meet a car containing bandits, pursue them and fire. When I arrive on the scene, my hopes will be fulfilled if you have shot off the top of their car and killed every criminal inside." Many members of the force, even in Wilson's time, adhered to that tradition. There were a number of cops with nicknames like "machine gun" Joe, Bob, or Bill—men who had used choppers to blow away criminals. An African-American cop nicknamed "Two Gun Pete" used both of his guns frequently. On the police side, it should be

---

7. Despite the corporate notion of win-win strategies, in mergers usually one CEO gets the corner office and the other gets his walking papers.

noted that some districts' station walls were festooned with pictures of murdered officers. In 1969, Jim Schaffer, the ex-major mentioned in Chapter 1, and his partner were literally blown apart by an individual who fired a rifle grenade at them.

Those who placed the convention in Chicago at a time of such national turmoil were defying history. Many people had urged that it be held in Miami immediately after the Republican meeting there. Miami was in a remote corner of the country, making it a lot harder for demonstrators to attend than Mid-continent Chicago, the transportation center of the nation. Daley, proud of his city and the bright and shiny police force O. W. Wilson had developed, assured President Johnson all would be well.

Within the Chicago police department, there were two schools of thought about how to handle the convention. One group, which had been favored by Wilson but was now out of power, believed that the demonstrators should be welcomed to the city, given a certain latitude, and even served complimentary coffee and Danish every morning. They realized that some people were coming to town to cause trouble, but they thought that if the city presented a good face, the moderates would not cooperate with the radicals and the media would not blame the police for whatever violence occurred. Superintendent Conlisk and his top aides, who bought into the federal warnings about one hundred thousand violent individuals descending on Chicago, believed that they should be given no concessions whatsoever. In any event, it was unlikely that Daley would have wanted to look soft in the face of so strong a challenge.

A week before the convention opened, the police department made a major mistake. It refused to allow the arriving demonstrators, who numbered less than a third of the amount estimated, to sleep in the public parks. Technically, the parks were closed at 11:00 p.m., however, the ordinance could easily have been waived. When police enforced it, they drove the demonstrators out of Lincoln Park onto the streets of the densely populated Near North Side nightlife district. There, battles broke out that were witnessed by thousands of Chicagoans and filmed by the media. The second major mistake came during convention week when the demonstrators were denied permission to march from the Loop to the convention site, seven miles away. The weather was hot, and it would have been very tiring to march. The area through which they had to pass was a maze of elevated railroad tracks, steep embankments and piles of waste material. Even those of us who had been raised there had no taste for scrambling over the terrain. Almost all of us had a memory of one of our boyhood chums who lost an arm, a leg, or even his life to a train. The area also happened to be Mayor Daley's political stronghold, so there would have been a lot of hecklers around screaming for blood. Any sensible marcher, finding himself in such an environment, would have stuck close to the police detail and been very happy to be escorted out of there when the march ended. Instead, after being refused permission to march, the demonstrators began battling with police in Grant Park, the front lawn of Chicago. Police leadership was not strong, and the rank-and-file was largely untrained for such situations. Outside law enforcement officials who were observing were stunned when they noted how individual police officers were breaking ranks and pursuing protesters. A maxim of military-type organizations is that it is essential to maintain unit cohesion. In that way, a smaller number of disciplined cops or soldiers can control an undisciplined mob.

The security arrangements on the convention floor were even more confusing than those in the field. In addition to a large force of plainclothes cops, there were federal agents and military intelligence operatives in the mix. I was second in command of the police detail, and one night, while I was checking our troops in before the convention assembled for the evening session, I asked a man who showed me ID whether he was a federal officer. He said that he was a federal agent working with the city police but that he was still in the army. I hope he was getting checks from all three. The fact that armed men, who were unacquainted with each other, were on that packed convention floor was not reassuring. Another time, an African-American man and woman, dressed as urban guerrilla fighters and sporting huge Afros, got into a battle with police officers and were dragged into a command center. It turned out they were military intelligence agents who, having to get a message quickly to their superiors, had resorted to the old trick of getting themselves arrested.

August 27th was Lyndon Johnson's birthday. It was planned that on that night he would suddenly fly into the Convention and receive the tribute of the delegates. A few hours before Johnson was scheduled to arrive, I sat watching songstress Anita Bryant and a full orchestra rehearse "Happy Birthday, Mr. President." As time went by, some of my officers came to me to say, "Shouldn't we be getting ready for the president's visit?" When I laughingly replied, "Don't worry about it," they thought that maybe I had lost my mind. Two days earlier it had become obvious that there was no way Johnson could enter the convention hall that night. Apparently none of the Democratic bigwigs or Johnson's aides cared to pass the information on to the top. The situation resembled the Vietnam experience. The responsible officials on the ground knew the war was going badly, but the depressing information was filtered out as it went up the chain of command. Finally, the White House learned the true situation from TV and the president's visit was canceled.

After working from midday till past midnight, I used to jump in my car and ride through the ghetto areas of the city. It was a hot, humid August, and thousands of people were sitting on doorsteps. No police were in sight, yet everything was perfectly calm. When the white demonstrators had first arrived in the city and appealed for support from blacks, they were turned down flat. The African-American leaders had no intention of being shields for the Ivy Leaguers and hippies. They divined correctly that it would not be the police deployed in the ghettos, but the United States Army. In fact, several thousand troops were at Fort Hood, Texas, ready to board planes for Chicago. It might have been the best thing if the troops had been sent in the first place. The commanding general of the Fifth Army, headquartered in the Chicago area, was Lieut. Gen. John "Mike" Michaelis, an outstanding figure in the U.S. army. As a lieutenant colonel in Korea, he and his "Wolfhound" regiment were routinely sent to the hottest spots on the line. It was commonly said of him, "He's either going to be a dead colonel or a live general." It turned out to be the latter.*** If the Army had been running security, there would have been a firm but fair hand at the controls. My contacts at Fifth Army informed me that Michaelis was chomping at the bit, waiting to be called. Instead, under the leadership that prevailed, the convention became a disaster.

The fiasco resulted in the federal prosecution of eight demonstrators, including such well-known ones as Abby Hoffman and Bobby Seale. Eight police officers, seven of them patrolmen, were chosen to stand trial for civil-rights violations. As one assistant United States attorney complained, "The whole thing is an exercise in futility." The juries will acquit the cops. Then the appellate courts will rule for the demonstrators, which is exactly what happened.[8]

Perhaps the real problem was that the Chicago police leadership did not realize they were going to be performing on a world stage, not just a local one. It was a mistake that the NYPD, which policed the capital of the world, never made. Chicago in 1968 was a turning point in American history. It increased the bitterness between the liberal anti-war crowd and "my country right or wrong" blue-collar Americans. The latter deserted the Democratic Party in droves and not for forty years would a northern Democrat be elected

---

8. The morning after the convention ended, I sat in an upscale café across from Grant Park with a journalist who later became a national TV star. The restaurant still contained broken glass on the floor and an odor of tear gas from the previous day's rioting. We were the only customers. My friend was depressed at the prospect of Nixon's winning the presidency. Nor, as someone close to the Kennedys, was she thrilled with Humphrey as the Democratic candidate. I, in turn, reflected the attitude of most Chicagoans that things weren't so bad because no one had died. In a city where there had frequently been a number of people killed in disturbances, this was an understandable reaction. But Chicago was not the whole of America, and I knew that around the country many people would have a very different opinion.

About this time, a well-known journalist came into the restaurant to buy something, and my friend invited him to join us. In making conversation, I asked him how he thought the election would turn out. He looked at me as if it were 1865 and I had just asked, "Other than that, Mrs. Lincoln, how did you like the play?" He quietly replied, "The election is over."

president. Conservatism would replace liberalism as the dominant faith in America for a generation, and bitter divisions between its citizens would continue and grow worse.

Chicago, the political convention center of the country, did not hold another one for twenty-eight years. No one dared to do it until President Clinton broke the ice in 1996. Jim Conlisk remained police superintendent until 1974. Again, it was an example of how a mayor's wrong decision in selecting a police chief can tarnish his entire record. Mayor Daley's image changed from that of a wise, old-fashioned politician who put his support behind liberal icons like Jack Kennedy to some kind of American fascist, like "Bull" Connor.

Professional policing, as preached by O. W. Wilson, did not take hold in Chicago. The city had always been a freewheeling town, where dropping a little cash got things done quickly. This heritage was not going to be wiped out in three or four years by some professor who, when he arrived, did not know how to find State Street or had ever met a ward boss. Within the police department, the lessons of the Wilson era confirmed the conventional police wisdom. Reform administrations do not last long, and those who cooperate with them will be punished when conditions returned to normal.

Chapter 6

Nixon's Schemes Fail, Webster Saves the FBI

If 1968 was a watershed year in American politics, one major reason was the escalation of crime and the waves of disorder that swept the United States in the 1960s. Four years earlier, there had been a warning that this would happen. In 1964, the Republicans had nominated Arizona Senator Barry Goldwater for president. In the election, President Johnson and the Democrats were able to convince the country that a Goldwater victory would mean an escalation of the Vietnam War, and he was overwhelmingly defeated.[1] During the campaign, however, Goldwater's complaints about crime and disorder resonated with a number of voters. At first, liberals dismissed his assertions as racist or a distortion of the facts. However, some Democratic leaders realized that Goldwater was not far off the mark. Big-city mayors, who controlled police departments, were hearing from their chiefs as well as the citizenry that crime was rising significantly. When a congressman would go back home, many people, including a number of blacks, complained that it was no longer safe to walk the streets. In 1965, the Watts riot shocked the country. There had not been an outbreak of that magnitude since Detroit in 1943.

The solution to the crime problem that the conservatives offered was basically a get-tough campaign by which cops locked up the bad guys, judges sentenced them to prison and the states ensured that there were enough cells to accommodate them. On the liberal side, some criminal-justice scholars

---

1. Whereupon Johnson escalated the war himself.

argued that the supposed increase in crime was a "statistical artifact" due to better reporting. Other liberals conceded that there was a problem, but that the solution was to meet the needs of the disadvantaged, particularly blacks.

President Johnson expected to run for re-election in 1968. He was too astute a politician to tell people who had been mugged or shot that they were "statistical artifacts." However, he was not about to substitute "lock 'em up" for "The Great Society" social welfare programs. He wanted a report that would express a consensus that all sides could agree on. So he appointed a commission of distinguished citizens and leading experts chaired by former Attorney General Nicholas deB. Katzenbach to study the crime problem and lay out a solution. It was not a task commissions are generally able to perform.

In any diverse group, there will be differing opinions. The commission members may be unable to agree on the facts. Is the glass half-empty or half-full? Is it the best of times or the worst of times? Some simply express the conventional wisdom of their specialty. Most of the time, elite opinion prevails over a voice from the field, even though the latter might know more about the subject. Commission member Kingman Brewster, who, as president of Yale, dwelt in an ivory tower, was sure to have anything he said receive respectful attention in the *New York Times*.[2] Johnson, like any president, would have some of his people planted within the commission, and his advisers would attempt to steer it toward findings the administration could live with. Only by compromise and papering over disagreements would a commission be able to produce a report that most people could accept.

The United States had not had a national crime commission since 1929, when President Hoover appointed one chaired by George Wickersham, who had been attorney general under President Taft. That commission was basically charged with studying the effects of Prohibition and whether the "noble experiment" should continue. Its findings were parodied by Franklin P. Adams in a famous piece of doggerel.

> Prohibition is an awful flop.
> We like it.
> It can't stop what it's meant to stop.
> We like it.
> It's left a trail of graft and slime,
> It don't prohibit worth a dime,
> It's filled our land with vice and crime.
> Nevertheless, we're for it.*

---

2. A few years after the commission met, a number of Black Panthers were brought to trial in New Haven, the seat of Yale University. At that time, Brewster expressed the opinion that a Black Panther could not get a fair trial anywhere in America. Shortly after he made the remark, the Panthers were acquitted by a jury.

A key figure on that commission was police reformer August Vollmer, but his views had little influence, even within the law enforcement community, because he did not have the respect of the big-city chiefs. In contrast, the report of the committee, chaired by Harvard law professor Zachariah Chafee, on police third-degree tactics had enormous influence because it was embraced by the legal community.

In 1965, America's most influential criminal justice official would not condescend to be on Johnson's commission. J. Edgar Hoover, from his office in the DOJ, had long been the nation's most powerful cop. His power lay partly in his ability to block other people from getting things done that he did not approve of. The irony was that the man had created what became probably the best law enforcement organization in the world, but in so doing made it more difficult to improve American police.

Sometimes the remarks of the commission leaders were humorous. The chief of a major city force, when asked the leading problem faced by the police, said it was "responding to a robbery in progress when it was raining. Everyone in the street is running and the police have to figure out which one has a gun." If, before the Normandy invasion, Gen. Eisenhower had said the leading problem his troops would face was German snipers, he might have been removed as supreme commander.

The corrections experts working with the commission were a well-educated group with considerable experience in their own field. Their report placed great weight on the government investing heavily in treatment programs as a means of dealing with criminal behavior.

One great difference between the police and correctional fields was that the latter was considered a respectable subject for academic study in college departments of sociology and psychology. At Harvard, criminology even found a niche in the law school. On the other hand, as O. W. Wilson's experience at Cal-Berkeley had demonstrated, police studies were much less welcome. John Jay College of Criminal Justice of the City University of New York had been established in 1964 because, with the baby boom coming to an end, fewer schoolteachers would be needed. So the university administration sought to make up the shortfall in educational students by increasing the number studying policing. However, within the university, John Jay was often regarded as a glorified police academy where professors taught students how to put on the handcuffs.[3]

3. The regular faculty all held doctorates from the major universities, and every discipline was represented. Some of them, like the historians Blanche Cook and Trumbull Higgins, political scientist Harold Laswell and literary critic Dwight Macdonald, were top figures in their fields. John Jay's location in Manhattan was a place where a scholar could interact with the leading figures of the world—something that could not be done in

The Organized Crime Task Force had been formed late because President Johnson did not want one. Fighting the mob was former attorney general Robert Kennedy's issue, and Johnson was not about to push the ideas of his most likely opponent in the 1968 Democratic primaries. Finally, pressure from some of the commissioners, like Lewis Powell, president of the American Bar Association and a future United States Supreme Court justice, forced the administration to appropriate a modest sum of money to investigate organized crime. When the task force recommended legalizing electronic eavesdropping, Johnson refused to accept the full commission report. Not until crime commission leaders threatened to toss it over the White House fence while cameras filmed the moment did LBJ give way.

The final report of the commission concluded that crime was indeed a problem. Its principal recommendation for controlling it was more "Great Society" type social programs. As for police, it offered better training and enhanced community relations programs. It did not propose any specific anti-crime strategy; rather, it implied that if the cops were more professional, this would translate into crime reductions.

Following up on the president's commission, the Department of Justice created the Law Enforcement Assistance Administration (LEAA) to dispense federal funds for the purpose of improving American criminal justice along the lines contained in the report. While the money caught the eye, LEAA provided an opportunity to create a federal center for police research and innovation away from the control of J. Edgar Hoover. In 1968, many "experts" and public officials were eager to help the LEAA spend its dollars. Then there was a change in the script. The Democrats were not going to be disseminating the money. In March, Johnson, undone by the Vietnam War, dropped out of the presidential race. In June, Robert Kennedy was assassinated. In August, the battles at the Democratic convention in Chicago turned off the electorate. When President Nixon took office in 1969, it was his administration that had the LEAA money to spend on projects they favored.

In 1969, I was preparing to leave Harvard and return to the real world when I got a call from a Kennedy supporter I knew, who surprisingly had taken a job in Nixon's LEAA. He asked if I would be interested in working in the new administration. He told me I could head any of several LEAA divisions that were aimed at reforming the criminal justice system. When President Nixon had replaced President Johnson, a new command had been installed at main Justice. The new attorney general was John Mitchell, a Wall Street bond

---

Hanover, New Hampshire, or Ithaca, New York.

lawyer who worked in a firm that Nixon had joined after his defeat for governor in California.

On November 15, 1969, I was scheduled to observe what would be the last great anti-Vietnam march in Washington. I arranged a visit to DOJ on the 14th to discuss my employment. That day I also went over to the District of Columbia police headquarters, where I was shown their new pepper fogger gas machine. It was reputedly able to clear the streets of thousands of demonstrators within a few minutes of being put into use. It had failed in previous tests because the operators pumped the handle too hard, thereby causing the machine to jam.

The next day a young Harvard law grad, serving as administrative assistant to one of the top officials at the Justice Department, escorted me around Washington to facilitate my observation of events. After all, I was soon to be a DOJ honcho myself—or so I thought. Our first port of call was a briefing at Mayor Walter Washington's office. The two of us entered the room unannounced and unchallenged and sat down to listen in. As briefings go, it was on a par with those given before a Shriners parade. I mused that if this was the level of command competence, we might be in for a long afternoon.

Our next stop was a military briefing being provided for a three-star general. The old man (a term of respect in the military) immediately spotted us and asked his aides who we were and what we were doing there. They explained that I was a veteran of the battle at the Chicago Democratic convention. So I was welcomed. I was not entirely comfortable with the identification provided for me, since I did not think the police performance at the convention was something to boast about. Having participated in military briefings, I quickly realized that this one was first-rate. I was particularly interested in the array of technology they had available, such as helicopters, closed-circuit TV, etc. Photos from Army observation planes could be fed right into the briefing room in real time.

Listening to the discussion, I found it obvious that the plan for containing the demonstration, if things got rough, was that the armed forces would take complete charge of security operations. No one was going to leave the protection of the White House or the Capitol to a mere police force. As mentioned earlier, I always felt that if Lt. Gen. Michaelis had been put in overall command at the Chicago Convention, the situation would not have turned out as it did.

Finally, we headed for the Department of Justice, which was to be the focal point of a protest by ten thousand radicals including the Weathermen. Probably the most militant organization in the United States at the time, they had made no secret that they were going to raise a ruckus there. Outside the building, security guards were turning away Department of Justice employees unless they carried a special pass for that day.

The main march had gone well. Turnout was on the order of two hundred thousand, with most people there to protest, not riot. Inside the building there was a company of U.S. paratroopers in battle dress, with helmets, rifles, gas masks, etc. If there was any serious trouble, they would have sprung into action and, in the unlikely event that they were not sufficient, the Army could immediately reinforce them by using troop-carrying helicopters. Down another hall, there was a group of FBI agents with machine guns. When DOJ employees attempted to enter, they were told that the area belonged to the FBI, not the DOJ. Obviously, Hoover was still maintaining that he ran an autonomous operation.

Since I had no pass and my guide lacked a special one, we were left waiting outside the building. Suddenly a top official of DOJ came out, recognized me and explained to the security guards that I was a Chicago expert. Leaving my guide behind, I followed the official into the building and was taken to the office of Attorney General Mitchell, who was temporarily out. Now I was worried. I was not on any official assignment, just seeking information for myself, and I certainly did not belong in the inner sanctum of the attorney general of the United States. I could see my DOJ career ending before it had started.

When Mitchell and a few of his deputies gathered to discuss the situation outside, nobody paid a bit of attention to me. Apparently it was the old rule. People assume that if you are there, you must have the right to be there. Eager to get away from the room and to observe the march, I went out on the attorney general's balcony. As I did, the protesters were marching around the building and, on two occasions, hauled down American flags and hoisted Vietcong banners. The police removed them and restored the Stars and Stripes. Just then someone tapped me on the shoulder and asked if he could join me on the balcony. It was Mitchell. Simultaneously, the pepper fogger began dispensing gas. This time the machine did not jam; I could hear the protesters coughing and choking. Then some of the gas began drifting up to Mitchell's outer office, which was filled with government employees who also began coughing. A few years earlier, during a siege, I had been hit with gas fired by friendly forces and for a while, though I was conscious, was pretty much out of the battle. This time I felt nothing—why, I do not know. Perhaps because I stood still while others were moving around. The staff members were looking at me, and some were whispering that I was that fellow from Chicago, where cops ate tear gas for breakfast. By nightfall most protesters were on their way out of town.[**]

As it turned out, I was not to become a DOJ employee. It was obvious that the Kennedyites would not last long in the new administration. If I came in as one of them, I would be dismissed when they were. So I decided not to accept the offer. Instead of Washington, I ended up back in Chicago, where it was made very clear that, having gone to Harvard, I could not expect the red carpet to be rolled out. Cut adrift, I adopted Harvard as my home, and I joined the staff at the MIT-Harvard Joint Center for Urban Studies. The campus was still in ferment. However, most of the young revolutionaries that I knew in Cambridge were friendly enough toward me. I did less well with some of the Harvard establishment.[4]

* * * *

When Richard Nixon became president, he faced the same problems as every other administration—how to get the bureaucracy to carry out his policy initiatives. As President Truman said of incoming President Eisenhower, "Poor Ike, he'll think he's still in the Army and all he has to do is press a button and say, 'Do this, do that.' But when he does, nothing will happen."

Nixon wanted to be seen doing something about crime. He also wanted a law enforcement agency that the White House could count on the way FDR could with the FBI. Hoover was still on the scene, though, and he would not put his agency at the disposal of Nixon. Shrewd operator that he was, Hoover knew Nixon was likely to fail as president or, worse, might try to take control of the Bureau by retiring him.

In federal law enforcement, each agency concentrated on its limited mission. None of them had a broad enough mandate to function as a general police agency. In some instances, it would have been illegal or unconstitutional. However, an exception had emerged. Drugs became such a huge problem that it touched almost every aspect of American life. High-school and college kids were among the biggest users, so parents were frightened. Because addicts had to scramble to find money to support their habit, drug use was connected to

---

4. It wasn't until a decade or two later, when some of the "radicals" were coining money on Wall Street, that they tried to avoid me. I think it was because they felt a little embarrassed. They could have handled the situation with the same line the European elite use "not to be a socialist at twenty shows a lack of heart. To be one at thirty shows a lack of head." However, some members of the Harvard faculty and administration never quite accepted me. I came to understand why O. W. Wilson had lost his deanship at Berkeley: because the chancellor thought cops were Neanderthals. One staffer complimented me by saying that before she met me, she thought police were "men of savage instinct and dubious intellect." It was the equivalent of telling a black man, "You are not like the others of your race." At least she did not claim that some of her best friends were cops. When people would ask me, "Why did you decide to become a cop?" I always answered, "Well you see, when Pater died, he left the estate in great disarray, so it was necessary for me to seek employment and since a position in commerce would have been déclassé, I joined the public service." My Harvard sojourn did not last long.

other crimes, such as robbery, larceny and burglary. At least, that was the wisdom of the time. The facts were a little more complicated. For example, did addicts become criminals or did criminals become addicts? In some places, drug use had killed off the members, or damped down the passions, of some of the toughest street gangs.

Nixon's staffers began to look at using drug enforcement to achieve a decrease in overall crime. If there was to be a concentrated drive against drugs, it would have to include the Department of Justice's Bureau of Narcotics and Dangerous Drugs BNDD (formerly known as the Federal Bureau of Narcotics, or FBN), Treasury's Customs and the IRS, as well as state and local cops. Since each agency balked at cooperating with the others, one way to achieve coordination was to make them all responsible to the White House. The hidden agenda was that the new organization was also slated to become a Nixon administration investigative agency—i.e., a presidential secret police. It included among its staff some former CIA operatives. In Eisenhower's time (under Allen Dulles, whose brother John was Secretary of State), the agency was loyal to the president and John Foster Dulles. When Johnson was president, he appointed as director a clueless former admiral whom the CIA staff shot down at every opportunity. Later, when the Nixon administration stumbled over Watergate, both the FBI and CIA refused to cover for the White House plumbers.

Jack Ingersoll, who headed the BNDD, would not go along with being a White House pawn, so he was scheduled to be replaced. Gene Rossides, a New York lawyer and former college football star, who directed law enforcement for the Treasury, also would not cooperate with the White House. For a while, the Nixonites foisted G. Gordon Liddy, later of Watergate notoriety, on Rossides as an assistant, but eventually Liddy was moved to another agency and later was fired.

The keystone of the White House plan was the creation of a new Office of Drug Abuse Law Enforcement (ODALE), which was to concentrate on low-level, easy-to-make drug arrests. In this way, the total number of arrests would rise considerably, thereby boosting the administration's statistical performance. Ironically, the corrections experts in the Nixon administration were trying to cut down on imprisonment, while persons concerned with drug activity were trying to vastly increase the number of arrests and ultimately the incarceration rate. Ingersoll and Rossides learned about the plan when President Nixon appeared on a television program the night of December 21, 1971. The show was supposed to portray White House operations, but it was carefully planned, and at the scheduled moment, Nixon stepped in front of the cameras and announced his reorganization plan. Ingersoll resigned, and John Bartels, an assistant U.S. attorney from New York, took over his agency, which was renamed the Drug Enforcement Administration (DEA), while another former New York assistant U.S. attorney, Myles Ambrose, ran ODALE.

ODALE included a number of strike forces, each with its own prosecutors. It looked like an organization that could accomplish a great deal. In action, however, things quickly went wrong. Raids are among the most difficult operations to carry out. It is not uncommon to break into the wrong location, subject innocent people to searches and make a number of other errors. ODALE kicked off operations in 1972. In 1973, one of its task forces made a series of raids in southern Illinois, just east of St. Louis, Missouri. Agents who conducted them were accused of breaking into private homes and putting guns to the heads of innocent residents. In one instance, they reportedly imprisoned the occupant of a house for seventy-seven hours while they ransacked the place. The walls were smashed, windows were broken and property was confiscated. None of the raiding parties had search warrants, and apparently they had entered various houses by mistake. Ten law enforcement officers from the DEA, the Internal Revenue Service and the St. Louis Police Department were indicted (though they were later acquitted). As a result of the widespread publicity given to the affair and U.S. Senate hearings on them, ODALE was discontinued. In any event, it would not have lasted long, because in 1974 Watergate put an end to the Nixon administration and most of the people involved in redesigning drug enforcement and political policing. Not until 1977, when journalist Edward Jay Epstein published his book *Agency of Fear*, was the plot revealed. Had the book come out a few years earlier, it would have been a bombshell. In 1977, it was overshadowed by Watergate.

One consequence of the Vietnam War, Watergate, and various disasters of the Johnson and Nixon administrations was that many Americans lost confidence in the integrity of their government. In the law enforcement sphere, this manifested in a new wave of doubts about the investigation of the greatest murder case in United States history, the assassination of President John F. Kennedy. Such has been the impact of the crime that, even today, most people are familiar with the basic facts in the case. On November 22, 1963, the president was shot and killed while riding through the streets of Dallas, Texas, in the backseat of his open limousine, and Texas governor John Connally, sitting in front of him, was wounded. That same day, Lee Harvey Oswald was charged with the murder. Two days later, Oswald himself was shot to death by Jack Ruby in Dallas police headquarters, while a national TV audience watched.

The murder of the president naturally led people to ask what Oswald's motive was and what forces might be behind him. His own murder caused many to believe that the two killings were part of a larger plot. In December,

President Johnson appointed a commission of seven prominent Americans, chaired by U.S. Chief Justice Earl Warren, to investigate the president's murder. In September 1964, the Warren Commission, as it was popularly known, issued a report which concluded that Lee Harvey Oswald carried out the assassination without the assistance of other parties. At first, the report was acclaimed by the media and was widely accepted by the public. Then doubts began to surface. One puzzling matter was that Jack Ruby, the owner of a strip joint, was allowed free entry into Dallas police headquarters on the days when Oswald was in custody. Ruby's background and connections suggested possible organized-crime involvement in the case. Oswald was reported to be a strong supporter of Cuba's Fidel Castro, raising the possibility of some kind of foreign plot. President Kennedy was unpopular with certain right-wing circles in America, some of whom espoused violence. In 1968, the assassinations of Sen. Robert Kennedy and Martin Luther King, Jr., added to suspicions that there was an ongoing plot to kill liberal leaders.

Nearly half a century after the murder, a majority of Americans still do not accept the official version of the case. One reason may be that the actions or inactions of law enforcement turned a fairly straightforward crime into an enduring mystery. Had the criminal investigation process followed a different pattern, the case might have been resolved to general satisfaction. It had begun in a relatively ordinary fashion. When the president was shot, police rushed to the sixth floor of the Texas Book Depository building, which observers identified as the place from which the shots had come. They confiscated a rifle near a window, and, based on witnesses' interviews, came up with Lee Harvey Oswald as a suspect. The police radio broadcast an alert to be on the lookout for Oswald. When Officer J. D. Tippett attempted to question a man he suspected might be the suspect, he was shot to death. Police responding to the scene of the shooting were told by witnesses that the gunman had run into a nearby theater. Officers entered and, after a struggle, seized Oswald.

Following interrogation by Dallas police officers, led by the head of the homicide squad, Capt. Will Fritz, though Oswald denied killing the president, he was charged with murder. The next major step would have been for him to be brought to trial. There he might have pleaded guilty on the advice of counsel in order to save his life. At the time, the electric chair was used regularly to execute Texas murderers. If he chose to contest the charge, the state's evidence would have been subject to a rigorous examination by skilled attorneys for the defense. The trial would have been extensively reported on and, in addition to the judicial finding, the American people would have made up their own minds about the case. The murder of Oswald foreclosed those possibilities. In the aftermath of Oswald's death, Dallas police were subjected to intense criticism.

However, their shortcomings reflected weaknesses in American law enforcement generally. Had Kennedy been shot in another city, the same events might have occurred. One problem was that American detectives were not as professionally competent as their European counterparts. In conducting criminal interrogations, they had never embraced the principles of forensic psychology. A further complication in the Dallas investigation was the division of duties in law enforcement. The assassination of President Kennedy was not the first such event in American history. Between 1865 and 1901, three American presidents had been gunned down. Yet the murder of a president had not been made a federal crime. Not until after McKinley's assassination, in 1901, did Congress legalize the informal practice of assigning Secret Service agents to guard the president. The rationale had been that Americans did not want their presidents surrounded by royal guards and accorded any special status. This may have been acceptable in the nineteenth century. In the post-World War II era, when the American president became the most powerful leader in the world, with his finger on an atomic trigger, it made no sense that it was a federal crime to climb over a fence to enter into a nuclear facility but not to attack the ultimate controller of the nuclear arsenal. Thus the investigation of the Kennedy murder was left to local authorities. This presented a major problem. In a presidential assassination, political factors, foreign and domestic, had to be considered. Yet local cops and prosecutors were often unaware of them and, in some instances, could not be told about them because they were state secrets.

At the federal level, three rival agencies had a role in presidential protection. The United States Secret Service, an arm of the Treasury Department, was charged with guarding him and, in addition, maintained a protective research unit to gather information on possible threats. However, presidential protection and national security were not the prime duty of the service. Rather, it was financial crimes like counterfeiting and fraud. The FBI, a bureau of the Department of Justice, did not guard the president but enforced most of the country's national security laws. As part of this responsibility, they were expected to be aware of threats against the president. A third agency, the CIA, which officially had no jurisdiction in the United States, not only collected intelligence abroad but, counter to its charter, in the United States as well. If there was a foreign plot against the president, the CIA might have been the first to know. During the various investigations, it was revealed that two members of the Warren commission, FBI director J. Edgar Hoover and former CIA director Allen Dulles, had not revealed certain information to their fellow commissioners. Hoover neglected to tell them about a threatening letter

Oswald had sent to an FBI agent, and Dulles remained silent about the agency's attempts to overthrow Fidel Castro.

The Dallas Police Department, which conducted the actual investigation, was a typical American police force of the time. In 1946, when the Chicago mob was in an expansionist mood, it cast its eyes far afield. A Texas drug dealer named Paul Jones approached some Chicago organized-crime leaders about backing a lucrative gambling operation in Dallas. A new county sheriff was about to take office there and, seeing an opportunity, the Chicago bosses authorized Jones to start negotiations with him. Jones got in contact with a lieutenant from the Dallas Police Department, who introduced him to the sheriff-elect. Jones told the sheriff that all his backers wanted was one big place hidden out in county territory, rather than half a dozen joints scattered throughout the city. For this he proposed to pay one hundred fifty thousand (1946) dollars per year. The negotiations proceeded so well that a Chicago mob lieutenant, Pat Manno, was brought down to close the deal. In Chicago, Manno was an overseer of the policy (numbers) racket, which the mob was rapidly taking over from African-American operators. So he was experienced in Mafia mergers and acquisitions. To sweeten the pot, Manno pledged mob support to the sheriff in going after ordinary criminals who might commit robberies and burglaries. Unbeknownst to Jones and Manno, their meetings with authorities were being recorded and photographed. Shortly after Manno flew back to Chicago, Jones was arrested and given three years in prison for attempted bribery. Efforts to extradite Manno to Texas failed.

In 1946, at about the same time Chicago mobsters were planning to move into Dallas, a petty Chicago dive owner named Jacob Rubenstein (*aka* Jack Ruby) moved to Dallas. There he ran strip joints Chicago style, enforcing order with his fists or a blackjack. Some researchers have claimed that he was sent to Dallas as part of the Chicago incursion; others believe he already had personal reasons for relocating to Dallas. Whatever, Ruby never held any position in the Chicago mob, although he could be characterized as a loose associate. In 1963 he was still around Dallas, where his strip joint was a hangout for cops, who were treated by Ruby as honored guests. That Ruby could have run a rough joint in Dallas without some kind of local arrangements of the folded green variety is hard to imagine.

Friday night, Saturday and into Sunday after the president was shot, Ruby was allowed free access to Dallas police headquarters. On Sunday the police agreed to allow TV to film a perp walk of Oswald as he was being transferred to the county jail. It was the standard kind of accommodation that many police departments would have made; but if FBI agents had been handling the case, they would not have allowed outsiders to frequent their headquarters or staged a perp walk. Ruby, standing in the crowd watching as Oswald walked through, drew a gun and shot and killed him. Many people, unaware of how loosely police affairs were handled in America, drew the logical conclusion that that cops had allowed Ruby to kill Oswald in order to silence him. When Ruby died of cancer in jail three years later, at the comparatively young age of fifty-five, many people believed that he too was murdered to keep him quiet.

Bookshelves groan under the weight of volumes that purport to explain the events in Dallas. Probably the most influential interpretation has not been a book but a movie, *JFK,* directed by Oliver Stone. It laid the blame for the assassination on U.S. government agents and right-wing forces. Most accounts of the case tell you more about those relating them than they do about the crime. If the author leans to the left, the assassins are agents of the government; if he leans to the right, it's Castro or Moscow; if they are organized-crime experts, it is the mob.

To a neutral observer, the circumstances of the case suggest that it was not carried out by a highly professional group, such as a foreign or U.S. intelligence agency. Organized groups prefer to attack the target at a location that he normally frequents so they can carefully plan their operation. They would not have chosen a distant city where there was no normal presidential routine to familiarize themselves with. On November 22, 1963, any number of things could have happened that would have precluded Kennedy's passing the Book Depository when he did. For example, the officially announced route of the motorcade might have been altered because of time considerations that suddenly arose. The notion that assassins could hide shooters on a grassy knoll with crowds around is also difficult to accept. On the other hand, there are examples of lone individuals who have shot, or shot at, visiting presidents in other cities. Sara Jane Moore and Lynette "Squeaky" Fromme each tried to assassinate President Gerald Ford during separate visits to California; Sirhan Sirhan killed presidential candidate Robert Kennedy in Los Angeles.

It is also hard to believe that the mob was behind the killing, although with them many pieces of the puzzle seem to fit. However, organized-crime figures both before and after the assassination of Kennedy were subjected to electronic eavesdropping by federal and other law enforcement agencies. While some gangsters suggested it would be desirable if the president or his brother were killed, there has never been any mention of an actual plot or naming of the killers.

At this late date, the case will never be solved to general satisfaction. Even after Castro is no more, were a file to be produced in Havana showing that the Cuban intelligence service organized the assassination, most people would believe it was a fake. Like the Pearl Harbor attack, the Kennedy assassination will be debated for decades.[5]

* * * *

Among its many mistakes, the Nixon administration also lost a great opportunity to revamp the FBI. The death of Hoover threw the agency into disarray. The president appointed L. Patrick Grey to head the Bureau. A retired naval captain who became a Department of Justice lawyer, Grey had not made much of a mark in either field. He also worked as an administrator in Nixon's 1972 re-election campaign. As an ex-military man, Grey was used to saying "yes sir" to his superiors. As White House chief of staff, General Al Haig, would later tell Attorney General Elliot Richardson, when he refused to fire the Watergate special prosecutor, "Your commander-in-chief has given you an order." In Richardson's case, he chose to resign rather than acquiesce.

The Watergate scandal broke on Grey's watch, leaving him torn between carrying out the investigations without political interference and seeking to placate White House aides such as H. R. Haldeman, John Ehrlichman, and John Dean. Grey, as an outsider, had no support in the Bureau, and Hoover's former number two-man, Mark Felt, angry at being passed over for the directorship, began feeding derogatory information to the press. Years later, when Felt confessed to being "Deep Throat," most knowledgeable law enforcement professionals were not at all surprised. He had long been suspected. Grey did not last long. He resigned and pleaded guilty to destroying some records. Felt was later convicted of authorizing illegal break-ins at the offices of radical groups in New York City. Ironically, former president Nixon testified in defense of Felt. Later, Felt was pardoned by President Ronald Reagan.

In 1973, Clarence Kelley, chief of police of Kansas City, Missouri, and formerly an FBI SAC, was named director of the Bureau. Kelley was seen as a man of integrity who would pose no threat to the FBI management hierarchy. Unlike Hoover, Kelley was willing to take on public corruption cases, and on his watch the Bureau began to hire women and more minorities.

In 1978, under the Carter administration, Kelley was succeeded by another Missourian, William Webster, judge of the United States Court of Appeals in St. Louis. Webster came out of a different background than most G-men. He had attended elite schools and been a partner in a leading law firm. However, as a former United States attorney and judge, he had been able to observe the FBI's work. Under Webster, the Bureau undertook the ABSCAM investigation,

---

5. For further analysis of the JFK case, see Appendix A.

where an agent, posing as an Arab sheik looking for favors from politicians, paid bribes to seven members of Congress, including U.S. Senator Harrison A. Williams, Jr., of New Jersey. Those targeted were Democrats, and it took courage for President Carter's attorney general, Griffin Bell, to allow the investigation to proceed, since it would do a great deal of damage to the president's party. Official Washington judged Webster to have done a very good job at the FBI and in 1987 he was appointed to head the CIA. The fact that Webster was a Brahmin meant he would not be derided by CIA agents as a "gumshoe cop."

The greatest success of the FBI was in breaking the power of the American Mafia. In the 1970s, the Bureau began to assign a large contingent of agents to work on organized-crime cases, some of them operating in an undercover capacity. It was a practice Hoover never permitted, fearing that it would lead to corruption. At about the same time, a former Kennedy justice department prosecutor, Notre Dame Professor Robert Blakey, "invented" the Racketeer Influenced Corrupt Organization (RICO) law. While invention is not a word normally used to describe the enactment of a statute, the RICO law that Blakey designed was a truly new instrument that made it illegal to participate in an organization or enterprise involved in a pattern of racketeering. A pattern could comprise as few as two of thirty-four common state and federal crimes, committed within a ten-year period; and on a RICO charge an individual could be convicted of both the substantive crime and conspiracy, with a maximum of twenty years for each offense, and a life sentence if murder was involved.

Many lawyers felt that the statute was unconstitutional. Previously, prosecutors could not introduce evidence that defendants had been involved in crimes other than the specific ones they were charged with, nor could they allege that the defendant was part of a criminal organization. Under RICO, past crimes could be cited to prove that the defendants were members of a racketeering organization. Even if they had been acquitted on the other charges, it did not matter. The crux of the law was carrying out the activity on behalf of a criminal organization. It took a decade for Blakey to teach lawyers how to use RICO. When he tried to explain it to the federal prosecutor's office in the Southern District of New York, in the midst of his presentation the U.S. attorney himself, Whitney North Seymour, Jr., terminated the meeting, calling it a waste of time. When Blakey finally did sell RICO, it became the foremost weapon in the FBI's battle against the mobs.

Armed with this new tool, the government went after the key elements of the mobs in their principal strongholds like Chicago, New York, and Las Vegas. In Chicago the mob's core strength was its political influence, particularly in the courts. One major operation, initiated in 1980, was called "Operation Greylord" (after the grey wigs worn by English judges, who are commonly addressed as "m'Lord"). It led to the FBI installing the first legal bug ever to be placed in the judge's chambers of an American court. The Cook County Circuit Court was cited in a federal indictment as "a criminal enterprise."

"Greylord" began in traffic court, where the bribes were penny-ante sums, and moved to the more prestigious divisions that dealt with felonies and major civil matters. A frequent tactic used in the investigation was the creation of fake cases, which could be presented to the courts. In one instance, a man whose briefcase was snatched pursued the thief through the streets, tackled him and held him until police arrived. To the responding cops' surprise, all the witnesses were eager to come forward and tell what they had seen. It was quickly determined that everyone involved, including the "thief," was an FBI agent.

The sting cast also included Judge Brocton Lockwood, a Downstater who was temporarily sitting in the Cook County court system, and an assistant state's attorney named Terry Hake, who was described by associates as someone who "had the face of an altar boy and the demeanor of an Eagle Scout." Lockwood, dubbed the "hillbilly judge," wore cowboy boots that contained a concealed microphone. Hake paid bribes to various individuals around the court, after which he would report to the FBI. When the investigation ended, twenty judges, fifty-seven lawyers and sixteen police officers or deputy sheriffs had been convicted of various crimes.***

Another case was known as Gambat, for "gambling attorney." A young lawyer taped politicians, judges and mob figures he did business with. This led to the fall of Chicago's First Ward Democratic organization, which had been a key link between politicians and organized crime since the nineteenth century. Every day the ward leadership met at a reserved a booth in a restaurant across from city hall, so the FBI placed a bug there. Until it was discovered by a busboy, it produced many interesting conversations. The Bureau also had a hidden camera aimed at the table. The leader of the First Ward organization, Pat Marcy, died while awaiting trial; other members were convicted and imprisoned. Mayor Richard M. Daley took advantage of the case to redraw the ward boundaries excluding the lucrative Loop business district, which the ward had feasted off for decades.+

A by-product of Gambat was the indictment of mob hitman Harry Aleman. Aleman had been prosecuted in 1977 on what appeared to be an open-and-shut murder case. However, the judge, who was known as a "tough on crime" jurist, took a ten-thousand-dollar bribe to acquit Aleman. The public uproar after the acquittal led to the judge's being defeated for re-election. Revelations by the lawyer-informer resulted in Aleman's being placed on trial again, although many lawyers believed that this was a violation of the double-jeopardy rule. Aleman was convicted, and the verdict was upheld by the U.S. Supreme Court, which ruled that Aleman had never really been in jeopardy because the original case had been fixed before trial. Aleman was sentenced to a minimum of one hundred years in state prison. The crooked judge, who was then living in Arizona, killed himself after his role was revealed.

In 1983, Joe Bonnano, boss of New York City's Bonnano family, published his autobiography, in which he described the operations of the New York mob commission composed of the heads of the city's five families. The new U.S. attorney for the Southern District of New York, Rudy Giuliani, read the book and decided that if Bonnano could write about the commission, he could prosecute it. He then proceeded to do just that. In February 1985, the FBI arrested the top leadership of all five New York mob families. Among them were Paul Castellano, boss of the Gambinos, Tony "Ducks" Corallo, head of the Lucchese family, Carmine Persico, leader of the Colombos (formerly the Profacis), and Rusty Rastelli, current boss of the Bonnano family. Anthony "Fat Tony" Salerno, who law enforcement believed was the top man in the Genovese family, was also hauled in. The real boss, Vincent "The Chin" Gigante, pretended to be mentally unbalanced, doing such things as walking around his neighborhood in Greenwich Village in a bathrobe and mumbling incoherently. A number of lesser figures were also arrested.

The principal focus of the investigation was the mob's control of the construction industry—especially concrete suppliers, who engaged in a regular system of bid rigging. During the trial, Castellano was murdered by an ambitious sub-boss named John Gotti. Rastelli was severed because he was facing charges in another case. The prosecutors played extensive tapes from the defendants, thereby convicting them from their own mouths. All were given one-hundred-year sentences. Later both "Chin" Gigante and John Gotti would also fall.

By 2000, no one wanted to be named boss because he would immediately be targeted by the government and a cell would be fitted out for them in "Club Fed." The mobsters were even afraid to meet because they knew the room would be bugged and some of the people at the meeting would be government informers.[++]

Las Vegas, which had been built up in the postwar era with money from Jimmy Hoffa's Teamsters Union, became a cash cow for organized crime. Vegas was an "open city" that any mob family could operate in. All they had to do was to secure Teamsters loans, which they got through bribery. Even after Jimmy Hoffa was sent to prison in 1967, his successors continued to do business with the mob. When Hoffa was released in 1971, a provision of his parole barred him from holding union office until 1980. Jimmy would not accept it and engaged in a war with his successors and also brought suit to invalidate the parole restriction. In addition, Jimmy threatened to reveal secrets of organized crime's dealings with the union. In 1975, he disappeared.[6]

Not content, the four mobs that controlled Vegas—Milwaukee, Kansas City, Cleveland and the senior partner, Chicago—instituted "the skim," where a mob henchman siphoned money off the top of the gambling profits. In an investigation that extended across the country, the government managed to bring down some of the leaders of the organized-crime families in those cities. The FBI also snared Allen Dorfman, a multimillionaire who ran the Teamsters Pension Fund. An FBI bug picked up conversations among Dorfman, Roy Williams, who was about to be named general president of the Teamsters Union, and the boss of the Chicago mob, Joe Lombardo. In one of them, they discussed a property deal with United States Sen. Howard Cannon of Nevada in return for his blocking a bill that would have changed trucking rates. Dorfman, Lombardo and Williams were indicted. Some Justice Department lawyers believed that Cannon, too, should have been. However, he was allowed to testify as a government witness. Dorfman was murdered in the Chicago area because of fears that he might turn government witness. Lombardo and Williams were sent to prison. Cannon was defeated for re-election by the Nevada voters. Because of the government drive against the mobs in Vegas, they lost control of their casinos and were replaced by large corporations.

In the period starting with the 1968 election of President Nixon, federal law enforcement was beset by many troubles. Not until the 1980s did it manage to right itself by winning major victories over the Mafia and in bringing the FBI out of the doldrums.

---

6. For an analysis of the Hoffa disappearance and the persons involved, see Appendix A.

Chapter 7

Contrasting Command Styles:
Murphy of New York, Rizzo of Philadelphia

In some ways, the two men's careers were parallel; in others, they couldn't
have been further apart. They were born in the same year to police families,
and both were white ethnics of the Catholic faith from large Northeastern
cities: one was a South Philadelphia Italian, the other a Brooklyn Irishman.
Both served in the Navy. Both were married before they joined their city's
police departments. Frank Rizzo was a burly, six-foot, three-inch man who
stood out physically, even among cops, and was a forceful, take-charge type.
He was ambitious, but like other big cities, Philadelphia had never had an
Italian at the head of its police department, and Rizzo, who lacked even a high-
school diploma, was less educated than most men who became big-city police
chiefs in the second half of the twentieth century. Despite the odds, he made it
to commissioner and then mayor. In office he was the hero of the white
ethnics who were in the process of becoming Reagan Democrats, and he was
not afraid to incur the enmity of various civil rights groups or the *Philadelphia
Inquirer*.

Pat Murphy was short and slim for a cop. His manner was reserved and he
enjoyed studying, earning both bachelor's and master's degrees. Murphy
dreamed of being police commissioner, but his ambitions went even further: to
becoming FBI director. Murphy would head three American police forces
before becoming NYPD commissioner. In New York City he sought to appeal
to liberals and papers like the *New York Times*. In the 1970s the two would
become national figures and represent two opposite styles of police leadership.

Until the 1950s, Philadelphia was as much a machine-run town as Chicago, although because the machine in Philadelphia was Republican, it didn't fit the classic image of a corrupt political organization. Somehow it managed to contain both Mainline aristocrats and working stiffs. Rizzo's father had come to the city from Calabria as a fourteen-year-old and settled in the Italian enclave of South Philadelphia. At the age of twenty-two, with the help of his local Republican committeeman, Ralph Rizzo became a city police officer. At the same time, he continued practicing his trade of tailor, which is why he and his children were always neatly turned out. Frank Rizzo was born in 1920 and, like the other three sons in the family, was brought up very strictly. One of his brothers became a cop; another joined the fire department and rose to commissioner.

Although Rizzo was powerfully built and handy with his fists, he was not a gang member, nor did he acquire a criminal record. In 1938 he joined the navy and served as a seaman on the cruiser *Houston*. After a year of service, he was found to have a form of diabetes and medically discharged. The United States was just beginning to emerge from the Depression, and the prospects for a young blue-collar man were limited. Frank worked construction, then on the open hearth at a steel mill. At twenty-one he married his sweetheart. At twenty-three, with the support of the Republican Party organization, he became a Philadelphia cop.

The police department that Rizzo joined reflected the city it served. It was not dynamic or noted for efficiency, and it was hit by periodic scandals. It contained few Italians, and these were often tarred by the stereotype of being mob connected. However, that label never attached to Frank or his father. In Frank Rizzo's youth, organized crime in the city was run by the Irish and Jews. Not until about the time he joined the police force did the Italians begin to take over.

During his early years on the job, young Frank was just a lowly foot cop pounding a beat in the Tioga section of North Philadelphia. Anyone who knew him at the time would have forecast that, like his father, he would spend his entire career as a uniformed patrolman. Still, Rizzo, well groomed, uniform pressed and shoes shined, always stood out from his peers. Sometimes a politician driving by an intersection where Rizzo was spending part of his tour of duty directing traffic would be so impressed with the look of the young officer that he would ask, "Who is that cop?" To which the reply was "He's Ralph Rizzo's boy." That meant he came from a good family and was reliably Republican. In 1950 the safety director of the city (equivalent of commissioner in New York) made Rizzo an acting sergeant and assigned him to South Philadelphia to help clean it up.

Pat Murphy, who was also born in 1920, was one of seven children of a Brooklyn police sergeant. Two of his brothers also became officers. Pat was the quiet son, the one who was meant for the priesthood. But World War II came along, and he found himself a Navy pilot. During the war he married his sweetheart, and by the time he returned from the service she was expecting their first child. No doubt Murphy, as an ex-officer, could have entered a management training program or, if he had gotten a college degree, a profession. But he needed money badly, and as he later would say, he decided to "join the family business." He began pounding a beat in the rough Brooklyn waterfront neighborhood known as Red Hook. Whereas Rizzo frequently had to use his fists to subdue rowdy drunks, Murphy stopped altercations with words—though in a mob-heavy area like the Hook, bad guys knew it was not wise to become known as a "cop fighter." After a short stint on the beat, Murphy was made a plainclothesman. In New York, that was the term for a vice cop, who, unlike detectives doing criminal investigations, did not receive grade ratings or the extra pay that went with them. While officially a lesser post then detective, in reality plainclothes was a much sought-after assignment. Gamblers and other organized-crime figures threw money at plainclothes men and it was not twenty-dollar bills but wads of hundreds. Within sixty days, Murphy asked to get out of the unit.[1]

Good at the books, Murphy studied hard, and in just eight years he made lieutenant. This set him apart because most police officers never advanced beyond patrolman. He also began to take college courses and was transferred to the police academy as an instructor. Then Murphy encountered one of those little disasters that occur in the civil service system. He flunked the captain's exam. Perhaps he had taken it for granted that he would pass easily. Whatever, he had to wait nine years to become a captain. A new police commissioner, Mike Murphy (no relation), who had taken a liking to Pat, pushed his career promoting him quickly to deputy inspector. Pat then left to be the chief of police of Syracuse, New York and when he returned to New York City, Commissioner Murphy made him a deputy chief.[2]

In 1965, the candidate of the reformers, John Lindsay, was elected mayor of New York City. Pat Murphy thought he should be considered for police commissioner, but Lindsay already had a man, Howard Leary, police commissioner of Philadelphia. So Pat left the department.

John Lindsay was everything that Pat Murphy was not: tall, handsome, outgoing, a WASP aristocrat who went to Yale and became a lawyer in the

---

1. In that short a time, he would not have been offered any money. The plainclothes squads kept new members in the dark until they were sure they could be trusted.
2. Despite the title, it is four grades below commissioner.

Department of Justice before being elected to Congress from the city's "silk stocking" district, the wealthy enclave on Manhattan's Upper East Side. His brother became the head of one of the country's major banks. The mayor's choice of Leary was based on his desire to install a civilian complaint review board (CCRB) to hear citizens' beefs against cops. At the time American police chiefs did not favor the establishment of such a board. The exception was Leary, who had no choice because Philadelphia already had one. Leary's and Rizzo's rise in Philadelphia was the result of a reform movement in the city of brotherly love. In 1951, liberal Democrats took over the city government from the Republican machine. Given the shortcomings of the local GOP and the changing demographics of the city, it would never come back. In 1952, a reform commissioner named Tom Gibbons promoted Rizzo to command of a district. The moving force behind the boost was Frank's dad, Ralph, who had mentored young Sergeant Gibbons when the West Philadelphia Irishman had worked in the South Philadelphia station. Later, Frank Rizzo was put in charge of the downtown area known as Center City.

That job brought Rizzo to public attention because of raids he ordered and frequent battles with street toughs. Rizzo always personally led his men, known as "Rizzo" Raiders," and because of his swashbuckling persona became known as "the Cisco Kid," after the hero of western movies. There were complaints about his being too rough, but even though there was a liberal reform administration in city hall, he was not removed from his post. It was important for the city administration that the downtown area be perceived as safe, so Rizzo was allowed a relatively free hand. As crime soared in Philadelphia, the "Cisco Kid" was promoted to be one of four deputy commissioners of the department and put in charge of field operations.

Howard Leary was a different sort. He held a law degree and generally worked in administrative jobs where he went by the books. Unlike Rizzo, he was not a street commander. The men's clash at the 1964 Philadelphia riot has already been described. Even then, the handwriting was on the wall. Deputy Commissioner Rizzo was the future, whereas Leary was out of touch with the times. The reform mayors of Philadelphia eventually left and were succeeded by a professional politician named Jim Tate. He realized that Rizzo was the right man to help the administration appeal to many Democrats, who had become disillusioned with their party. In February 1966, Leary jumped at the chance to be commissioner in New York because he realized he would soon be removed in Philadelphia. In May 1967, Rizzo was installed in room 318, the commissioner's office at police headquarters, a building known as the "Round House" (because of its twin cylindrical architecture). Two months later, Newark and Detroit burned within a week of each other, leaving twenty-six dead in the former city and forty-three in the latter. Other American cities were also swept by violence. Philadelphians fully expected that something similar would happen in their town. Rizzo put hundreds of cops on municipal buses and sent them roaming through the city or stationed them at strategic locations.[3] Some people objected to the show of force, but most Philadelphians loved it. A poll showed that eighty-four percent of the respondents, including a majority of blacks, approved of Rizzo's actions. More importantly, Philadelphia did not experience any major civil disorder.

Rizzo personally was present every time there was a serious incident. After a police sergeant was assassinated by Black Panthers, Rizzo declared an all-out campaign against them. He mobilized the entire police force with his favorite unit, the Highway Patrol, as the spearhead. Almost immediately, two Highway Patrol officers spotted a stolen car driving through the city. They did not know that the occupants were stickup men from Washington who had disarmed, kidnapped and later released two District of Columbia police officers. When the Philadelphia officers stopped the car, the criminals opened fire and both policemen were severely wounded. One, the son of former commissioner Gibbons, was so badly injured that he had to be put on permanent disability pension. Rizzo held an informal press conference and challenged the Panthers to meet him at a local park. As it turned out, the Washington gunmen were not Panthers but ordinary crooks. Still, the public applauded the "Cisco Kid."

Even hardened criminals feared Rizzo. When a bunch of inmates rose up and got control of a Philadelphia jail, Rizzo raced to the scene from a banquet, still wearing his tuxedo, with a club stuck in the cummerbund. He did not waste time with sugary words. He told the prisoners, either surrender or he would blow up the building. It is doubtful that he intended to do so, but they thought he did and promptly gave up. As police commissioner, Rizzo behaved the same way he had when he was cleaning up Center City a decade earlier. The law was the law, and cops should never back down in the face of those who broke it. He was also the rare high police official who personally led his men into dangerous situations. Modern police brass avoided that sort of thing, not necessarily because they were afraid of being injured but because they feared the damage a mistake could cause to their career.[4]

The appointment of Howard Leary as New York police commissioner was one of those instances where the mayor picks the wrong man to head the

---

3. Unlike the 1968 riots in Chicago, where cops broke loose on their own, Rizzo maintained tight control of his troops. No one moved unless Frank gave the order.
4. I never crossed paths with Rizzo. I have a hunch he would not have liked me, and if I had worked for him the feeling would probably have been mutual. However, in a situation where my partner and I had to go into an apartment after three killers with guns, I would have been very happy to have a man like Frank Rizzo leading us.

police force, as a result of which the reputation of his administration is badly damaged and his own personal image is tarnished forever. City hall believed they could use Leary as a front man to install a civilian complaint review board, then send him packing. Their real choice for commissioner was Sanford "Sandy" Garelik, a career cop who was closely connected to the small but influential Liberal Party.[5] The problem was that the Jewish Garelik was not part of the in-group at headquarters known as the "Irish Mafia." Lindsay knew better than to start what New Yorkers call a "tribal war" in the NYPD. Garelik could not be the man to get rid of the old-line Irish bosses. That would have to be done by the Irishman Leary. Garelik would get the number-two post, chief inspector,[6] and city hall would deal with him on everything important, eventually promoting Garelik to commissioner. In practice, Leary outmaneuvered both Lindsay and Garelik. As a result, he was able to remain commissioner for over four years, and it was Garelik who left to run successfully for city council president (the number-two job in the city on paper, although it was not in reality).

When Lindsay attempted to install a review board, the PBA, claiming it was a charter change, forced the city to place the proposal on the ballot, where it was defeated. Despite being brought in to take the lead in installing a CCRB, Leary was equivocal. His position was essentially that he was for it before he was against it, or "I feel very strongly both ways." During the campaign against the board, the PBA ran commercials showing a young white woman walking down a dark street. The subtle message was that if a CCRB were adopted, she would not be safe because the police would be handcuffed. A furious Lindsay attacked the union for racism.

Leary knew little about the NYPD. He continued to reside in Philadelphia and was chauffeured to work in New York each week. He did not have the lines of communication in the department to people who would tell him what was really going on. It became a house divided, with the Lindsay-Garelik partisans on one side and Leary's people on the other. In one instance, the chief of detectives refused to turn over a report to Garelik, so the chief of internal affairs made a midnight raid on the detective bureau to retrieve the report. The chief of detectives had been tipped off, and the two chiefs ended up swapping punches.

---

5. By World War II, New York State's traditional third party, the American Labor Party, led by Congressman Vito Marcantonio, had allegedly become dominated by American Communists. So a group of powerful liberal, anti-Communist labor leaders set up a new party as a replacement. In the 1965 election, the Liberals proved very helpful to Lindsay.

6. Although technically the first deputy commissioner was number two, the chief inspector, who was the highest-ranking police officer, was traditionally de facto number two. Not until the 1970s would the first deputy come to surpass the chief inspector, whose title was changed to chief of operations and later to chief of department.

A third power center was the office of the first deputy commissioner John Walsh, the man who was in charge of fighting corruption. Walsh, who had been appointed three commissioners back, was fireproof because of his relationship with the Manhattan district attorney. Such was the byzantine nature of the NYPD that New York City had virtually three separate commissioners— more than that when one of Lindsay's young aides would decide to give orders to the police department.

Two bold young cops, Frank Serpico and Sergeant David Durk, went directly to a number of high police officials and aides to the mayor to complain about corruption. The response of the brass varied from warning them that they might end up floating in the East River to "I'll get back to you," which they never did. In addition, Lindsay did not want to depress police morale because he needed the police to handle the city's racial protests without employing excessive force. Nor, like any mayor, did he want headlines about a police scandal. Finally, after the whistle-blowing cops went to the *New York Times* and stories appeared, Lindsay tried to damp down the fallout by appointing an in-house commission, including Leary, to investigate the charges. That would not wash, and an outside body, under distinguished attorney Whitman Knapp, conducted the investigation. Leary quietly resigned and went off on a European vacation. Some of the police officials and mayor's aides who had refused to act on Serpico and Durk's complaints eventually received high posts in other law enforcement agencies or were appointed judges. In contrast, Serpico caught a bullet in the head while making a drug raid and retired on a disability pension, while Durk spent the rest of his career as a pariah.

In 1970, Lindsay was gearing up to run for president as a Democrat, so members of his new party advised him to name Pat Murphy as police commissioner. After Syracuse, Murphy had gone off to Washington to fill a newly created post as public safety director, which gave him control over the police chief, who had been taking his orders from Congress. As director, Murphy managed to make some changes in the department. He named Jerry Wilson, a career Washington policeman who was open to new ideas, as chief. In Washington, Murphy worked closely with Atty. Gen. Ramsey Clark. When the Law Enforcement Assistance Administration (LEAA) was created, Clark chose Murphy to be the first head of the agency. After the Republicans took over Washington at the beginning of 1969, Murphy was replaced at the LEAA. Roman Gribbs, the mayor of Detroit, snapped him up to be his police commissioner. Although Gribbs begged Murphy to remain in Detroit, Murphy accepted Lindsay's offer and took over Teddy Roosevelt's old desk.

As a former New York cop, Murphy was well aware of the NYPD's internal problems. One was the policy of not holding anyone responsible for misconduct or failure to perform except the individual offender. He changed that to one of command accountability so that if a police officer got into trouble, it was deemed to be equally the failure of his commander. At the heart of corruption in the city was the so-called "pad system," whereby those who wished to break the laws against gambling, vice, etc., would arrange to get on a payoff list so that they would not be raided. Every month collections were made, and in some eras the money went high up in the department, sometimes even as far as the commissioner's office.

Murphy beefed up the department's internal affairs unit and set them to looking for corruption. With the new policy of command accountability and an aggressive internal-affairs unit, the top brass had to rethink the pad system. A division inspector or borough chief who allowed gambling and vice to operate in his area might be held responsible and lose his job. Murphy was not afraid to dismiss from their posts individuals whom he had risen with in the police department and who were sometimes personal friends. Many of the top brass forced out were not on the pad, but were deemed not to be up to the responsibilities of their post. In some instances, men who had devoted their lives to the police department burst into tears when told they were out. In one instance, a chief stormed into Murphy's private office and had to be restrained by other cops from attacking the commissioner.

Under Lindsay, the RAND Corporation, a highly regarded national think tank, had been invited to study the management and operations of the police department. Murphy enlarged upon their recommendations, introducing a number of innovations, but they rarely went beyond the experimental stage. With great fanfare, he created a model precinct on the Upper West Side. Within a relatively short time it became just another police station. It was said of the highly touted community patrols that they simply wrote "Neighborhood Police Team" on the door of their squad cars and went on working in the usual fashion.

In 1971, angry because some back wages awarded to them by an arbitration panel had yet to be paid, cops reported for duty at their stations but declined to go out on patrol. Some police commissioners would have suspended anyone who refused to perform his duty; some mayors would have called for the National Guard. Instead, Murphy replaced patrol cops with other members of the department. Detectives received extra pay and were thought to have generally desirable jobs. However, they were not under civil service and could be dropped back to patrolman by order of the commissioner. So Murphy assigned the city's three thousand detectives to man the patrol cars. It was cold in New York at the time, keeping some criminals off the streets, and with the detectives and superior officers patrolling and answering calls, there was no crime wave in the city. Eventually, the matter was settled with a promise to pay the award. Later, Murphy was to make a number of changes to downgrade the detective bureau, incurring the sleuths' special enmity, since they felt they had saved him in a time of crisis.

Another major crisis of the Murphy administration came as the result of a false call of a 10-13, "police officer needs assistance," at a Harlem mosque originally run by Malcolm X and at the time by the Reverend Louis Farrakhan. Police officers rushed to the scene and, when denied admission, forced their way in. Some of the mosque members locked the door behind them and attacked the officers. One police officer was fatally wounded with his own gun; another was badly beaten. When additional police arrived, a disorderly crowd gathered out on the street. Instead of police breaking down the doors and searching for the assailants, high-ranking officials on the scene accepted the word of some local leaders, including politicians, that if the cops went away they would bring the suspects into the precinct. However, nobody was ever brought there. This angered the rank-and-file, who denounced both Mayor Lindsay and Commissioner Murphy for backing down from cop killers for political reasons.[7]

The Lindsay era was a time of turmoil. The battle over the control of schools made the conflict over the Civilian Complaint Review Board look like a tea party. Specially chosen outside administrators, some of them minorities, were appointed to supervise schools in inner-city neighborhoods. The powerful teachers union, the leading municipal labor organization, refused to accept this. As a result, Lindsay not only had the PBA against him but a large portion of the city's other unions, who stood in solidarity with the teachers.

Murphy could have chosen to distance himself from Lindsay by pointing out that he was a career New York cop, not a politician or an out-of-towner, and by demanding that a grand jury be impaneled to look into the actions of police officials, politicians and citizens at the Harlem mosque. J. Edgar Hoover died in office while Murphy was police commissioner. Naturally, the Nixon administration did not choose Murphy as Hoover's successor, but if a new president were elected in 1972, the story might be different. Alternatively, Murphy harbored the ambition of succeeding Lindsay as mayor, so his public statements were much more attuned to liberal ideology than the views of his own rank-and-file.[8] Murphy's strident liberalism hurt him in the police world.

---

7. The dispute has gone on for 40 years, with some ex-officers still attempting to get some retired police officials punished over the affair. Whatever happened, it was clear that a policeman performing his duty had been murdered and no one was brought to justice for it.

8. A British police official who spent six months studying American policing once asked me why Murphy invariably wounded his men with every order he wrote. The answer was simple. The orders were not written for the rank-and-file but for how they would play in the *New York Times*.

The International Association of Chiefs of Police refused to elect him to a vice presidency, which was the usual stepping-stone to president of the organization. The New York State Chiefs tried to expel him from the organization because he had made critical comments about policing in general.

Often reviled as an ultra-leftist, Murphy had a personal life that was quite different from his public persona. He lived with his wife and children in a working-class area of Staten Island, not a chic Manhattan neighborhood. His recreation at night was to go for long bike rides accompanied by his dog, not socializing with the city's celebrities. He had been a wartime pilot, and his eldest son was badly wounded while serving as a paratrooper in Vietnam. Those who knew Murphy personally (as I did) liked him. Had he stayed in Detroit with Mayor Gribbs, he might have done better in the long run. In New York, Lindsay did not like Murphy because the commissioner would not let the mayor dictate to him. Later, Murphy would write that Lindsay interfered more in the police department than any other mayor he had ever known. When Lindsay announced in 1973 that he would not run for a third term, Murphy left the police department to accept a job as head of the Ford Foundation-financed Police Foundation in Washington, DC.

In 1971, Frank Rizzo was elected to the first of two terms as mayor of Philadelphia. He named a trusted subordinate as police commissioner but, de facto, remained the city's top cop. In 1978, as his second and final term in city hall was winding down, there arose another of those confrontations between police and blacks that marked his administration. A black militant who called himself John Africa, né Vincent Leaphart, established a compound in West Philadelphia for his followers. A sort of back-to-nature group, known as MOVE, they were prone to broadcast from loudspeakers shouting obscenities or threats, dumping garbage in the backyard (thereby drawing rats) and maintaining seventy-five howling, uncared-for dogs. Occasionally they brandished rifles and shotguns from the windows. This did not make them popular with their neighbors, many of whom were blacks.

When John Africa had to leave town because the feds were looking for him on a weapons charge, his lieutenant, Delbert Africa, took over the group's leadership. Despite a previously negotiated agreement that the group would leave, Delbert decided that MOVE would not move. So the police were ordered to evict them. Rizzo mobilized six hundred cops to handle the assignment. The police ordered a bulldozer to knock down barricades. Fire hoses then pumped streams of water into the houses. The police commissioner, Joe O'Neill, asked for volunteers from the Highway Patrol willing to enter the compound. To the taunts of the MOVE members, cops started forward. Shortly after 8 a.m., shots began coming from MOVE. One police officer was hit, then another and then a fireman. The police commander on the scene ordered a cease-fire. Then there was another burst of bullets. One hit a fifty-two-year-old officer, a former Marine who had survived combat landings during World War II and Korea. He was killed by a round that penetrated just below his flak vest.

Eventually the MOVE members began to surrender, and Delbert Africa climbed out with his hands up. When he got within reach, he was allegedly beaten and kicked by several officers. Nine MOVE members were found guilty of the officer's murder and given long prison terms. MOVE did finally leave the neighborhood, but the saga was only beginning.*

After Rizzo's mayoralty ended, one of his eventual successors was Wilson Goode, an African American. In 1985, with John Africa back in Philadelphia, MOVE was occupying another house with the usual bullhorns, garbage, rats and threats. Finally the citizenry had enough. Goode ordered the police to get rid of the MOVE compound. The managing director of the city (a retired Army general), the police commissioner and fire commissioner designed a plan to accomplish the mission. Before dawn on May 13, 1985, the police approached the area and by bullhorn ordered the MOVE members out. The original plan was to knock out one of the MOVE bunkers with a crane. When the crane failed to work, cops went to plan B. They would use explosives to put a hole in the bunker. The mayor was informed and did not object. At 5:27 p.m. a Philadelphia bomb squad lieutenant, riding in a Pennsylvania state police helicopter, dropped a satchel on the roof of the MOVE compound. There was an explosion and fire, which spread to other houses. When the conflagration was finally put out, the bodies of six adults and five children were found in the rubble of the MOVE house. Sixty-one neighboring homes had been destroyed, and Philadelphia was leading the news all over the world. Although there was an investigation, no one was ever punished for dropping a bomb in the heart of an American city. Frank Rizzo mused that if he personally had ordered it, he would have spent the rest of his life in prison. Rizzo sought the mayoralty again in 1983 but was beaten. In 1991, while canvassing another run for mayor, he died of a heart attack.

In New York, the legacy of the Murphy administration was mixed. His attempts to institutionalize command accountability and eliminate the "pad" were successful. In an earlier time this would have been a huge accomplishment, but the world had changed. Drugs had become the chief corruption problem. In the past, police officers saw drug money as dirty and gambling as clean. Most of them had grown up in a blue-collar environment where horses, dice and cards were common and considered largely harmless. Now cops were set down in inner-city neighborhoods that were totally unfamiliar to them. It wasn't long before they considered drugs part of the landscape. Some cops also became users of "recreational drugs," so their tolerance for the product increased.

After a while, groups of young cops began shaking down drug dealers—in some cases even selling drugs themselves. The big brass had no idea how to handle drug rings involving patrolmen. In some instances, if headquarters heard reports that cops might be doing business with dealers, they simply transferred them. All that would mean was that the culprits would lie low for a while until the matter was forgotten; then they would go back into business.

Mayor Lindsay never again held public office, and when he tried to win the Democratic nomination for the Senate, he finished with a mere twelve percent of the vote. His handling of the police department had harmed him considerably. Even worse was his approach to the school system. Many New York families, their relatives or friends had daughters who had gone into the school system as teachers with stars in their eyes (like the Sandy Dennis character in *Up the Down Staircase*). When these women began telling people how threatened they felt in the schools, it had a tremendous impact on a normally liberal electorate.

In New York a worse catastrophe than the drug explosion was the fiscal crisis of 1975, which led to fifty thousand workers, three thousand of them police officers, being laid off and a five-year freeze on hiring cops. By 1980, the three municipal police forces (city, transit and housing) had lost one third of their strength and crime had risen to new heights.

Pat Murphy garnered no support for his attempts to become FBI director or New York City mayor. From the Washington-based Police Foundation, he spent a number of years seeking another police job. One time he was certain that he was going to be named police superintendent of Chicago, but it was highly unlikely and did not come about. After he retired from the foundation at the compulsory age of sixty-five, he took a job working for the National Conference of Mayors. He mistook it for a policymaking post, and when he spoke out on some issue he was fired by the chairman of the conference, Mayor Richard M. Daley of Chicago. Murphy lived on, dying in 2011 at the age of ninety-one. Lindsay's fate was worse. For a long time he was unable to support himself and had to exist on gifts from friends. Mayor Giuliani restored him to the city payroll so he could receive health benefits. In 2000, Lindsay died in a South Carolina nursing home.

The turmoil of the '60s and early '70s produced some outstanding police administrators. Unfortunately, they did not last long enough to make a major impact on the profession. The most prominent was Tom Reddin. In 1967, within six months of Los Angeles' Chief Parker's death, Reddin was named as his successor. At the time, everyone agreed he was the right choice. Reddin was the son of a New York millionaire who lost his money drilling for oil in Oklahoma. After knocking around the West for a few years and serving in the Navy, Reddin join the LAPD in 1940 and rose rapidly. A six-foot, four-inch, two-hundred-fifteen-pound burly Irishman, he had a winning personality. As chief he established a good relationship with everyone, from conservative mayor Sam Yorty to ultraliberal attorney general Ramsey Clark.

When Reddin stepped into the chief's job, leadership in American policing was virtually nonexistent. Parker had died; O. W. Wilson was four months away from voluntary retirement; Cincinnati chief Stanley Schrotel had retired the previous year and gone into the corporate world. Seventy-two-year-old J. Edgar Hoover was a spent force who no longer intimidated people as much as he had previously. He died in early 1972.

Reddin touched every base locally. He and his wife regularly socialized with wealthy Angelenos who formed part of the liberal elite. This did not sit too well with some of the old-timers in the department. He opened up lines of communication with many black militants, further disconcerting some LAPD members. But he retained the confidence of most officers. When problems arose in the department, Reddin handled them well. After Senator Robert Kennedy was murdered while campaigning in that city in June 1968, Reddin went forty-two straight hours without sleep. Possibly this was because he recalled the rumors that, six years earlier, Chief Parker had allowed a cover-up in the death of Marilyn Monroe, and he wanted to make sure that no such charges were leveled against him.

Some observers thought that Reddin, who had performed capably in high positions, was not comfortable with the number-one job. He worried about his health and the prospect of dropping dead in his early '60s like Parker. His salary was thirty-two thousand dollars a year, and when a local television station offered him five times that much to be a commentator, he accepted. It was a mistake. Relaxed in informal settings, he was stiff and awkward on TV. After he was let go as a commentator, he ran for mayor but was badly beaten. He then opened a private security agency. Unlike Parker, Reddin managed to live to eighty-eight years of age, so perhaps his decision was a correct one. But many people thought he harbored regrets.** His successor was Ed Davis, another 1940 recruit, who displayed much of the hard-line outspokenness of Bill Parker.[9]

9. Davis did grow in the position. As chief, he refused to accept gays on the force and in his speeches attacked them with harsh rhetoric. Later, as a California state senator, he was a spokesperson for the gay lobby in Sacramento and the lead sponsor on their bills.

E. Wilson "Bud" Purdy was a Michigan boy who, on the same day in 1942, graduated from the state college school of police administration, received his lieutenant's commission in the army and married his sweetheart. After four years of wartime service, finishing up as a captain of MPs in the Philippines, he joined the FBI. Purdy was the embodiment of the clean-cut, strait-laced, middle-American that J. Edgar Hoover favored as an agent. After the usual early career rotation of FBI offices, Purdy was assigned to Miami and eventually headed up the satellite office in St. Petersburg. It was not the most glamorous and challenging assignment in the Bureau, but St. Petersburg was a great place to live. After thirteen years with the FBI, Purdy accepted an offer to be chief of police of that city.

In 1962, Purdy got a big break. He was appointed commissioner of the Pennsylvania State Police. This was a large, well-established organization with a long history. Purdy had been a trooper himself for a year in Michigan while he underwent his college training, so he was not unfamiliar with a state constabulary force. The commissioner's job in Pennsylvania had always been filled from the ranks of the state police, with one exception. In 1937, when the motor patrol force and the older state police were merged, it was felt that it would be too difficult to appoint someone from one of the forces over the other. So a retired rear admiral was brought in to head the joint operation. Given the military tradition of the troopers, it was thought that they would respect a flag rank officer of the regular services. They did, as long as he did not stay too long.

Pennsylvania reflected the rough-and-tumble ethos of politics in a large Eastern state, and commissioners in the past had received their share of harassment from politicians. Purdy was not used to this, but initially he had the support of the rank-and-file. The powerful Fraternal Order of Police union could have blocked his nomination in the state senate. Instead they threw their support to him. The view of the police union was to give Purdy a chance to see what he would do.

Criticism of the state police reached its height every fourth year, when a gubernatorial election was scheduled. When that came in Purdy's time, troopers were accused of conducting illegal wiretapping. All of the top members of the force denied that such a thing occurred, but a low-level detective, seeking to clarify the situation, admitted, "Well, we do some wiretapping." That was all the opposition needed. That and a number of other minor charges were combined, and eventually Pennsylvania Governor William Scranton asked for Purdy's resignation. He received it at 5:30 on Good Friday afternoon, 1966. However, the governor had already cut the commissioner off the payroll at noon and refused to allow him any severance pay or money for sick leave. It was a nasty blow to a decent man with a wife, three children and very little money.

Luckily, Purdy was well known in the law enforcement field, and he was not unemployed for long. Dade County, Florida, was organizing a metropolitan police department to replace its sheriff's office. Although it did not include the city of Miami, it would be a major force. Purdy accepted an offer to head it. He remained for thirteen years and enjoyed a high reputation in law enforcement. Then a new political regime decided to dispense with his services.***

Jack Ingersoll began his police career in the Oakland, California, department, which at the time was a highly rated force. After reaching the rank of sergeant, he was invited to join the field staff of the International Association of Chiefs of Police, then probably the leading consulting group in the law enforcement field. In 1966, he was appointed chief of police in Charlotte, North Carolina, where he earned a reputation for developing a superior organization. Word of his ability got around, and he began to be a sought-after figure. In 1968, the newly elected mayor of Boston, Kevin White, offered Ingersoll the job of police commissioner. The only problem was that the previous commissioner was still in the post. A newspaper reporter revealed White's negotiations with Ingersoll, and the deal had to be canceled. Atty. Gen. Ramsey Clark then asked Ingersoll to help him revamp the Bureau of Narcotics. Under his direction, the Bureau was merged with the drug abuse investigating arm of the Department of Health and Welfare. Ingersoll was appointed to head the new Bureau of Narcotics and Dangerous Drugs (BNDD). Unfortunately for him, he was sacrificed to the machinations of the White House scheme to create ODALE. In 1973, he resigned and went to work in the private sector for IBM, where he remained for many years.+

American law enforcement in the '70s might have been very different with Reddin as chief in Los Angeles and national leader of the profession, a man like Ingersoll running the Boston police and Purdy in a major command, either in Miami or somewhere in his native Midwest, like Detroit. Instead, two of them were out of law enforcement completely, and Purdy had to fend off political criticism. Because of America's failure to create a system for developing police chiefs and placing them in the right job, the best people either did not come to the fore or did not last if they did.

* * * *

Another problem that emerged in the 1960s was the rise of police unions. In New York they were given huge concessions by Mayor Lindsay, making them virtually as powerful as the police commissioner. At first it was difficult for sergeants, lieutenants and captains to change the way they traditionally handled their patrolmen. Some tried to ignore the unions, and continued to rake erring officers over the coals. But that type of captain would soon get a message from headquarters that there was a new order in the department and that he'd better get with it. In some cases, it was not the erring cop who got transferred out of a precinct, but the captain. A lazy captain could justify allowing his cops to do virtually anything by pointing out that it was in the union contract (though an arbitrator might not have bought the union interpretation).

In 1976, to protest a wage freeze, many off-duty officers began picketing the police commissioner's house in Queens, blocking traffic on the Upper East Side and urinating on the lawn of the mayor's official residence, Gracie Mansion. When Muhammad Ali and Ken Norton fought for the heavyweight championship at Yankee Stadium in September, fifteen hundred militant off-duty cops showed up. They roamed about like high-school kids at a pep rally shouting while four hundred on-duty cops ignored them. Three high-ranking chiefs were knocked down and slugged by protesting cops as they alighted from their official vehicle. In the melee, the chief of the department lost a valuable diamond ring. Local gangs from the South Bronx decided to get in the act and began attacking the beautiful people as they arrived at the championship fight. Howard Cosell, then the reigning TV sports broadcaster, had his toupee snatched off.

The incident spelled the end of the NYPD career of a man who many people believe was the greatest police commissioner New York City *never* had, Anthony Bouza. He had been born in the Basque country of Spain and raised in Brooklyn. After Army service, the six-foot, four-inch young man spent his time partying and getting into fights. His married sister worried about him and persuaded him to take the police test. Within a few months, he was assigned to a youth-gang squad in Manhattan, then to the detective bureau. Over the years he picked up bachelor's and master's degrees and more promotions. He read Sartre, hoped to be a writer and in fact authored a novel about one of his cases, though he failed to find a publisher. He also commanded the Bureau of Special Service Investigations (BOSSI), which was the department's hush-hush unit that investigated alleged subversive activities.

In 1976, Bouza was an assistant chief in command of the borough of the Bronx. Already many observers had picked him as a future commissioner, although that is not always a good designation to have because the incumbent commissioner finds it upsetting. The higher brass decided to make him the scapegoat for what happened at Yankee Stadium, and he was forced out of the department. He still had many admirers, however, and he was quickly appointed deputy chief of the city's three-thousand-officer transit police force.

In 1979, the city administration decided to again make him a scapegoat, this time for rising subway crime. Although he was only deputy chief of the transit police, he lost his job. However, he was immediately hired as chief of police of Minneapolis, where he remained for eight years. He was a prolific author and familiar figure on TV, and his outspoken ways and liberal views both attracted many admirers and closed many doors to him. Thus another man who might have headed one of the large police forces, such as New York, Los Angeles, Philadelphia or Chicago, eventually ended up out of the profession.[++]

The behavior of police officers in the 1970s probably would not have occurred in any previous decade. But by then cops were not their father's police force. Few World War II veterans were still in policing. By the end of the '70s, anyone under fifty would not have been old enough to have served in the war. America was prosperous. Memories of the Depression had faded away. Some cops still joined up for security; for others, it was because they preferred the excitement of police work to a job in a factory or an office.

Another change was that cops did not look like cops as much as they had in the past. The most obvious difference was that there were a growing number of female officers. Height requirements had been dropped to accommodate women and ethnic groups, whose average height was on the low side. Most police officers initially regarded women as being of little help if any kind of trouble developed. So when a patrol car with a male/female team received a disturbance call, another car would unofficially back them up. It was similar to the case of other minorities who had survived early stereotyping. In their time, Italians, Jews, even American-born Irish were often thought to lack what it took to be a cop. By the end of the century, the new cop minorities with their own stereotypes attached would be Asian and Middle Eastern.

Many police chiefs of the 1980s adopted the social-science view that police could do nothing about crime. That provided them with an excuse to avoid blame for any increases in their city. Pat Murphy joined that school of thought. He even signed on to a report by a well-known think tank (no longer in business) which argued that prisons should essentially be closed or at least limited to no more than fifty inmates in any state. In California or New York, that would not have been enough cells to house multiple murderers.

The South, once the backward element of policing, continued to surprise with the progress it made. The most colorful figure in American policing was Reuben Greenberg, an African-American of the Jewish faith who was chief in Charleston, South Carolina, the old citadel of the Confederacy. Greenberg, a tough law-and-order cop, had a somewhat unusual method of patrolling the city. He navigated its streets on roller skates. Although his name was often suggested for appointment as chief in a Northern city, nothing came of it.

In the 1970s, the greatest sign of progress I personally noted in race relations occurred one day in Atlanta. There, another ex-cop and I joined a black police captain for lunch. We went to a truck stop with a Confederate flag hanging outside and motorcycles filling the parking lot. Inside were a bunch of well-muscled truck drivers and bike enthusiasts with plenty of tattoos. My initial thought was, "We're probably going to have to fight our way out." On the contrary. There were no hostile remarks, the waitress was polite and took our order immediately, and everything went fine. A decade earlier a restaurant owner in Atlanta, Lester Maddox, was issuing pick handles to his customers so they could slug any blacks who tried to come in. Thanks to the publicity this engendered, he was elected governor of Georgia. Now, it was not just that blacks (or mixed groups) were served in a predominantly white restaurant; it was that they were treated like any other customer.

Chapter 8

Chaos: Cops Lose the Streets

A fundamental test of the efficiency of urban policing is whether individuals and goods can move through the streets with a reasonable degree of safety. In eighteenth-century London, noon was the society dinner hour because no one went out in the evening unless accompanied by an armed escort. After Robert Peel's 1829 establishment of a police force, public safety increased to the extent that the dinner hour could begin at 8:00 p.m., and escorts were not required.

American cities, which copied London's policing arrangements, experienced a similar improvement, although there were always a few areas like the Lower East Side of Manhattan, San Francisco's Barbary Coast or Chicago's Near West Side that were unsafe to venture into, especially after dark. In the 1960s, many big-city districts that formerly were safe began to experience huge increases in crime and disorder. These manifested in several ways. One was a rise in the number of conventional crimes, such as murder, robbery and burglary. In the country at large, the figure for murder (the most accurately reported crime) rose 200% between 1960 and 1980. In big cities like New York, Los Angeles, Chicago, and Philadelphia, the increase was even greater. The number of murders in New York increased 350% (390 to 1826). Other crimes also rose significantly. Overall, crime went from something people read about in the newspapers to a frequent occurrence in their own neighborhoods, often among their own family and friends. A second development was the proliferation and increased violence of gangs—particularly those involved in drug trafficking, who became more numerous and bolder in their operations. In many big cities, drug gangs ruled half the neighborhoods. The third was the growing hordes of "street people"—drug addicts, vagrants, mentally ill—who used city sidewalks as bedrooms and bathrooms and often harassed passersby.

Emerging problems were dealt with by efforts that were as confused as they usually were when police encountered new situations. Pre-1960 crime-fighting largely involved patrol cars cruising and responding to 911 calls and teams of detectives investigating major cases. While not a particularly effective system, it had worked reasonably well in an era of low crime rates. From the '60s on, though, patrol cars spent the bulk of their time racing from one call to another, filling out reports or applying Band-Aids. Detectives could only handle the biggest cases—i.e., the kind that made the newspapers. In 1969, one of President Johnson's study commissions, headed by Milton Eisenhower, set forth a frightening prediction about how American cities would look in the near future.

> High-rise apartment building and residential compounds protected by private guards and security devices will be fortified cells for upper middle and high in-come populations living at prime locations in the City. Central business districts in the heart of the City surrounded by mixed areas of accelerated deterioration will be partially protected by large numbers of people shopping or working in commercial buildings during daytime hours, plus a substantial police presence, and will be largely deserted except for police patrols during nighttime hours. Streets and residential neighborhoods of the central City will be unsafe in different degrees and the ghetto slum neighborhoods will be places of terror with wide-spread crime, perhaps entirely out of police control during nighttime hours.*

By 1980, the Eisenhower Commission forecast constituted a description of life in many U.S. cities.

In the postwar era, the youth gang problem was the first to draw significant public attention. In New York, starting in 1955, under Commissioner Steve Kennedy, a career cop and lawyer who had replaced his Brooklyn accent with Shakespearean tones, the police department took a hard line. Kennedy said, "Apply the law and apply it vigorously. It's not your job to become bemused with the vagaries of the why-oh-why school. The policeman has a job to do, and if he does it honestly and intelligently, he gains respect. That's a damn sight more important than being liked." Recalling his own youth, Kennedy noted that cops never asked him, "Are you happy?" Instead it was, "Look, bud, do this," and "if you didn't do it, you got belted."

Also starting in 1955, Mike Delaney's gang squads in Chicago not only apprehended offenders but also stressed prevention and treatment. Then, as youth gangs became front-page news in the 1960s, other units got into the act. Superintendent Wilson's embarrassment over the failed gang truce did not teach the department a lesson. The new gang "experts" had to learn the hard way what worked and what did not.

In 1970, a few nights after I graduated from Harvard and headed back home, some Cambridge cops, whom I had known, were stunned to hear that I had been killed by a sniper in Chicago. Actually, it was a young sergeant with a last name similar to mine, whom I had never met. I heard, though, that he was an outstanding individual. He and his partner had been playing baseball with some young kids in the courtyard of the Cabrini Green Housing Project, then the hottest of hot spots in the city. An older gang member decided he didn't like cops on his turf, so he got a rifle and killed the two of them. In the old days of the youth gang squads, we might have been aware of this possibility and headed it off.

The most famous gang in America was the Blackstone Rangers, whom I had known when they were young teens hanging out on the corner of 65th and Blackstone. The Rangers were products of an urban ghetto in ferment. Living amid violent conditions, many young men opted to join a gang as a form of protection. The gangs, in turn, fought to control their turf. In the mid-'60s, the Rangers were drawn into the political affairs of their local Woodlawn neighborhood. As a result, they became involved in a federal grant program designed to prevent riots. While helping to "keep the ghetto cool," they acquired considerable political savvy. Under a dynamic leader named Jeff Fort, their power grew. In 1967, Senator McClellan's investigations committee heard testimony from former gang members that the Rangers were extorting money from individuals involved in an unemployment program. Fort was sent to jail for the embezzlement of federal funds. While there, he began calling himself Prince Malik and formed a group called the El Rukns, which he identified with the Black Muslim movement (though there was no real connection). In this new incarnation, the gang became major drug traffickers. In the 1980s, Fort was sentenced to thirteen years in prison for participating in a cocaine distribution conspiracy.

In the early 1980s, the tide of crime appeared to be receding. Then, when the crack explosion hit American cities, it shot up. Easily ingested, the cocaine derivative was both potent and cheap. A kilo could be purchased for less than twenty thousand dollars, melted down and sold for several times that amount. The only other piece of equipment that anyone needed to go into business was a firearm, preferably a machine gun. As was said, "Anyone bold enough to shoot a gun qualified as an entrepreneur." Many of the youth gangs entered the drug business and became major entrepreneurs. A Chicago group, the Black Gangster Disciples, had an estimated thirty thousand members and ran a one-hundred-million-dollar-a-year drug business. In the 1990s it engaged in extensive political activity, registering voters and supporting candidates in city elections. When its leader, Larry Hoover, sought a parole—he was serving two life sentences for murder—many politicians backed him, including a former Chicago mayor. In 1997 the federal government convicted Hoover and many of his members on drug conspiracy charges.

In the drug wars of the '80s, gangs employed methods that made the Mafia look like Boy Scouts. They would use automatic weapons to spray a street corner, not only killing the intended target but also hitting five or ten by-standers. The tactic was meant to terrorize people and to demonstrate that the gangs were in charge. Innocents gunned down were referred to as "mush-rooms" (because they popped up underfoot). In some neighborhoods, gunfire could be heard all night long, and shots went through the windows or walls of private residences. Little children sometimes slept in bathtubs to protect them from bullets. Nursery-school youngsters were taught to drop down flat when they heard a popping noise. The murder figures, already extremely high, rose dramatically. By 1990, New York City recorded two thousand two hundred and forty-five.

Even worse than the youth gangs that had become big-time drug dealers were the international cartels, which played the largest role in American drug trafficking. The most prominent were the Colombian-based Cali and Medellín cartels. When cocaine became popular, the Colombians were ideally situated to dominate the trade. They were located near coca-producing areas such as Bolivia and Peru, and their position on the northern coast of South America—facing both the Caribbean and Pacific—facilitated their ability to smuggle the drug into the United States. Using Cubans, Dominicans and other Latin Ameri-cans as middlemen or street distributors, the cartels dominated the cocaine trade. Their marketing activities, such as developing cheap crack, helped to make the drug popular, and their incomes soon exceeded that of the wealthier Mafia groups. The leader of the Medellín cartel once offered to pay off the entire national debt of Colombia in return for being released from custody. The Colombians' use of violence was worse than that of other drug gangs. Women, children and infants were deliberately killed. Victims' throats were slit and their tongues pulled through and left to dangle—a practice known as "a Colombian necktie."

Some urban neighborhoods lived under a reign of terror. Beginning on New Year's Day, 1988, a 17-year-old East Harlem crack addict, Leslie Torres, killed five innocent people and wounded six others in the space of eight days. He had no previous record. Crack, according to Torres, made him "feel like God." His rampage took place just north of the chic Upper East Side. If it had occurred a few blocks south, it would have made the headlines, accompanied by demands for the city to be put under martial law.**

About the same time, a Guyanese immigrant, Arjune, started reporting on crack dealing in his Queens neighborhood. One of the gangs found out about it, and at 4:30 one morning his house was firebombed. He called the police, jumped in a patrol car, rode around the neighborhood with them and spotted one of the bombers, who was arrested. Ten minutes later, two more Molotov cocktails were thrown at his house. As a result, the police put an officer in a car sitting outside Arjune's home as security. At 3:30 on the morning of February 25, 1988, a 911 operator received a call of an officer shot. When patrol cars arrived at the scene, they found a twenty-two-year-old uniformed police officer, Eddie Byrne, slumped in the front seat of his police car with the top of his head blown off. A local drug gang had done what the Mafia had never dared to do in New York—assassinate a police officer.***

The crime sparked an all-out drive against the gangs. However, it was clumsily handled. The police department fell back on the customary device of forming special squads, known, in this instance, as Tactical Narcotics Teams (TNTs), to sweep through the affected neighborhoods, making large numbers of arrests. Soon the jails were so full that the city had to buy prison barges to hold the excess inmates, and the chief judge of the State of New York declared an emergency in the clogged court system. What had happened was that when TNTs removed one set of dealers from the street, another group, lured by the large sums of money that could be made, was ready to go to work for the drug kingpins. In the end, crime continued to rise. New Yorkers had had enough. In 1989, after twelve years in office, Mayor Koch was defeated in the Democratic primary by David Dinkins, who went on to win the general election. His administration would introduce a new method of policing. Instead of mass roundups it would emphasize working with the community.

The worst-hit gang city in the United States was Los Angeles. In the 1980s, the South Central area was largely populated by low-income African-American families. Unemployment and poverty were rife. Out of this milieu rose two rival gangs, the Crips and the Bloods. Each had its own color: Crips, blue; Bloods, red. Crips wore a certain type of sneaker with a blue stripe on each side. Bloods had their own sneakers, black with a red stripe on each side. For someone with red to go into a blue area was to court death, and vice versa. Even innocent citizens who happened to be wearing one of those colors and inadvertently wandered into gang turf were occasionally murdered.

The LAPD, under Chief Daryl Gates, responded, like New York, by deploying its forces in special units, such as CRASH (Community Resources Against Street Hoodlums). CRASH officers cruised South Central looking for gang members and responding to gang incidents, which frequently involved shootings with fatalities.[1]

Most Angelinos did not worry about problems that were confined to the ghetto areas. Although South Central was only a twenty-minute drive from Beverly Hills and other elite areas, the city was laid out in such a way that these locales might as well have been twenty hours apart. Then, in 1988, an Asian-American woman, Karen Toshima, was caught in a crossfire between the Crips and the Bloods and killed. It happened in Westwood Village, near UCLA, close to the respectable areas of Los Angeles. Immediately a crackdown was ordered.

Chief Gates sent his forces out on a series of gang sweeps, which, in conjunction with the sheriff's office (which also maintained anti-gang units), rousted thousands of young men. Roundups, sweeps, dragnets—whatever they were called—were an old police tactic. They would work for a time because gang members would stay off the streets to avoid being picked up. But they had little permanent effect.[+]

The question might be raised: had Delaney of Chicago methods, which combined enforcement with outreach, been employed in places like New York and Los Angeles, would it have stopped the gang situation from getting out of hand? The answer is that a handful of cops cannot stop a national trend. But if the correct strategies and tactics had been followed, the results might have been less calamitous.[2]

* * * *

Street disorder did not receive the same level of publicity as gang warfare, but it was often as vexing to the public. Police departments and the courts groped for answers and provided few. Once the streets of American cities were

---

1. The movie *Colors,* with Sean Penn and Robert Duvall as CRASH cops, is a good representation of the unit's work. Eastern police chiefs would never call the unit's vehicles CRASH cars. Police wrecked enough vehicles without encouraging them by using that kind of identification. Nor would they use the word "hoodlum," which was politically incorrect. Detroit called its anti-crime unit STRESS, for "Stop The Robberies, Enjoy Safe Streets." New York designated its comparable group the street crime unit (SCU). By this time Chicago had a gang intelligence unit (GIU) which took over some of the work of the old youth bureau.

2. The same was true in other categories. The 1968 Democratic convention might have witnessed less conflict if a softer line had been followed by the police. Note also the October 1969 "days of rage," where the Weathermen ran wild through the streets of Chicago. I had been away at Harvard for a while. After I was gone, there was a change in the command arrangements. A young lawyer was put in charge of handling civil disorder, with the cops taking orders from him. He had no police training, but he was a member of a powerful political family. During the course of the event, he attempted to apprehend a Weatherman by tackling him. The attorney was left paralyzed for life.

orderly except for certain skid-row districts where drunks, panhandlers, street-walkers and vagrants congregated: areas like New York's Bowery or Chicago's West Madison Street. By tradition, cops in such districts gave the street population fairly wide latitude, but if the so-called "bums" tried to hang out in other parts of town, the police would run them in on charges of disorderly conduct or vagrancy. In New York, when winter approached, some vagrants deliberately courted arrest by panhandling in nicer sections of town, where they hoped a cop would grab them and a judge give them 90 days in a warm cell on the island (the city jail on Blackwell's Island).[3]

Sometimes skid-row areas would exist side by side with the ritzy parts of town, but the twain did not meet. In the song *The Bowery,* the singer declares:

> Oh, the night that I struck New York,
> I went out for a quiet walk;
> Folks who are "on to" the city say,
> Better by far that I took Broadway;
> But I was out to enjoy the sights,
> There was the Bow'ry ablaze with lights;
> I had one of the devil's own nights!
> I'll never go there anymore.
> The Bow'ry, the Bow'ry!
> They say such things and they do strange things on the Bow'ry
> The Bow'ry! I'll never go there anymore!

Chicago, in addition to West Madison, had two other skid-row areas: South State, which ran south of the central business district known as the Loop, and North Clark, which was adjacent to the city's "Gold Coast," where the rich society people lived. Despite their proximity, South State was kept away from the Loop, and North Clark was never allowed to intrude on the Gold Coast.

The police were an integral part of the skid-row scene in ways that were beyond a patrolman walking along twirling his nightstick (something that was never done in Chicago because it was thought to look stupid). Chicago often had manpower shortages, and workers for temporary labor jobs were hard to find. Companies would send a contractor and a truck to West Madison to recruit itinerants for a day or two's work. Some men of the area were willing, but they were concerned that at the end of the day they would not get the promised wages. So a cop (often a detective), whom the vagrants knew and

---

3. O. Henry, the great chronicler of New York life in the early 20th century, described this routine in "The Cop and the Anthem." The film version, with Charles Laughton as the vagrant, is contained in the movie *O. Henry's Full House* (1952).

trusted, would vouch for the labor contractor's bona fides and even have him show that he was carrying a large roll of bills so he could pay off workers at the end of the day. (Flashing money on West Madison was never done without a cop present.) With that assurance, the vagrants would climb aboard the truck.

During the first half of the twentieth century, one cop who worked in the State Street area was the legendary Sergeant Murphy, whose name was chalked on every wall in America where vagrants congregated.[4] It advised them, if they landed in Chicago, to check in with Murphy, who would give them a handout and help them in other ways. It was said that he never turned anyone down. Murphy was not an eccentric millionaire who had become a police officer so he could do good deeds. His police district included mission societies who provided shelter and a meal for vagrants. It is likely that the societies kept him supplied with money to disburse because they knew he was honest and would use it to help people in need.

A few cops continued Murphy's work, occasionally giving handouts that came out of their own pockets. Some were deeply religious, others were just kindly people. Fellow cops referred to such an individual as a man who "should have been a priest." Some others had not been near a church in twenty years or were not at all kindly. Yet, like certain gamblers, they would always be willing to help people in need. Perhaps it was a gesture meant to bring them luck. As with so many things that could or should have been done, the police department never created a system to handle its dealings with the vagrants and the needy.

In the 1950s, New York Inspector Conrad Jensen operated his Manhattan precinct as though it were a mission. Parker's Los Angeles police department ran its own jail system, including a large farm for alcoholics. It was the job of the county sheriff to operate jails, not the city police, but Parker was seeking a semi-social service response to the problems of public intoxication.

Over time, the ACLU and similar organizations began suing to strike down or narrow laws and ordinances that were used to control street disorder or even street crime. Some of the blame for this situation rests with police. Most cops did not want to deal with petty disorder. When citizens complained to them about street people using their hallways for bathrooms or that they had been harassed by a beggar (usually a young, physically fit individual who in some cases had been trained and costumed for the role), they got little

---

4. Men of the road had a secret code of their own which scholars found fascinating to study. It would advise the fraternity which trains to hop on and which cities to head for or, conversely, which to avoid. It would also include items of information such as how to get a handout in a particular city.

sympathy. A frequent response of police officials was that they were too busy fighting crime to deal with the matter.[5]

Some police departments allowed officers to use the disorderly conduct or vagrancy statutes when it was inappropriate. A cop who wrote a traffic ticket and got an earful from the motorist might charge him with "discon." The courts held that a motorist protesting a ticket was not disturbing the peace of the public and, in any event, a cop was not part of the public. A few judges would still uphold a disorderly conduct charge if the motorist called the officer an SOB or some similar term.

The common law traditionally included the crime of "night walking" under disorderly conduct. An 1871 Illinois court decision delineated police authority in this area:

> Police officers have the authority at common law to arrest and detain in prison for examination persons walking the streets at night when there is reason to suspect felony although there is no proof of a felony having been committed. The reason why night walking and lurking about the premises of peaceful inhabitants in the nighttime is disorderly conduct is because such conduct cannot in general be for any but a bad purpose and tends to the annoyance and discomfort of peaceable citizens, who have a just right to be exempt from such disturbances.[++]

The problem was that, in some instances, police exceeded their legal authority. When the "dragnet" was out, organized crime squad cops would go into a bar where a known gangster was enjoying a beer, take him off his stool and lock him up. As the judge would tell the officer in such cases, "He wasn't disorderly—you were." Gangsters with five hundred dollars in their wallets were charged with vagrancy (no visual means of support) even though they were millionaires who owned legitimate businesses. On the other hand, it was lawful for police to detain individuals, loitering about or cruising through neighborhoods late at night, who could not give a legitimate explanation for their presence. However, judges began dismissing even these sorts of arrests.

Starting in the '60s, the prevailing notion in the courts became that street people should not be criminalized for following alternative life-styles, or because of the failures of society. A federal judge, in declaring the New York anti-loitering statute unconstitutional, wrote that begging should have the same protection as First Amendment Freedom of Speech requirements—i.e., that

---

5. One Eastern city police lieutenant declared that he was too busy investigating murders to be worried about such minor things. When I inquired about how many murders he had investigated during the previous five years, the answer was none.

begging was essentially communication. According to the judge, "The beggar has arguably only committed the offense of being needy. The message one or 100 beggars send society can be disturbing... The answer is not in criminalizing these people...but addressing the root cause of their existence." If police told aggressive beggars to move on, there were groups ready to go to court and sue them.[6]

In 1982, Harvard political scientist James Q. Wilson and his research partner, George Kelling, published an influential article in *The Atlantic Monthly* in which they posited a relationship between disorder and crime. They argued that police had all but decriminalized such things as graffiti, loud music, drunkenness and urinating in public. The neglect of these problems, they contended, created conditions in which disorder and crime flourished. They called their theory "Broken Windows" because it was similar to the situation where a broken window, if left unfixed, seemed to encourage people to break the remaining windows. Wilson and Kelling traced the vicious cycle whereby, when the laws were not enforced, low-level disorder increased and law-abiding citizens, who heretofore had constituted a critical mass to deter crime and disorder by their presence, would become frightened and forsake the area. Eventually, the neighborhood would become so lawless that felons would begin to commit serious crimes there, because they felt there would be little police interference. Kelling and Wilson argued that the only way this cycle could be broken was for the police to take enforcement action against low-level disorder.[+++]

In New York City, the poster boy for disorderly street people was Larry Hogue, whom the press labeled the "Wild Man of Ninety-sixth Street." Hogue, who was tall and powerfully built, was receiving military disability pay as a result of having been struck in the head by an airplane propeller (though not,

---

6. It has been my observation that many people who take a tolerant view of street disorder express a different opinion when it's acted out in their own backyard. I recall a man who headed a major civil liberties group and was himself a former Communist leader. (I did not learn this fact from J. Edgar Hoover or Joe McCarthy but from the man himself, who proclaimed it at the top of his lungs.) Some teenagers in his neighborhood were bouncing basketballs when they went past his house or left bottles on his lawn—common behavior of boys growing up in certain parts of the city. From time to time, he complained to me about it, and I brought them in for a reprimand—not a euphemism for use of force. Members of the youth bureau, under court order, were allowed to function as a sort of examining magistrate. This permitted them to write up a case and dispose of the charges informally. Alternatively, they could file a complaint with the circuit court, which handled cases up to and including murder. It was not the place where bouncing basketball charges were customarily heard. By the same token, police were not granted unlimited discretion. Felonies and certain graver misdemeanors had to be referred to the court unless the parties were very young. It was a system that both social workers and cops approved of. However, Mr. Civil Liberties was never satisfied. He claimed the whole thing was part of a Communist plot to harass him for having broken with the party, and he continually demanded that I crack down. I don't know if he believed what he told me. All I can say is, if those boys were Communists, I was a Martian.

as first reported, in Vietnam). He was a constant threatening presence at the intersection of 96th Street and Broadway. On one occasion, he threw a young woman in front of a moving car. Repeatedly arrested, he was just as repeatedly released by mental health officials, who deemed him "not dangerous." There seemed to be no legal basis for holding him. In December 1992, his story was told on *Sixty Minutes*. Interviewed during one of his periodic incarcerations, Hogue made it clear that he had no intention of leaving the neighborhood or changing his ways. After the national television program, medical authorities suddenly decided that Hogue should remain in custody after all. But a state court judge overruled them, advancing his own diagnosis. Hogue was not mentally ill, said the judge; he had an "attitude problem."^

Across the country, many cities sought to apply the "broken windows" theory. In Baltimore, the police began to take notice of the so-called "homeless." The majority of them were alcoholics and a significant number were mentally disturbed. At first, police training amounted to fifteen minutes in preservice recruit academy instruction. A federal district judge, in denying the city's motion to dismiss a suit against the municipal anti-panhandling ordinance, noted that the training of the officers may have been sufficiently inadequate to constitute "deliberate indifference" to the population being policed, and thereby to provide grounds for a civil rights suit against the city and the police department.

The volume of disorder also contributed to Baltimore's crime problem. It was one of the cities hit hardest by the crack explosion; between 1985 and 1993, the number of murders rose from two hundred and thirteen to three hundred fifty-two (a sixty-five percent increase). This was a rate of murder per one hundred thousand higher than New York, Chicago, or Los Angeles. To deal with the city's problems, the police commissioner instituted special foot patrols to handle homeless and other street people as well as stepping up regular law enforcement. The Civil Liberties Union brought a legal challenge against the city and private business programs as "an effort to expel an entire class of citizens from the downtown area of Baltimore City based on their appearance and homeless status." The federal judge did dispose of some points in favor of the defendants. He held that the fundamental right to privacy and personal autonomy did not extend to a "right to eat, sleep, or perform other essential activities in public." He ruled that a police officer's order to a panhandler to move on or cease panhandling did not constitute a "seizure" under the Fourth Amendment. However, he was more sympathetic to the suit against the city anti-panhandling ordinance, and some elements of the judge's decision were actually interpreted as ruling that the police could only enforce the law against crimes and that there should be virtually no interaction between them and emotionally disturbed individuals, drunks, youths, etc. Even many social workers had never favored that view. They were happy to see the police intervene if it was to make referrals to welfare agencies.

San Francisco cops always had a reputation for being tough. A sin city since the Gold Rush days, it had the politics and policing of a traditional East Coast metropolis. In the postwar era, its mayors were respectable businessmen like Roger Dearborn Lapham and George Christopher. In 1956, it was Christopher who appointed Frank Ahern, the city's star detective, as chief of police and Ahern's partner, Tom Cahill, as deputy chief. Ahern died of a heart attack in 1958 but was succeeded by Cahill, who served until 1970.

In the early 1970s, violent radicals conducted a virtual war against the San Francisco police. The decade began on a bad note when, on January 1, 1970, a police officer was murdered in the city's Tenderloin district. A few months later, another officer was assassinated while sitting in his marked police vehicle writing a parking citation. A third was slain by a bank robber. A sergeant was killed by a bomb set by leftist political radicals against the assembly room window at Park station. The following year, Black Guerrilla Army members invaded the Ingleside station and killed the sergeant manning the desk. At the funeral of one dead police officer, a pipe bomb placed against the church's wall exploded.

In 1974, a local radical group known as the Symbionese Liberation Army kidnapped Hearst newspaper heiress Patty Hearst. To everyone's surprise, the kidnap victim soon joined her captors in robbing banks to obtain money for the revolution and releasing tapes explaining how her political views had changed and she was now Tanya, a radical heroine.

In 1975, George Moscone was elected mayor with the support of leftist groups, minorities, and gays. Among his supporters were the Reverend Jim Jones of the Peoples Temple. Moscone appointed an outsider, former Oakland chief Charles Gain, to head the San Francisco department. This did not go over well because Oakland, across the bay, was a force that San Francisco cops always thought inferior to their own.

In 1978, City Supervisor (equivalent to a city council member elsewhere) Dan White resigned but then had second thoughts. He went to city hall and asked Mayor Moscone to let him withdraw his resignation. When the mayor refused, White shot and killed him. He then went down the hall and killed Supervisor Harvey Milk, a leader of the gay community. At the time, the city was already reeling from the mass suicide of Jones and his congregation in Guyana, South America. Authorities there found 909 dead bodies. Jones had begun the slaughter by having his gunmen kill San Francisco Congressman Leo Ryan, who had gone down to investigate Jonestown.

In 1979, although White was tried for two murders, he was only found guilty of manslaughter and sentenced to eight years in prison. It was the case where the famous "Twinkie defense" was raised; i.e., White's mental equilibrium was supposedly affected by his having eaten too many Twinkies. When the verdict was announced, gays from the Castro district began marching on city hall. When they arrived, there were only a handful of cops on duty and the protesters started damaging the building. They then turned over police cars and set fire to them. Finally, police reinforcements gained control of the area. That night a police team entered a gay bar in the Castro district and roughly dispersed the patrons. The gay community in the area broke into rioting, and eventually a San Francisco deputy police chief ordered the police to withdraw from the Castro district. As the police were retreating, they were followed by a jeering mob. Rank-and-file San Francisco cops bitterly resented the events of what came to be called "the White Night Riot" and denounced the deputy chief who gave the order. The chief himself would later characterize the affair as "the inevitable eruption in a long-simmering conflict between the San Francisco that had been and the city that was about to be—the death throes of the old San Francisco, you might say, amid the birthing pains of the new."

It was not surprising that the new San Francisco became the most liberal city in America, and its law enforcement policies reflected that. The city adopted generous social service policies, but conditions on the public streets deteriorated significantly. According to George Kelling, the Downtown Civic Center became a "shantytown." Local citizens dubbed it "Camp Agnos," after the mayor, Art Agnos, who refused to break up the encampments of the homeless in public spaces and parks until housing he deemed adequate was created for them. Parks, rail terminals and parking garages were essentially taken over by street people.

Rarely discussed was the notion that many street people do not want housing, jobs, or other services. If one has actually spent time among them, it is clear that more than a few are there by choice. They do not desire to live a middle-class life-style. Well-known Americans of earlier generations, such as the writer Jack London, chose to live as a hobo without prompting hand-wringing.

In 1991, Camp Agnos was a major issue in the mayoral race between a former police chief, Frank Jordan, and the mayor. Jordan was victorious, and he set up programs to deal with the homeless. However, a federal judge ruled that a restriction on begging and panhandling violated the First Amendment free-speech rights and the equal-protection clause of the Fourteenth Amendment.

The 1995 mayoral election was largely a referendum on Mayor Jordan's homeless policies. His opponents generally condemned them. The *San Francisco Chronicle,* in endorsing Jordan, noted:

> There was a time when Jordan's critics attacked him for what they called criminalizing homelessness. Homeless advocates still say this, but the political pack seem to have clued into the fact that rap doesn't play well with voters.
>
> Remember Mayor Art Agnos? He didn't want to move the homeless without first providing enough services. The result: when the homeless broke the law, the police were paralyzed. The Civic Center became the Mecca of America's unwashed. The decision to not use the police turned San Francisco into a magnet for people who just want to hang out, not work, do drugs and soil the City."^^

However, Mayor Jordan lost a runoff election. Since then the city's policies have become even more liberal.

Of all the police problems that faced the country as the twentieth century drew to a close, street disorder may have been the worst. Gunmen eventually got caught and jailed. But court decisions were making it virtually impossible to enforce the rules of a civilized society. The peril of unchecked public disorder was recognized over a century ago by one of America's great radicals, Henry George, author of *Progress and Poverty,* who wrote:

> Let the policeman's club be thrown down or wrested from him, and the fountains of the great deep are opened, and quicker than ever before chaos comes again. Strong as it may seem, our civilization is evolving destructive forces. Not desert and forest, but city and slums and country roadsides are nursing the barbarians who may be to the new what Hun and Vandal were to the old.^^^

Chapter 9

New York Community Policing and Gates' LAPD Style Both Fail

As in most fields, there are fashions in policing. The predominant style in 1945 was traditional, which worked to the satisfaction of most people in the classic industrial cities. In the 1950s the professional model of policing, favored by police and political reformers, was adopted in some locales. When the waves of crime, disorder and riots swept across the country in the 1960s, neither system seemed to have an answer. The political power of the individuals who controlled traditional policing was of no help in dealing with the problems of the time. No professional police expert, like O. W Wilson or Bill Parker, could wave a magic wand and make the troubles go away.

Police departments, such as that in Philadelphia under Frank Rizzo, met the challenges by becoming like Marines, who were tougher and smarter than those who appeared to be threatening public safety. In the nearly twelve years during which Rizzo ran the police department, Philadelphia did not experience a major riot, and the public felt safe, if for no other reason than cops seemed on top of the crime situation. The problem was that minorities did not like the way Rizzo and his police treated them.

In New York, Pat Murphy was able to achieve lasting gains against corruption. But the police department under Mayor Lindsay, both before and during Murphy's tenure, was not spared riots and rising crime rates. Programs like model precincts, neighborhood teams and efforts to make police more sensitive all showed few results. If the image of Philadelphia police was Rizzo, with a club in his cummerbund and his elite highway patrol unit standing by awaiting the order to charge, in New York it was Lindsay mouthing platitudes while Murphy's commanders released cop killers.

In the '70s, some police administrators and academics attempted to create models of policing that could reduce crime without alienating the people they were meant to help. Often the models went under the vague heading of "community policing," which Chief Daryl Gates of Los Angeles characterized as "a bunch of cops grinning at people, patting kids on the head and handing out lollipops." That was not the intention of most advocates of community policing. They realized that cops sometimes needed to be social workers, but that policing had to come first.

Beyond the generalities, however, proponents of community policing never fully agreed on what it was. They were sure they wanted to get away from the 911 system, where patrol car crews applied Band-Aids and then moved on to the next call, but they were not sure what they were going to create in its place. Some envisioned that under community policing, cops would identify neighborhood problems and devise solutions to them. In line with Wilson and Kelling's "broken windows" theory, they would try to reduce low-level disorder, thereby encouraging law-abiding citizens to use the streets and the ill-disposed to behave or make themselves scarce. This, in turn, would lead to a significant reduction in serious crime. It all made sense—on paper.

In September 1989, David Dinkins defeated the three-term incumbent New York mayor, Ed Koch, in the Democratic primary. Crime had soared to astronomical levels on Koch's watch, and drug dealers ruled half the city's neighborhoods. Koch's TNT program (set up following the murder of Officer Eddie Byrne, as described in Chapter 8) had loaded the courts and jails without producing any real decrease in drug sales or crime. Although his defeat was the result of many factors, it could reasonably be seen as a vote of no confidence in his handling of the crime problem. Two months after Dinkins defeated Koch in the primary, he narrowly beat out the Republican candidate, former United States attorney Rudy Giuliani, who ran on his reputation as a tough law enforcer. Thus the election of Dinkins, the city's first African-American mayor, could not be characterized as a call for hard-line law enforcement. The public wanted something in between. On the recommendation of a screening committee (of which this writer was a member), Dinkins chose Houston police chief Lee Brown, who had introduced community policing ideas in that city, to head the NYPD.

A native of Oklahoma, Brown had moved to California's San Joaquin Valley with his sharecropper parents. He went on to a state college, where he played football and then joined the San Jose Police Department, eventually rising to sergeant. During that time he also earned a doctorate in criminology from Berkeley. Next he was appointed sheriff of Multnomah County, Oregon, which surrounds the city of Portland. The county police department was one of the few in America that required its recruits to possess a bachelor's degree. Brown then became chief of police in Atlanta, serving at the time when twenty-three children were murdered. In 1982, he was made chief in Houston, America's fourth-largest city. During his career he had become well known in law enforcement circles and in 1990 was serving as president of the International Association of Chiefs of Police (IACP), the first African American to hold the post. His election to the office was significant. A number of police leaders, like Pat Murphy, had never been able to win the job because they were deemed too liberal. Brown was regarded as a progressive law enforcement administrator who also respected the traditions of the profession and got along well with its leading practitioners.*

If Brown's concept of community policing were to work, it had to satisfy a large segment of the New York population, not just experts. Yet much of the appeal of community policing was based on certain beliefs, some of them near mythical. Essentially it derived from a longing for the lost home of one's youth, an older America where an omnipresent beat cop provided both protection and friendly counseling.[1] This was not always an accurate picture. The type of neighborhood where community policing seemed ideal was one like the West End of Boston, which was described by Herbert Gans in his book *The Urban Villagers*. Gans examined the effects of the destruction of the area, in the 1950s, to make way for a dreary group of public buildings known as "Government Center." Even after the neighborhood was leveled, many of the former residents continued to mourn for their lost home.** Jane Jacobs caught the imagination of a wide audience with her 1961 book, *The Death and Life of Great American Cities*. She argued that traditional urban neighborhoods provided not only an invigorating environment but also a large measure of safety, because its residents and shopkeepers watched over each other. By the '60s, though, a small, densely populated, tightly knit community such as the West End was not where most people lived. Jacobs' own neighborhood, Greenwich Village, was an exceptional place.***

---

1. For an idealized portrait of a community cop, circa 1916, see the movie *A Tree Grows in Brooklyn* (1945). In it, the officer, played by Lloyd Nolan, is not only a helpful friend to a family, but ends up marrying the young widow, played by Dorothy McGuire.

By the middle of the twentieth century, urban villages were usually made up of particular ethnic groups, because new immigrants found it easier to adjust to America if they resided among people who shared their language and culture. But their children did not wish to live in those environments, confined to the restricted lives of their parents. They preferred mainstream America. Frank Rizzo, as an adult, did not reside in South Philadelphia, but rather in middle-class Germantown (which was not German).

Middle-class Americans were not interested in spending a lot of time gossiping with their neighbors (their own friends were spread across the city) or having a heart-to-heart with the local beat cop. If they wanted police, they called them. If they had another legal problem, they called their lawyer.

The duties envisioned for community policing officers were somewhat broad. They were to deal with problems ranging from dirty streets to gangs shooting up the neighborhood and to know everyone. The idealized beat cop seemed to have pounded the pavement twenty-four hours a day, seven days a week, over ten or fifteen years. The actual cops who patrolled a neighborhood, mostly in cars, worked eight-hour shifts, with a couple of days off every week, and were frequently detailed away on special duties. Thus, within a one-week period, eight or ten different officers might patrol a particular neighborhood. Many also had no intention of staying on a beat any longer than they had to. It was a constant complaint at community meetings that as soon as people got to know a local cop, he was transferred out.

Whatever omissions there were in the planning and whatever possible problems there might be, community policing at least sounded good. Any politician who promised to get more foot cops in his district never suffered at the ballot box. The public wanted a new approach to law enforcement—one that would be effective but not too heavy-handed. So why not try community policing?

By the late '70s, most police chiefs in America claimed to be doing community policing—even Daryl Gates, who, on occasion, denounced it. One chief, when asked what his program consisted of, would say he had two headquarters detectives working full time on the problem in his city of half a million people. In practice, they went out to neighborhood meetings to give safety tips, like what type of lock to buy. In places where there was a well-developed community police program, it usually contained certain common features. It stressed decentralized organization, participatory management by rank-and-file officers and an all-out effort to win the confidence of local residents. Substations were opened to bring cops closer to the neighborhoods, and special teams were formed to staff them. Usually, they were freed from the control of the regular police hierarchy and from responding to radio calls.

Team commanders, often mere sergeants, were given the flexibility to change working hours, or shift their officers from cars to foot, uniform to plainclothes and back again. In the rest of the department, only a captain had the authority to do that. Teams were expected to operate in a collegial fashion, with each member offering ideas on how to solve problems. Community policing officers were encouraged to take a broad view of their duties, ensuring that other city agencies respond to non-law-enforcement complaints such as litter-strewn lots and abandoned cars. It was pretty heady stuff. Low-level cops were going to transform whole neighborhoods—a task that had defied mayors and the U.S. Department of Housing and Urban Development. In practice, team members spent a lot of time at meetings, sharing coffee and cake with residents. It was a way to meet people in a more relaxed setting than a crime scene; however, among veteran officers who were left to do the routine work of responding to brawls and reports of shots fired, community policing was derided as a waste of time. In most cities, community policing failed because it was carried on separately from the regular police operation. In some places, documentary films were made about such experiments. However, by the time anyone got to see them, the substation had been closed, the team abolished and the department was embarked on some new initiative.

Sometimes books appeared about community-type policing that were a bit embarrassing. The authors would eulogize a local police chief who had cooperated with the research, often describing him as "innovative"—the highest compliment in American social science.[2] However, by the time the book appeared, the chief had been fired and, in a few cases, was in jail. In one of the latter instances, it would have taken any experienced law enforcement officer about five minutes to realize that he should not have any dealings with that particular chief. In another case, the chief was an outstanding professional and his fall was a shock to those of us who knew him.

Many big-city precincts held a community meeting once a month. They were usually presided over by the captain and contained a regular cast of characters: the heads of local civic organizations who wanted to get a picture of themselves making a speech to put in their monthly newsletters, a few people unhappy about some incident that had occurred and folks who wanted to bring up issues that more properly belonged before the United Nations Security Council. Talk was endless and busy people did not care to participate in such

---

2. If the social scientists knew what some chiefs they praised really thought about them, they would have been shocked. In the police world, unless you have worn the uniform you are never really accepted as a member. Academics particularly are seen as people who live in an ivory tower whereas cops value knowledge of the streets. In private, even educated police reformers ridiculed academics. It is interesting to note that the Academy has allowed some police chiefs into their ranks, while the reverse is not true.

events. The captain was usually friendly, anxious to get his ticket punched so he could move on to a higher post in the department. The community affairs officer was a college-educated young patrolman who was liaison to neighborhood groups. Of course, neither the captain nor the community affairs officer was what the people in the street called "the real police." The real cops were the ones that showed up at midnight when there was a call of shots fired. When they arrived on the scene, their chief concern was not to make everybody happy but to ensure that a gunman didn't put a bullet in them. In such tense and dangerous situations, cops tended to behave in their traditional fashion.

One feature of community policing that was rarely commented on was that some of the most dangerous assignments were given to untrained civilians. Many programs encouraged citizen patrols, who were expected to go out in the street and be the "eyes and ears" of the police. This could make the local drug gangs very angry. In some neighborhoods, it was unwise to be labeled as a "snitch." A woman on Manhattan's West Side became known for her complaints about drug dealers in her neighborhood. After she was murdered, a corner youngster sadly commented, "She did right, but she did it dumb."

The cities that served as experimental laboratories for community policing varied. The two leading ones were Newark, New Jersey, and Houston, Texas. The former was a medium-sized municipality with three hundred and eighty thousand people in an area of nineteen square miles. Its population was mostly poor and nonwhite. Newark had never really recovered from the disorders of 1967, and because of the riot, the city received many government grants and was open to experiments. It also had an outstanding public safety director in charge of its police force. Hubert Williams was a career Newark cop who as a sergeant spent a year in a special course at Harvard, then earned a law degree at Rutgers. He would eventually replace Pat Murphy as president of the Washington-based Police Foundation, where he would serve for many years as a gray eminence of American policing.

Houston was a middle-class, predominately white city which grew rapidly in the postwar era. By the 1980s, it had one million eight hundred thousand people sprawled across five hundred and fifty square miles. Its police chief was Lee Brown.

Newark's experiment was designed by police administrators and academics as part of the regular police organizational structure. Its rationale was that enhanced attention to street disorder would lessen public fear and encourage people to use the streets. Though not stated, it was a logical concomitant of "Broken Windows" that this would eventually cause serious crime to decline significantly.

Newark's methods were a mixture of conventional policing and new approaches. Cops carried out intensive patrols and enforcement against street disorder. Among the innovations were: the establishment of a storefront police station to bring the department closer to the citizenry, the issuance of a newsletter and a door-to-door survey to learn of individuals' problems. Officers would then be assigned to assist in solving them.

One typical small, but eye-catching, tactic was the police department bus crackdown. Riding public transportation in a high-crime city is not always relaxing. It takes people through neighborhoods that they would not normally go into, and they are never sure who will board the vehicle. On a bus, hustlers and hoodlums had a captive audience. In Newark there were complaints that not only were riders harassed but passengers drank, played loud radios and used drugs. In the community policing program, a team of officers would suddenly board a city bus and warn riders that those who were in violation of city ordinances would have to stop their activities or leave the bus. They then passed through, scrutinizing the passengers, ejecting some riders and occasionally making an arrest. It was always interesting to watch the passengers when the cops appeared. Most riders smiled and were glad to see them. A few riders frowned and invariably got off at the next stop. A bus with cops on it constituted a reverse captive audience of criminals. When the police boarded, a citizen might point out a rider who had tried intimidating him or her into handing over money. With the vehicle moving, the suspect could not run away.

Evaluations of the Newark program were mixed; that was a common phenomenon in experiments. There were both positive and negative findings, but not really enough time or number of cases from which to draw any firm conclusions. They did suggest that police could effectively reduce levels of social disorder by employing intensive enforcement tactics. A large proportion of people interviewed remembered the police visits and problem-solving efforts as positive. Far more people in the target areas reported seeing visible police patrols than in comparable neighborhoods—although in any experiment there is also the familiar "Hawthorne effect," where the mere fact that it is going on causes it to receive favorable ratings from respondents.

The Houston program was largely created by the cops who were working in it. Not surprisingly, police teams were given a high degree of autonomy from the command structure. Houston, too, had storefronts, newsletters and problem-solving efforts. One complaint was that in such a sprawling, impersonal, middle-class city few people knew police. So the experimental areas adopted a tactic called "beat integrity," whereby dispatchers tried to keep local cars in their same patrol area at all times rather than sending them into other areas as they had previously done. Of course, this delayed response to calls in the non-experimental areas. The statistical ratings for the Houston program largely confirmed what many social scientists suspected. Experimental programs worked best where most of the population is already sympathetic to the police. As sociologist Al Reiss noted, it is easier to work in an area where there is a single dominant group than in one where there are diverse groups competing for power and resources.

One of the problems with community policing was that it was always an experimental program carried out by a relatively small group of officers. In New York, Commissioner Brown promised to institute community policing methods in the entire NYPD. To support the program, the city and state were asked to appropriate funds to increase the three municipal police departments—city, transit and housing (which would soon be merged)—from thirty-one thousand to thirty-seven thousand officers. Many experts on government predicted that the program, known as "Safe Streets," would never be approved by the state legislature. To their surprise, it was swiftly authorized. A number of people helped to ensure this outcome, but in the final analysis it was Gov. Mario Cuomo who did the heavy lifting.[3] Strangely, he never took any credit. Perhaps he did not want every interest group coming to him demanding its own earmarked program. The simple fact was that in 1990 the governor and Mayor Dinkins realized that crime was destroying New York City and that no other program—housing, transit, etc.—would work as long as crime was out of control.

Brown's approach to community policing was more academic than dynamic. He was a man who thought deeply and held strong convictions. He spent half an hour early every morning meditating in his office, and he stated publicly that his three heroes were: Gandhi, Jesus and Martin Luther King, Jr. His aides always referred to him as "Dr. Brown." Such a title may have been impressive in academic circles, but in the streets of New York it sounded analogous to Dr. Pepper, a popular soft drink.

Despite the notion that the entire department would carry out community policing, that never really happened. The bulk of the police force, already on the job, learned little about the initiative beyond a few announcements amid the confusion of roll call. Before Brown's arrival, there had been a handful of officers in each precinct assigned to community policing duties. They were known by the name CPOP (for Community Patrol Officer Program). Other cops often ridiculed them as social workers and referred to them as "C-Moms." Some of this attitude carried over to the new program. In an effort to

---

3. Full disclosure: I was one of the principal advocates of the program, utilizing TV, print and other forums to point out its virtues.

raise the status of community policing within the department, Brown began giving out awards to officers for the success they achieved in making their neighborhood a better place. At an honors ceremony in October 1991, the commissioner bestowed a Cop of the Month award on a captain who had saved a man's life by shooting and killing an assailant who had been holding him hostage at knifepoint. This was the traditional kind of police work honored at such occasions. The second award went to a patrolman who had saved twenty-five wedding dresses. He was recognized for calming the angry customers of a bridal shop that had closed without notice and then for mediating between them and the store owner. Brown called it "an act of compassion and initiative which was the very epitome of 'problem-solving policing.'" The rank-and-file reaction was expressed by one officer interviewed for the *New York Times,* who exclaimed, "He won it for *that?*"+

A disproportionate number of community policing cops were young. Often they had never held a real job and still lived with their families. Some had never set foot in a ghetto until they arrived in one wearing a blue uniform. Suddenly they were thrown up against armed gangs. An African-American officer in the Bronx, known for his effectiveness against local drug dealers, attributed his success to the fact that, unlike many of his peers, he was from the inner city, not "East Cupcake, Long Island."++

The bulk of precinct cops continued to man radio cars answering 911 calls, although in the original plan for community policing that Brown's aides had prepared, it was stated that the department would no longer be an "incident-responding bureaucracy." Instead, officers would get to know their beats and become familiar with "its people, their concerns, the crime problem, the make-up of the blocks, the crises of daily living and the support systems available to help people live better." In practice this proved impossible. 911 calls, which totaled six million annually, often involved emergencies, crimes in progress or disorders that required police cars to be sent at once. In other instances, if a CPOP cop encountered a problem, such as an alcoholic husband who beat his wife, what could he do about it that a decade of treatment by professionals had not managed to accomplish?

Sometimes the rhetoric that would accompany community policing, such as "empowering the powerless," made it sound as if cops were going to lead marches on city hall. Community police teams never became more than an adjunct to a reactive 911 system, and they had virtually no impact on the crime rate. Drug dealers did not stop selling or shooting because the neighbors complained about them. "Officer Friendly," hurrying from meeting to meeting with his thick "beat book" full of neat reports, did not scare them either.

In 1991 a major riot broke out between blacks and Jews in Brooklyn during which a Hasidic man was stabbed to death. For three days, disorder raged unchecked while police stood by. The mobs in Crown Heights meant business. When a well-known columnist, Jimmy Breslin, came out to the riot scene in a taxi, he was dragged out and his trousers were ripped off. On the fourth day, when Commissioner Brown himself arrived to inspect the area, a mob of black youngsters attacked his car. If the chauffeur had not been able to radio a 10-13 call for emergency reinforcements, Brown might have experienced a fate worse than Breslin's. In the same vicinity, a thrown bottle narrowly missed Mayor Dinkins' head. His security detail advised him to leave the area because they estimated that at least a dozen people in the crowd had guns. Finally, First Deputy Commissioner Ray Kelly, who had essentially been kept on reserve at headquarters, interjected himself into the situation and led the police forces in restoring order in the neighborhood.

In 1992, another riot broke out in the largely Hispanic Washington Heights section of upper Manhattan, a prime drug-dealing area. It was claimed that a plainclothes officer had killed a young drug dealer while he was lying on the ground begging for his life. Mayor Dinkins, seeking to prevent the disorder that sometimes occurred at funerals of individuals killed by the police, authorized the city to pay for the slain man's burial and the family's air fare back to the Dominican Republic to attend a memorial service. Eventually it was disclosed that the charges against the cop, leveled by so-called "witnesses," were totally false and that drug dealers, angry about police crackdowns, had been behind the riot. However, Dinkins was labeled the mayor who "paid for a drug dealer's funeral." In 1993, he was defeated for re-election by former United States Attorney Rudy Giuliani. It was clearly a call for tougher law enforcement.

In 1992, when a ring of drug-dealing cops, led by an officer named Michael Dowd, was uncovered by Long Island Police, Brown did not respond in the traditional style—by talking tough and demoting police brass. Soon the papers were full of allegations of a cover-up. Commissioner Brown announced his resignation, citing the ill health of Mrs. Brown, who had been stricken with a fatal illness and wanted to return to Texas, where she would die within a year.

In New York, Brown came across as one of those nice guys who, in the words of baseball manager Leo Durocher, "finish last." Not a local, he had failed to realize that the town demanded decisive action and quick results. With blacks and Jews fighting in the streets of Brooklyn, there was only one possible response. Send an army of cops there (thanks to the "Safe Streets" plan, Brown had an army) and stop the trouble immediately. When corruption surfaces, the rule is: "cut off heads or lose your own."

After Commissioner Brown left, Acting Commissioner Ray Kelly ordered an assistant chief to do a survey of the community policing program; his report was devastating. According to him, community policing was a make-believe force viewed with widespread scorn by members of the real force. The latter operated around the clock. The community cops worked straight days. The chief reported that some of them took advantage of the flexibility of their work to run personal errands and disappear for long intervals during their duty hours. Often they had been recruited with the promise of straight day tours and weekends off to get them to volunteer. A survey found that CPOP cops (supposedly embedded in a neighborhood) were not much better known in the community than regular cops. A model precinct was established in Sunset Park, Brooklyn. Two years later, a survey determined that few local residents or business people were even aware of the program. In a poll of five hundred civic activists in the precinct (the people most likely to know the police), only a fourth could remember any contact at all with their beat officers.

In the years that followed the New York experience, no other city managed to develop a major community policing program. It was too difficult to break free from the 911 system, and it did not mesh well in cities where proactive anticrime strategies were a high priority. In practice, it also neglected to anticipate various hurdles. Northwestern University Prof. Wesley Skogan, who studied and designed many community anti-crime programs, observed that "in the absence of a guiding legal code to enforce in traditional fashion, police would have to develop ways of discovering the problems and priorities of local residents. As many concerns would involve events and conditions not clearly within the purview of the criminal law, this would inevitably lead the police into uncharted territory, where their training and experience would not offer them much of a guide to action."+++

The Washington-based Police Foundation, headed by Hubert Williams, who had been involved in early community policing experiments, issued a report warning cities that there was no model plan or template for community policing and that much of what was claimed for it was unproved. Williams urged municipalities not to rush into such programs. Creating a workable community policing program would remain a task for the future.

* * * *

At the same time that Commissioner Lee Brown was confronted with riots in Brooklyn and Manhattan, Chief Gates of Los Angeles was going through a rerun of the 1965 Watts riot. This time it would spell the end of the Parker model in the Los Angeles Police Department.

Gates himself had been present at the creation. In 1949, at twenty-three, he had joined the LAPD. A year later he was assigned as a chauffeur/bodyguard for Parker. Gates was a quick study and discreet (he did not blab to the world about Parker's excessive drinking, which, as noted earlier, sometimes required Gates to carry his boss from the car and put him into bed). Parker made the young officer his protégé, counseling him on how to be a successful police leader. On occasion he would point him out to high-ranking officials as a future chief. By 1963, Gates was a captain.[4] At the time of Watts, he was an inspector, and he personally witnessed the confusion of the top command. In 1978, he finished first in the chief's exam. Like his predecessor, Ed Davis, he had Parker's outspokenness and a strong personality. As with any chief, he had the usual problems—rising crime, gangs, questionable police shootings. Whatever the problems, though, the LAPD could still lay claim to being the best in America, and it firmly believed it could solve its own problems its own way. A particular source of "outside advice" that Chief Gates never wanted to listen to was the city's African-American mayor, Tom Bradley, himself a member of the legendary police class of 1940 and a retired lieutenant.

In 1984, the Olympic Games were held in Los Angeles. Despite threats that there would be a replication of the '72 Munich games where eleven Israeli athletes and coaches were killed by terrorists, they went off smoothly. Afterward, it was widely believed that Gates, then approaching sixty and with thirty-five years' service, would retire and go off into lucrative private consulting work. However, in 1991, he was still chief.[5]

In March of that year, California Highway Patrol officers clocked a motorist driving on a freeway at over 100 mph. In a rerun of the Watts riot, they pursued him into Los Angeles, where they were assisted by city police officers. The driver of the vehicle was a physically imposing black man named Rodney King. Allegedly he resisted arrest and the police used force to control him. Some of the actions that followed were videotaped by a civilian living nearby. When the tapes were shown on TV screens, they did not look good. The Rodney King case quickly became a national story. The district attorney followed up by charging a sergeant and three officers with assault and civil rights violations. Gates himself was briefly removed as chief pending an investigation, but the city council voted to restore him to his post.

Because the defense contended that the officers could not get a fair trial in Los Angeles, the case was moved to Simi Valley, a distant small suburban town, where the residents did not resemble most Angelenos. Given the possi-

4. Forty percent of a promotional candidate's grade was based on ratings he received from an oral exam before a board of superiors. Being known as the chief's protégé was no doubt a plus with the board.
5. On Chief Gates, see Appendix B.

bility that an acquittal would bring civil disorder, the judge in the case agreed to withhold announcement of any verdict for two hours until police units could be deployed to deal with possible problems—although no one believed that there would be a not-guilty verdict.

However, at the end of April 1992, the jury found three officers not guilty and was hung in the case of the fourth. As promised, the court held the announcement for two hours. When the verdict was made public, the police were not ready. Crowds gathered in South Central and began rioting, looting and vandalizing. A white truck driver was dragged from his vehicle and beaten while television viewers watched and no police arrived to help him. In some instances, cops dealing with the mobs were ordered to advance to the rear on the double—i.e., run away from the mobs and go back to their police station.

Top brass were confused. The assistant chief in charge of operations had retired, so Daryl Gates personally directed the force, something he had not done for years. His performance was judged to be inadequate, and his field command post essentially failed to function. Eventually it took twenty thousand police, national guardsmen and U.S. soldiers to halt the rioting. The final death toll numbered fifty-eight.

Within a few months of the riot, Gates retired and was replaced by Philadelphia police commissioner Willie Williams, an African-American.

Even after the retirement of Chief Gates the troubles of the LAPD continued. In 1994 the fallout from the arrest and prosecution of celebrity athlete O. J. Simpson for the murder of his wife Nicole and her friend Ron Goldman reflected badly on the already demoralized department. The American public was introduced to the case in true Hollywood fashion by watching on national TV as Simpson, sitting in the back seat of a white Ford Bronco driven by a friend, rode down the highway with a squadron of police cars following. Simpson's lawyer had arranged a deal for him to surrender to the LAPD and be booked for the murders. At the time, I wrote off the fact that a murder suspect had been allowed to voluntarily surrender rather than being summarily arrested, as due to the fact that the Los Angeles police always accommodated celebrities. Though, like most police commanders, I would have never allowed such a thing.

Simpson made it to his Brentwood home where he sat in the white Ford Bronco for 45 minutes. He then went into the house for an hour while cops waited patiently outside. Finally, his lawyer arrived and persuaded him to surrender. A search of the Bronco found $8000 in cash, a change of clothing, a loaded .357 Magnum, a passport, family pictures, and a fake goatee and mustache. All could be taken as signs that he was about to flee.

After Simpson was indicted for the two murders, his case was transferred from the Santa Monica judicial district, where the crime had occurred, to downtown Los Angeles. At the time it was widely believed that District

Attorney Gil Garcetti had moved the case downtown to ensure that more blacks would be called for the jury pool. Garcetti claimed that it was because the Santa Monica courthouse had been damaged in a recent earthquake so the facilities were not secure or large enough to handle the media horde that would descend on it.[6] After Simpson's acquittal, much abuse was heaped on prosecutors and the judge in the case, Lance Ito, for supposedly mishandling the trial. Ito was specifically criticized for allowing the defense extreme latitude. I do not have the legal expertise or close familiarity with the California courts to offer judgment. Nor have I been impressed by the talking heads of television, including lawyers who have never tried a major criminal case.[7] However, I think it is safe to say that the work of the prosecutors and the judge will not be held up to future law students as a model to be followed.

It is the police performance in the case that concerns us and in the end this mostly revolved around a detective named Mark Fuhrman. Forty-two at the time, Fuhrman came from a typical background for a Los Angeles cop. After graduating from a small town high school in the state of Washington, he joined the Marine Corps where he reached the rank of sergeant. In 1975 he became a member of the LAPD, finishing second in his academy class. Unlike most big city detectives (though, like many other LA cops), he did not have an innate understanding of the culture of a big city and only became familiar with Los Angeles through the eyes of a police officer. In 1985 he became a detective sergeant.

Furhman and his partner were not the lead detectives on the case, that role was filled by two veteran Los Angeles homicide officers. The two conducted a formal interrogation of Simpson on tape which lasted a total of thirty-two minutes, hardly sufficient time for a detailed probe of the murders. Initially, though, the case appeared very strong. Blood found at the murder scene, on Simpson, and in his house was matched by DNA testing. However, based on controversial rulings by Judge Ito, the defense was able, in effect, to conduct a trial within a trial as to whether Mark Fuhrman was a racist cop and had, with the aid of other officers, framed the defendant. Contrary to California evidentiary rules, the defense was able to ask Fuhrman questions about any personal prejudices he might have and whether he had used the N-word. Fuhrman vigorously denied that he had done so within the previous 10 years. Later it was shown that that in 1986, while Fuhrman was being taped by a writer he was working with, he had repeatedly used the N-word and made statements such as "you can take one of these n------s, drag 'em into the alley and beat the shit out of them and kick them." When this was revealed, Fuhrman took the Fifth Amendment and refused to answer further questions. Eventually he was charged by the attorney general of California for perjury and was given a fine.

---

6. Though by 1994 the court had been repaired and had adequate space and security.
7. In my account of the Simpson case I have relied on the book *Outrage* by former Los Angeles prosecutor Vincent Bugliosi who won murder convictions against Charles Manson and his "family."

Fuhrman's words were used to bolster the notion that he had planted a glove with blood stains in Simpson's house. Fuhrman was also criticized for illegally entering Simpson's property. Many observers felt the defense conduct should have led to a mistrial. However, Judge Ito did not declare one.

In 1983, during an attempt to acquire a disability pension, Fuhrman had told the examining doctor that he beat up suspects, blacked out and became a wild man. At the time the LAPD refused to grant him a pension, believing he was simply looking to obtain a lucrative early retirement. In some police departments a man who made these statements would have been removed from street duty and placed behind a desk. If that had happened he would not have been involved in the Simpson case. Many observers of the trial felt that because of Fuhrman the defense was able to persuade the jury that the case might very well be a frame up, particularly given the history of mistreatment of blacks by police officers. Thus the mostly African-American jury was able to conclude that there was at least a reasonable doubt of Simpson's guilt. In the end, the case was essentially lost by the prosecutors, or perhaps won by the tactics of the defense lawyers.[8] However, much of the blame was transferred to the LAPD. When the families of the victims filed a wrongful death civil action against Simpson for committing the murders, the jury assessed punitive and compensatory damages of $33.5 million against him.

In 2002 the LAPD experienced a rerun of the Simpson case. Former film star Robert Blake was the leading suspect in the murder of his wife. Despite strong evidence, the police delayed arresting him for nearly a year. Finally, after they did charge him with murder, Blake was found not guilty. As in the Simpson case, the defense accused an LAPD detective of misconduct. Blake too was sued in a civil case and a judgment of $30 million was rendered against him.

Chief Williams' stewardship of the LAPD was largely unsuccessful and he was eventually replaced by LAPD assistant chief Bernard Parks, also an African-American. In the late 1990s, a major scandal erupted involving officers from the CRASH unit of the Rampart Division. Among the accusations was that they engaged in various crimes, including murder. In 2001, Mayor James K. Hahn declined to reappoint Parks as police chief. His replacement was William Bratton, late of Boston and New York. The federal government also required the city to sign a consent decree placing the department under a federal monitor. The various actions spelled the end of fifty years of Parker style policing in Los Angeles.

---

8. Commonly referred to as the "Dream Team," none of them really qualified for that appellation with the possible exception of F. Lee Bailey who was long past his prime years.

America's Top Cop

In 1945, J. Edgar Hoover was the leading figure in American policing. He had made his bureau into a world famous and highly acclaimed agency. Never a real cop himself, he often clashed with police chiefs, thereby blocking necessary changes in the profession. In the 60s Hoover failed to adapt his agency to the changed times and his influence waned considerably. By his death in 1972, he had lost most of his standing in American law-enforcement.

Police Reformers:

William Parker of Los Angeles

and Stanley Schrotel of Cincinnati

From 1950 to 1966 they led America's two most professional police departments. Both were much praised and frequently touted as successors to J. Edgar Hoover as director of the FBI. However, the magic they had wrought in the tranquil 50s no longer worked in the turbulent 1960s.

Two Southern Police Administrators:

Eugene Connor, Public Safety Commissioner of Birmingham, Alabama

and Herbert Jenkins, Chief of Police of Atlanta, Georgia

In the 1960s, "Bull" Connor became the national symbol of hard-line resistance to integration, using fire hoses and police dogs to break up protest marches. In the same era, Herb Jenkins (seated center) provided a model of how a restrained police department could help facilitate integration.

The Chicago Story

In 1960 O.W. Wilson (top left) Dean of the School of Criminology at the University of California at Berkeley was appointed superintendent of police of Chicago, Illinois. Wilson, a champion of police professionalism, managed to make a number of improvements in a police department that was often regarded as corrupt. However, he did not change the basic organizational culture.

Chicago cops clashing with demonstrators at the 1968 Democratic convention as the whole world watched. As a result of the police performance, the city that had once been the principal site of national political conventions would not host another one for twenty-eight years.

California Riots

Protesters being arrested for disrupting hearings of the US House Committee on Un-American Activities at San Francisco City Hall in 1960. The affair was the first major student protest of the decade.

Los Angeles police officers and a national guardsman being shot at during the 1992 riots following the acquittal of officers accused of beating motorist Rodney King. Fifty-eight people were killed during the disturbances.

Frank Rizzo, police commissioner of Philadelphia from 1966 to 1970 and mayor of that city from 1972 through 1979.

A swashbuckling street cop, Rizzo personally led his troops in controlling civil disorder. Here he arrives at the scene of a 1969 prison riot in evening dress carrying a nightstick in his cummerbund. His cops loved him but many citizens did not approve of his methods.

The slight, gentlemanly Murphy, though a career cop, largely confined his duties to administrative work. Though he did manage to end the city's century-old system of payoffs known as "the pad."

His liberal pronouncements did not endear him to his cops nor did it lead him to the job he desired, FBI director.

Patrick V. Murphy police commissioner of New York City from 1970 to 1973 (pictured in 1968 as Washington D.C.'s public safety director).

Texas Ranger Capt. John Klevenhagen. In seventeen years as a Ranger "Texas Johnny" was a modern version of an old West law man. He explained his method of operation with the statement "I never shot anyone who did not shoot at me first."

FBI Directors. Left to right, Robert Mueller, III, 2001 to date, Judge William Webster, 1978 to 1987, Judge William Sessions, 1987 to 1993, and Judge Louis Freeh, 1983 to 2001. Mueller and Webster were universally praised for their work in bringing the FBI into the modern age. Sessions had a relatively stormy tenure and was compelled to resign. Freeh ended up at odds with the man who appointed him President Bill Clinton.

Crimes that Rocked the Nation

The 1947 murder of Elizabeth Short, who became known as "The Black Dahlia," rocked the city of Los Angeles. The original police investigation was carried on in a confused and inept manner. Since 1947, the crime has served as the basis for several movies and numerous suspects have been accused of committing it, but the case has never been solved.

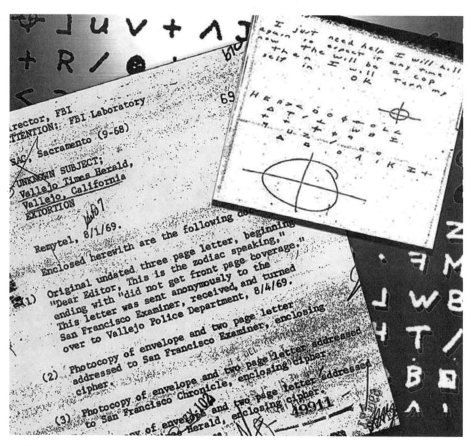

In 1968-69, an individual who styled himself The Zodiac shot seven people, five of them fatally in Northern California. During the hunt for him he taunted investigators by sending them letters and cryptograms which he claimed, if solved, would reveal his identity. Though one that was, did not. While a number of individuals were suspected of being The Zodiac, no one has ever been charged in the case.

In 1971, a man who signed his name "Dan Cooper" commandeered a Northwest Airlines plane in Portland, Oregon. Claiming he had a bomb, Cooper received two hundred thousand dollars and two parachutes. He then parachuted from the plane. Despite an intensive investigation, the hijacker (whose name was initially read as "DB Cooper") has never been found. Occasionally items have turned up in the area where Cooper would have landed, but none have been linked to him.

New York detectives escort David Berkowitz "the son of Sam." Between July 1976 and July 1977 he held the city in terror killing six people and wounding seven more in eight separate incidents. Berkowitz sent letters to newspapers claiming he was ordered to carry out the shootings by a dog who belonged to a man named Sam. Based on his writings many people speculated he was either some kind of artist or intellectual. When captured he turned out to be a nerdish clerk.

LAPD Detective Sgt. Mark Fuhrman pointing at evidence found near the body of Nicole Simpson, the murdered wife of sports celebrity O.J. Simpson. At O. J.'s 1995 trial the defense conducted a virtual trial within a trial as to whether Fuhrman was a racist cop who framed the defendant. Simpson's acquittal upset many Americans.

Bill Bratton, shown as chief of the Boston Transit Police in 1983, became a cop at twenty-three and by thirty-three had reached the number two position in the Boston Police Department. He sought the top job too avidly and had to leave the department. After heading smaller forces in the Boston area he took over the New York City Transit Police and turned them into a model organization. He returned to Boston to be commissioner and in 1994 was appointed police commissioner of New York City. He produced huge reductions in crime employing proactive strategies and a management control system known as COMPSTAT. In 1996 he was forced out by Mayor Rudy Giuliani. But from 2002 to 2009, as chief of police of Los Angeles, he repeated his crime-fighting successes.

The Greatest Police Administrators in Contemporary America

NYPD Commissioner Ray Kelly (fifth from left), carrying the body of an NYPD officer found at ground zero, 2002. Kelly is the only man ever to have served two separate terms as head of the NYPD. He was police commissioner in 1992 - 1993. Then he served in a variety of public capacities including Undersecretary for law enforcement of the U.S. Treasury. Appointed as commissioner again, following the 2001 attack on New York City, Kelly created the leading police counterterrorism system in the United States all the while reducing crime to historic lows. The symbol of American counterterrorism operations, Kelly is the first law enforcement official since J. Edgar Hoover to play such a large role in public life.

Chapter 10

Fighting Crime by the Numbers: Bratton Defies the Experts

As long as policing has existed, there have been developments in science, physical or social, that it was believed would have profound effects on law enforcement. Usually, they turned out to be less significant than anticipated. In the 1880s, Thomas Byrnes, the New York inspector who created the modern detective bureau that other American police departments have been modeled on to this day, initiated the practice of taking photographs of suspects and using them as a means of identification. Information of all kinds was maintained and filed systematically in Byrnes's photograph-and-records department. These were distributed to detectives, including some in other cities. Byrnes published much of his material in a book, *Professional Criminals of America*, that constitutes a "who's who" of the late-nineteenth-century underworld.*

Equally important in Byrnes's time was the Bertillon system of anthropometry (physical measurements, named for Paris police scientist Alphonse Bertillon), designed to classify crooks throughout the world. During the heyday of Bertillon, fingerprinting, known as the "Henry system," was introduced. Whereas Bertillon actually invented his system, Sir Edward Henry merely presided over the development of fingerprinting, first as inspector general of police in the province of Bengal, India, and then as commissioner of the London Metropolitan Police.

The Bertillon system was dealt two fatal blows. In 1903, two American prisoners at the federal penitentiary in Leavenworth, Kansas, William and Will West, were found to have identical measurements. Then, in 1911, the Mona Lisa was stolen from the Louvre. The Paris police were unable to solve the crime despite the fact that the thief had left fingerprints at the scene. Although both his prints and his measurements were in Bertillon's files, the prints had not been classified in a manner to permit identification and the measurements were useless, since, as the Paris press pointed out, "Unfortunately, this discourteous thief neglected to leave his measurements at the scene of the crime."[1]

Before taking over the NYPD detective bureau in 1906, Arthur Woods, a Harvard graduate, went on a tour of Europe to study that continent's detective methods and scientific policing, which were both miles ahead of American practice. Upon his return, he encouraged the use of fingerprints in New York City and later, as police commissioner (1914–17), he introduced scientific studies of murder and sex crimes.

By the First World War, American police were routinely using fingerprinting and photos in criminal identification and forensic science in crime scene searches. Yet the backbone of policing was still the plodding beat cop and the practical detective, who relied on informants rather than "scientific" methods.

When radio-equipped patrol cars came on the scene in the late 1920s, police administrators believed that the cars would make a major contribution to the fight against crime. They could respond rapidly to crimes in progress while other cars could surround the crime scene, preventing the criminals from escaping. Criminals, too, became proficient in the use of vehicles in carrying out their work and, viewed from a broad perspective, cars were as much value to them as they were to the police.

In contemporary times, various forensic methods such as the use of DNA have been touted as holding great potential for crime fighting. There have been spectacular results where crimes twenty or thirty years old were solved or innocent people exonerated; however, it is not certain whether this will significantly alter detective work. The FBI has yet to locate Dan "D. B." Cooper, the hijacker who, in 1971, parachuted from a plane in the Pacific Northwest.[2] An even bigger failure was the FBI search for its most wanted fugitive, Massachusetts crime boss and murderer James "Whitey" Bulger. Despite worldwide dis-

---

1. Bertillon also made the mistake of engaging in activities beyond his competence. He identified certain handwriting as belonging to the defendant in the case of Capt. Alfred Dreyfus. He explained to the French military court that it was written to disguise the fact that it was Dreyfus' handwriting—i.e., it was not his writing but he wrote it. Later it was proven that, in fact, Dreyfus did *not* write it. Because of the political significance of the case, Bertillon's reputation suffered a decline.
2. On the Cooper case, see Appendix A.

tribution of his photo, information on him and repeated pleas to the public, he was not arrested for fifteen years after the search for him began. In 2010, it was an acquaintance of Bulger and his girlfriend who turned him in to earn a two-million-dollar reward. When caught, he was living in a California apartment building like an ordinary citizen.

When computers were introduced to police work, they were used to compile crime statistics that had previously been tabulated by hand counts. As with any new device, extreme claims were made for the latest toy. It was said that before computers, police did not know what the crime figures were in their jurisdictions. Sometimes this was stretched to argue that they were not even certain of the pattern of crime, such as where certain offenses were committed most frequently and by what sorts of offenders. The truth was that every detective worth his salt knew which were the high-crime areas in town and which individuals and groups were most likely to be committing particular crimes. If a jewel theft occurred on Chicago's Gold Coast, detectives did not go to the nearby Cabrini Green housing project to look for the offenders. Similarly, if there was a mugging a block from the project, the police did not walk a few blocks over to the Ambassador East Hotel to see if one of the wealthy guests might resemble the mugger. In sum, while technology can be very helpful in certain areas, the skill of humans is still the key element in police work.

Some modern police research may have actually led to incorrect conclusions. The discovery that patrolling police seldom encountered crimes in progress was extended to an argument that patrol was a meaningless exercise. In reality, it resembled British naval tactics in the days of the Pax Britannica, when Queen Victoria's warships "showed the flag" in every corner of the globe to remind other nations that the "strong arm of England" was always present.[3] Those of us who grew up in an industrial city were always aware of the identification numbers of the cars that patrolled our neighborhood. As a police captain, when there was a crime surge in my district, I would order patrol cars to cruise past the usual trouble spots and give the evil eye to those hanging out there. Soon the neighborhood grapevine would be buzzing with the message "Beware, the cops are on the prowl." This damped down crime and disorder for a while.

Similar misunderstandings arose over the vast amount of time spent by patrol cars responding to disorderly conduct or other minor matters. Certain calls were screened out, but failure to respond to most of them would bring

---

3. The term was used, in 1850, by Britain's foreign secretary, Lord Palmerston, after he sent the Mediterranean fleet to seize Athens because the Greek government would not pay compensation to a British subject whose property was destroyed in a riot.

complaints to city hall. If citizens could not get a police response, they would feel less safe, and some would take on the police role themselves by going after their neighbor with a club, knife or gun. Big-city political bosses, from Frank "I am the law" Hague in Jersey City to Dick Daley in Chicago, believed that anyone in their city who wanted the police should get them—fast. In Hague's case, he would put in calls and wait at the scene, timing how long it took for cops to respond. Those who were too slow could expect to (literally) feel Hague's boot on their posteriors.

In the final analysis, it was not that police brass did not know about crime patterns; rather, field operations were not geared to coherent strategies. This was partly because they recognized that crime was not the highest priority with their political masters. As the saying went, no police chief was ever fired because of crime, only scandal. Academics always gave little credence to police being able to do something about crime. In the 1970s, the Ford Foundation turned over a large amount of money to a social researcher, Charles Silberman—a purported expert on everything from race relations to education—to provide wisdom on the criminal justice system. One of his recommendations was to "abandon the quixotic faith that there is a police solution to the problem of criminal violence."** In the 1980s, even some police chiefs adopted the view that police could do nothing significant to reduce crime in the long run. An American secretary of state who declared that nothing could be done to prevent wars because they arise from social, economic and political factors would be fired. Police chiefs who said they were similarly helpless about crime were considered enlightened.

The fallacy of this negative thinking was obvious to many police officers. It had never been embraced by the citizenry in general. If the police could not reduce crime, what were they there for? Like community policing, what came to be known by names like COMPSTAT was an effort to develop a police anti-crime strategy that would work over the long haul. COMPSTAT (computer-generated or comparative statistics), "Hot Spots" or "Impact Policing" was a combination of two factors: operational plans based upon refined crime data and police administrators who knew how to implement them.

* * * *

The arena in which COMPSTAT was developed was New York City, the place where community policing had been given its largest trial. In 1990, at the same time Lee Brown arrived from Houston as New York police commissioner, Bill Bratton came down from Boston to head the New York City Transit Police. Brown's appointment was national news, and in New York he became an instant celebrity and VIP. He held the most important municipal job next to the mayor. If a commissioner wished to play the Manhattan society game (most did not, preferring to go home to their wife and kids), he would be welcome at black-tie events where billionaires and movie stars would be delighted to converse with him.

On paper, the New York City Transit Police, a force controlled by the state but funded by the city, was a large and important department. Its four thousand officers (about as many as Lee Brown had commanded in Houston) patrolled the vital transportation routes of the world's greatest city. If the subways stopped running, so did New York. However, no elite New Yorker could even name the chief of the transit police, much less be interested in hearing what he had to say.

Periodically, the city or state revived a proposal to merge transit cops and the housing police, who patrolled the projects occupied by low-income New Yorkers, into the main city force. It was always rejected, because the Metropolitan Transit Authority (MTA) opposed it. Change in New York only came about because of scandal, riot or disaster. By 1990, a hurricane of crime had finally engulfed the city. In the subways it was anarchy. Boom-box radios blared, homeless people sprawled all over the trains, many slept alongside the subterranean tracks, where a number of them were run over or electrocuted every year. Gangs roamed the system mugging people. In the hurried response of city hall, the merger plan was revived. But the MTA had a new management, headed by Robert Kiley, who had held the same job with the Massachusetts Bay Transit Authority (MBTA), where his police chief had been Bill Bratton. Kiley had plans for revamping the subways, and he did not want to have to rely on the city police to secure the system. So he invited Bratton to be chief.

If Lee Brown was an unusual cop, highly educated with the manner of a minister, Bratton was, at first glance, a typical one. He was raised in the Boston blue-collar neighborhood of Dorchester, and from childhood his ambition was to be a policeman. After high school, he enlisted in the army as an MP. He spent a tour of duty in Vietnam as a dog-handler. His outfit was guarding an airbase the night the TET offensive began. Things got hot but only one member of Bratton's company was killed, the one on the post next to him. It was the beginning of a career of ups and downs and close shaves. Back home he became a telephone repairman until he could take the police exam. On the day it was scheduled, his car died as he set out for the school where the test was being given. Luckily he managed to call his sister, who lived a couple of towns away, and, wearing pajamas and floppy slippers, she rushed over. They got there just as the doors to the school were being locked.

Bratton was a good street cop. Once he responded to a situation where a robber was holding a hostage and suddenly found himself standing face to face with the criminal over gun barrels. When more help arrived, Bratton holstered his weapon and talked the man into surrendering. Despite this, he was not interested in being a detective. Top management was his goal. In the 1970s, as a lieutenant, he commanded a community policing unit which brought him into contact with Harvard academics.

Within ten years of joining the force, still a lieutenant and only 33, he was given the number-two job in the department. The police commissioner's post was obviously the next stop. Then came another of those incidents that would temporarily derail his career. During an interview with *Boston Magazine*, Bratton mentioned his hope of becoming commissioner someday, "be it one year or four." It was a cardinal rule in policing that a subordinate never expressed a desire for his boss' job. Bratton was moved out of headquarters to another position and eventually left the force to command the one-hundred-and-thirty-officer Boston Transit Police. He staged a partial comeback by becoming chief of the nine-hundred-officer Metropolitan District Commission Police, who patrolled the parks and boulevards in the area. But when the MDCP was merged with the state police and the motor registry police, Bratton did not get the top job. Again, he had suffered a major career setback. Kiley's summons to New York revived his fortunes.

Bratton took the demoralized transit cops and made them proud like Marines. He smartened up their uniforms and equipped them with 9-mm automatics. While every street hoodlum carried his "9," the NYPD did not allow its officers to have one. Bratton moved his cops away from guarding turnstiles against fare beaters and put them on patrol. George Kelling, co-author of "Broken Windows," was Bratton's adviser, so controlling disorder was a high priority.

Another colleague who became close to him was a transit detective lieutenant named Jack Maple, who was as unorthodox a cop as one could find. Maple had joined the transit police after graduating from a Queens high school. Most of his time was spent working in undercover units, hunting the muggers who roamed the system in wolf packs. Not infrequently, he was involved in a rough-and-tumble with the packs, and in one struggle narrowly missed being shot with his own gun. After getting divorced, Maple took his modest savings and went to live at the glamorous Plaza Hotel so he could experience the high life for a year. He became known to local reporters as a character. Had Bratton not come to transit, Maple probably would have retired as a detective lieutenant (a college degree was required to be captain, and he did not have one). Still, he had more ideas than a Harvard professor.

One of Maple's suggestions was how to deal with criminal fugitives. If a robber failed to show up in court, a warrant was issued and sent to the NYPD for service. There it languished at the bottom of a pile for months. Thousands of fugitives were roaming the city, committing new crimes and going home to sleep in their own beds. Bratton and Maple created a special squad which executed the warrants on the evening of the day they were issued. Its method of operation was to surround the fugitive's house. Then a team would enter and search the flat thoroughly. Sometimes, they caught the fugitive hiding under the bed or in a closet. Other times, they spotted him sliding down a drainpipe. Popular radio host Don Imus did a comedy skit on Bratton's tactics, mimicking the chief's pronounced Boston accent. In it, the Bratton character boasted of a supposed pilot program, a surprise visit by transit cops at 3:00 in the morning to recently paroled subway criminals: "We give them a little welcome-home pahty…we bring cake or a box of pastry, and invite them to put on a pot of coffee. Then we chat for a while, talk about "spahts," and what life was like in the joint."

Soon the transit chief became as well known as Lee Brown. Some city police administrators thought the Boston subway cop did not know his place. The social-service lobby publicly declared war on him because of his drives to get the homeless out of tunnels and off the trains. But Bratton had the public on his side. He also had his cops behind him. He had learned from management seminars that punishment-centered bureaucracies with their "don'ts" were out of fashion. He also learned management jargon. As chief he could address a group of CEOs in the language they understood—quarterly indicators, performance measures, etc. Half an hour later, he would speak to his troops at a district roll call. There he would begin by complimenting them on their good work, making sure to cite a few recent cases that had been well handled. Then he would tell a story illustrating some problem that had surfaced, while pointing up the need for a higher standard of performance. His manner was that of a loving father, gently chastising his son. When traveling around with him, I witnessed a phenomenon that I had never seen in American policing. Ordinary cops would come up to me and ask, "Will he stay? Will he stay?" as in "Say it ain't so, Joe." I had a feeling that chief of the transit police was not big enough for Bratton's ambitions, but I did not want to break their hearts, so I would give some sort of vague, upbeat answer.

In 1992, Bratton returned to Boston to take the number-two job in that department and quickly slid into the commissionership. It was obvious, though, that he had left his heart in what he called "Noo Yawk." In August 1992, when Brown resigned, Bratton sought to replace him. David Dinkins passed him over in favor of acting Commissioner Ray Kelly, the total opposite of Bratton but a man who in the early twenty-first century would rival him for the title of "Best Police Chief in America."

In November 1993, the pendulum swung back to Bratton. In a rerun of their 1989 contest, Rudy Giuliani defeated David Dinkins for mayor. Like all his predecessors, he wanted his own man for police commissioner. He chose Bill Bratton. It was a brilliant move except for one thing, Bratton was *his own* man. Though Bratton may not know it, he was almost fired before he was even sworn in. As police commissioner designate, he made a speech declaring: "We will fight for every house in the city. We will fight for every street. We will fight for every block, and we will win." It was the same speech he had made in Boston the year before, and neither time did he have to pay any royalties to the estate of Winston Churchill for the use of his phraseology. A New York tabloid headlined Bratton's statements as "I Will End the Fear." The public was thrilled and heartened by his pledge that in fact the police would do something about crime, not just make excuses. One person who was not pleased was Rudy Giuliani, who did not like to be upstaged—particularly since he was the mayor and the police commissioner his subordinate. Phone calls followed among New York criminal justice figures in which it was discussed whether Bratton should be denied appointment. As the Duke of Wellington said after Waterloo, "It was a close run thing, a damn close run thing." But Bratton was retained.[4]

New York not only had an unusual police commissioner but an unusual mayor. It was Giuliani's first elective office. While his many opponents might find it hard to believe, as a student and young lawyer, Rudy was essentially a quiet person. He attended a Catholic college and was active in the opera club. He then went to a top New York law school, where his grades were good enough to land him a job in an elite firm. Before that, Italian Americans had been scarce in such precincts. He married a cousin who became a college president. Eventually, though, the marriage was annulled and he wed TV reporter Donna Hanover.

In 1981 he joined the Reagan Administration's Justice Department, where he held the number-three post. He decided to leave that job for what was officially a lesser, though actually more important position: U.S. attorney for the southern district of New York. It was the most prominent prosecutor's office in the United States and an excellent stepping-stone if one had political ambitions in New York. With his new wife, he became very visible socially, and as U.S. attorney he prosecuted organized crime, white-collar criminals, drug

---

4. Full disclosure: I was one of those consulted about Bratton. Of course, I strongly supported him. I don't know whether my views counted a little or a lot.

dealers and everybody else in sight. One time he and New York senator Alphonse D'Amato went off on a well-publicized drug-buying expedition to demonstrate how widespread street-level dealing was.

When Bratton returned to Boston, he took Jack Maple with him. When he became NYPD commissioner, he made Maple a deputy commissioner. It was an unheard-of jump, as though a Coast Guard lieutenant had been appointed a three-star admiral in the United States Navy. Maple began churning out ideas in a very forceful manner. It was customary in the NYPD for the top brass to retire or be pushed out when a new police commissioner came in. All ranks above captain served at the commissioner's pleasure. Those who moved up under Bratton were among the best commanders in the department. As chief of the department he chose John Timoney, who would later head the police departments of Philadelphia and Miami. Other Bratton subordinates would eventually be in charge of the police in places like Baltimore, Newark and Chicago.

George Kelling, too, was a key figure in Bratton's team. Maple, a believer in hard-charging "lock 'em up" tactics, was not enamored of Kelling's "Broken Windows" theory. As he commented, "Rapists and killers don't head for another town when they see that graffiti is disappearing from the subway." Maple versus Kelling was the old detective-versus-patrol argument that had existed since the early days of policing. Despite Maple's doubts, increasing attention to the maintenance of order became a major priority of the NYPD.

"Broken Windows" and COMPSTAT were the two centerpieces of Bratton's administration. "Broken Windows" in New York was aimed at street hustlers, public drinking, using and selling drugs in the streets. It was not designed to eradicate the use of drugs, as critics often claimed. It was meant to close down the open-air markets which drew criminals to them like a magnet. In the course of frisking low-level offenders, sometimes weapons were found. Most important, it brought to the public a realization that government was again functioning at the street level. The media, though, frequently characterized it as "zero tolerance," as though nobody were allowed to do anything on the street.

COMPSTAT provided the drama at police headquarters. At intervals of four to six weeks, an entire police borough command (comprising eight or ten precincts), led by the two-star chief in charge, along with his assistants, would be assembled in the command center, or "war room," on the eighth floor of One Police Plaza, at 7:00 a.m. It had not been an hour of great activity at headquarters in years gone by. Commanders would be questioned on crime conditions in their particular areas of jurisdiction. In the room, long tables flanked by green lamps were set up in a horseshoe, facing a lectern. Sitting opposite the lectern in a central position were Deputy Commissioner Maple and Chief of Department Timoney (and later, after Timoney moved up to first deputy commissioner, his successor, Lou Anemone). A high-tech console flashed maps and graphs on overhead video screens. Commanders were called to the roster to make their presentation, then grilled with frequent reference to the map. Maple would wield a laser pointer like an accusing finger. In the sessions, many bosses were unable to discuss the most basic facts about crime in their areas. It was not that they didn't know, but they weren't used to presenting them in a succinct form, the way sales managers give their figures, past, present and projected, at a meeting.

Some precinct captains, when asked if they had talked to the detective squad lieutenant or the local narcotics and youth division supervisors about some problem, would reply that they had. Fortunately, these men and women were in the room, and they would be asked to join the captain at the podium and explain their collective plan. It quickly became obvious that they had not consulted on the problem. Anemone would question them often asking "who owns this," i.e., who was responsible for dealing with a particular problem. No one raised a hand. A detective lieutenant might explain that he had prepared a report on the case. Anemone would remind him that reports do not solve anything. Maple would occasionally flash a Pinocchio image on the screen, using his laser beam to make the nose grow as some commander struggled through his confused explanation. Like Winston Churchill, he would seize on particular numbers. For example, when Churchill learned that the Allied Army at Anzio had what appeared to be an excessive number of trucks, he declared, "We must have a great superiority in chauffeurs." Maple would point out that in Queens, where thirty percent of the population of New York lived, twenty-eight percent of the patrol force had not made an arrest in the first six months of the year. "Conscientious objectors," Maple called them.

Some of those at the podium became angry. A few virtually lost their commands on the spot. One precinct commander steeled himself for the ordeal with some early-morning nips of alcohol. It turned out to be a celebration of his retirement. Some bosses left the room and went straight to the pension office. Others might say, "I need more cops," confident that they would never get them. Anemone would ask, "How many?" To a captain, fifty might sound like a nice, impossible figure. That day, fifty cops were transferred to the captain's precinct. And if they did not bring down crime, that commander would probably be taking early retirement.

Giuliani also managed to merge the transit and housing police into the city force. The mayor was the kind who would not take "no" for an answer. He threatened to cut off the city's financial contribution to the system. Since state authorities were not willing to provide three hundred million dollars of their own money as a replacement, the merger went through.

Crime began to show amazing declines. By 1995, murder and larceny of auto had fallen by half, robbery and burglary by forty percent. Hustlers began to disappear from the streets and subways. Gunmen had to leave their weapons at home.[5] Foreigners who came to New York City noticed the sea change in public order. Nationally and internationally, the media began to refer to "the New York miracle."

The academic community was aghast. How could police operations bring crime down so much every year? Social scientists had declared they could not. Some embarrassed scholars then claimed it was a trick done with smoke and mirrors. But if murders were not really down from two thousand-plus to fewer than one thousand, where were the bodies? A few experts conceded that they might have been wrong. Some kept silent; others went right on denying the obvious. In 1994 a prominent professor stated, "The police do not prevent crime. Experts know it, police know it, but the public does not know it."*** As late as 1997 a distinguished panel submitted a report to the mayor of Philadelphia on how to improve his police force. In the entire one hundred fifty-seven pages, it did not once mention crime.+

Bratton's unique ability was to make both COMPSTAT and "Broken Windows" an integral part of policing and to persuade his troops to buy into it. Among his other management virtues was his ability to pick good subordinates and give them wide latitude to do their jobs. Anemone and Timoney were examples, and there were also men like Joe Dunne, who became the department's most outstanding field commander, and Pat Kelleher, its most brilliant administrator. Jack Maple went on to become a nationally recognized consultant on crime and was featured in news stories and on the cover of magazines. Unfortunately, he died of cancer at the age of forty-nine.

* * * *

New York was not the only city to show large crime reductions; Houston, San Jose and San Diego also did. Compared to New York, however, the last two did not have much to begin with. Crime went down generally in the United States. Much of the overall decrease, though, was due to the inclusion of New York numbers. In a comparison of New York with the nation, murder was down 38% nationally and 73% in New York. For robbery it was national,

---

5. One day two rival gang leaders suddenly met on a Brooklyn street. Both forgot they were not carrying a piece and went for their guns. One of the embarrassed pair raced away, while unwisely the other stayed on the corner to crow. The second man returned with a gun and shot the first man.

38%; New York, 70%; burglary, 40% vs. 72%; and auto theft, 33% vs. 78%. Experts like Franklin Zimring of Cal-Berkeley examined the figures carefully and concluded that a significant amount of the NYC crime reduction was due to police operations. In the twenty-first century, crime began rising again in the United States, but in New York it continued to go down. Viewing the New York experience, Zimring characterized it as the "greatest decrease ever to occur in any American city."

Just as scholars claimed that police could do nothing about crime, those who hold an opposite view trumpeted COMPSTAT, "Broken Windows," etc., as the answer to crime. The argument was bolstered when Bratton served as chief in Los Angles, from 2002 to 2009, and crime there dropped by a large amount. The question of what a police chief can achieve in crime fighting is a little like measuring the difference a baseball manager makes to the team's won/lost record. In New York, Bratton benefited from the vast increase in police strength and the absolute power the commissioner had over all members of the department above the rank of captain. He also had a large talent pool from which to pick his commanders. It is not clear he would have done as well in a place like Philadelphia, where all superior officers except four deputy commissioners have civil-service protection and belong to the same union as all other ranks. He might also have been stymied in some other cities where the mayors were weak and a different one took office every two years.

One aspect of COMPSTAT that was not generally commented upon was the fact that in police departments, as in most organizations, a relatively small number of people do a disproportionate share of work. Jack Maple estimated that number at about fifteen percent of the total complement, while some put it as high as twenty-five percent. Bratton managed to gain the confidence of most rank-and-file cops to an extent that few top bosses have ever achieved. Some observers claimed that he got fifty percent of the officers working, which was a tremendous accomplishment in an organization where employees are virtually fireproof because they have civil-service protection.[6] A police chief who has the numbers to free up active cops from routine duty to engage in a concerted attack on crime can secure large reductions in various offenses, particularly those that are carried out in public, like auto theft, shootings, robbery and gang violence. Because of the personnel increases under "Safe

---

6. Of course, no police chief is going to admit that one hundred percent of his officers are not giving top performance, because he will be accused of not doing his job and will be resented by the unions. However, World War II was fought by a minority of men in the service. Of 13 million Americans in uniform, a great many more were in Air Force ground, Navy shore duty or Army rear-echelon units than were in flight crews, warships and combat battalions.

Streets," Bratton always had sufficient officers for crime fighting. Though, he also managed to bring crime down in Los Angeles with a much smaller force.

On the diplomatic front, relations between Giuliani and the police commissioner deteriorated. They were in basic agreement on crime-fighting programs, and Giuliani particularly liked Maple for his feistiness in dealing with police critics. Giuliani was also one of the very few mayors who would have supported two key features of Bratton's program: command accountability and intensive policing. The superior officers' associations were constantly protesting to city hall about the way their members were treated at COMPSTAT meetings. Other than fiery, combative Fiorello La Guardia, fifty years earlier, any mayor before Giuliani would have told the police commissioner that it was alright to bawl out some errant commander, but not to institutionalize the practice. After all, police brass were men and women of influence in the city. Not Giuliani: his instructions were to keep the pressure on. Similarly, when complaints came in about police over-enforcing laws against low-level disorder, most mayors would have passed on word to the commissioner to cut back. Giuliani supported police initiatives one hundred percent.

But Bratton's high profile, including socializing in elite night spots with movie stars and other prominent people, rubbed city hall the wrong way. In October 1995, Bratton scheduled a parade to celebrate the one hundred and fiftieth anniversary of the founding of the NYPD. "Coincidentally," the day selected was Bratton's birthday. Giuliani canceled it. In January 1996, Bratton appeared on the cover of *Time* with an article giving him primary credit for the crime reductions. Giuliani could not cancel the magazine, but he could cancel the commissioner.

The truth probably was that it is more common for strong leaders to disagree than to agree. Eisenhower and Patton could not stand Field Marshal Montgomery, and vice versa. McArthur and Truman never saw eye to eye. Bratton signed a three-hundred-thousand-dollar book deal about his experiences in New York. City hall took him to task for not clearing the arrangement with them, and the corporation counsel launched a formal investigation. A number of other minor matters were also subjected to inquiry. In April 1996, Bratton resigned.

Mayor Giuliani named Fire Commissioner Howard Safir to succeed him. Safir was formerly in charge of the United States Marshals fugitive program. Most important, he was a friend with whom Giuliani could feel comfortable. During his mayoralty, Giuliani never appointed anyone from the command ranks of the NYPD or the fire department as commissioner of either force. As he explained later, he felt they would be more loyal to their departments than to him.[++]

Despite the dire predictions of many people, COMPSTAT continued to go on without Bratton and crime kept falling. Then, in 1997, a Brooklyn cop named Justin Volpe was assaulted while responding to a brawl outside a night-club. Volpe arrested a 32-year-old Haitian immigrant, Abner Louima, in the mistaken belief that Louima had punched him in the head. Later that night, while processing the arrest at the 70th Precinct station house, Volpe took Louima to the men's room, where he rammed a wooden broomstick into the prisoner's rectum. Despite the fact that it was a hot summer night in a busy Brooklyn precinct, supervision in the station was minimal and no one stopped him.

At first the case was covered up. Then a civilian complainant called the internal-affairs division and was essentially brushed off. She and others went to the news media. When the stories broke, Giuliani was compelled to appoint a citizens commission (including this writer) to look into the police department. Later he rejected its report.[7] Officer Volpe was eventually sentenced to thirty years' imprisonment. Other officers received lesser punishments.

Another mistake was to assume that the vigorous enforcement was the be-all and end-all of crime reduction and that if a pound of it was good, two pounds was even better. One of the spearheads of police enforcement under COMPSTAT was the Street Crime Unit (SCU), one hundred thirty hand-picked cops who cruised the city looking for armed robbers and other gunmen. Far from being a bunch of cowboys, they operated in a cool, systematic manner and their street stops were choreographed like a ballet. The goal was to take down gunmen without precipitating a shootout. The commanding officer, Inspector Richard Savage, was a street cop *par excellence* who spent his vacation times pursuing dangerous sports like mountain climbing. As unit commander, though, he was very cautious about who was let into the SCU. Candidates had to go through a trial period, and the squad had to vote on whether to accept them. Such votes were not based upon sentiment, because they were trusting the individual with their own lives.

When Commissioner Safir proposed to triple the unit in size, Savage objected on the grounds that it would bring unqualified individuals into the SCU and dilute the core group of experienced veterans. Safir went ahead with the plan and Savage opted to retire. In February 1999, four inexperienced members of the SCU (the senior man had spent only a year in the outfit, and the group was working together for the first time) were searching for a serial rapist when they observed twenty-two-year-old Amadou Diallo standing near

---

7. The mayor did not like some of the recommendations. The problem with committees is that they are com-posed of a cross-section of the community, and only through compromise and bargaining can such a committee produce a report that most members will sign on to.

the entrance of an apartment building in the Bronx. As they approached him, Diallo reached into his pocket and removed an object that at least one of the officers took for a gun. It turned out to be a wallet. Diallo was a hard-working, religiously devout immigrant from Guinea who shared an apartment in the building with three roommates. The cops opened fire and of the forty-one shots they loosed at him, nineteen struck their mark. The district attorney of the Bronx indicted them.

In reaction to the shooting, there were massive demonstrations throughout the city in which a number of prominent people, not normally given to marching, participated. Former mayor David Dinkins was arrested at one protest. The accused officers' defense team managed to get the case moved from the Bronx to Albany, where all the defendants were acquitted, sparking more criticism of the city administration and its police.

* * * *

Many cities noticed the huge crime decreases and demanded their own magic COMPSTAT system. However, some of them declared they did not want the New York version which they perceived as superiors brow beating subordinates. After witnessing a New York COMPSTAT session, one chief returned home and abolished his own recently installed COMPSTAT system, on the grounds that it was "unprofessional and demeaning."[8] Thus, when COMPSTAT was introduced in other cities, it often turned into a computer exercise with the command accountability part omitted.[+++] After all, no one wanted to embarrass some good old boy whose wife played bridge with the wife of the chief of police. So the results were not always spectacular.

New York was not the only place in the country where crime-focused policing was introduced. In the 1980s, as chief in Minneapolis, Tony Bouza implemented a number of programs designed by Prof. Lawrence Sherman (now of Cambridge University), who is generally considered America's leading expert on police crime fighting. In 1987, Sherman's research documented that over half of all reported crime and disorder occurred in just three percent of the property addresses in a major city. This permitted police to predict where crimes would occur with a far greater degree of certainty than in the past.

---

8. Folks from the hinterland are not used to what passes in New York for "spirited" discussion. By the same token, New Yorkers do not understand the conventions of Middle America. One former NYPD official, who became a police chief in the heartland, did not realize that when a local came to his office, he expected a few minutes of small talk before getting down to the matter at hand. As a result, the chief's stay in that city was short. When Lee Brown was NYPD commissioner, he did not understand that New Yorkers want things done yesterday.

From this theoretical base, Sherman developed a program in which police concentrated their resources where crime clustered, areas he called "hot spots." He also conducted research that determined that homicides, shootings, and other gun crimes could be reduced by intensifying the lawful use of police stop-and-search authority in high-gun-crime zones. In addition to Minneapolis, his ideas were also instituted in Kansas City and Indianapolis. As a result of Sherman's work, "hot spots" policing became an equivalent to COMPSTAT in New York.

After Ray Kelly again became police commissioner, in 2002, he instituted "impact" policing. In this program the NYPD "pinpointed" small high-crime areas—i.e., the local "hot spots"—and concentrated police patrols there. When crime started to spike in any location, police designated it an "impact" area and deployed extra personnel there to engage in intensive patrol. Thus, despite predictions that crime would go up in New York because it had already reached the lowest possible level, Kelly was able to keep the numbers going down. In addition, by refining police deployment, Kelly was able to partially offset the loss of several thousand officers because of financial cutbacks.

The crux of the crime-fighting programs developed by Bratton, Sherman and Kelly has been to maintain police focus on the primary mission. This contrasts dramatically with the pre-1990 period, when some police leaders waved the flag of surrender by announcing that they could not significantly reduce crime. Whether the police strategies are called COMPSTAT, "hot spots," "impact" or some other name, the concept played a significant role in the dramatic reduction in crime that occurred in some American cities over the past twenty years.

Chapter 11

Terrorism: Kelly in Command

On September 11, 2001, a terrorist attack on the United States was not unexpected. Even the target was not a surprise. It had been blown up before. On February 26, 1993, two men parked a rented Ford van in the public garage beneath the twin towers of the World Trade Center complex. The van contained an explosive nitrate compound packed in cardboard boxes, tanks of compressed hydrogen gas and containers of nitroglycerin. The driver and his passenger then lit a twenty-foot-long fuse and left the vehicle. At 12:18 p.m. the explosives went off,[1] blowing a one-hundred-eighty-five-foot hole in the basement of the north tower, causing damage seven stories up and knocking out the complex's emergency command post. Many people were trapped on upper floors.

Scores of police and fire units raced to the scene. Mayor David Dinkins was in Japan, so police commissioner Ray Kelly functioned as de facto head of the city government. Kelly was a man of the two worlds he had inhabited all his adult life: the NYPD and the U.S. Marines (where he had risen to colonel). He also held advanced degrees in law and public administration. Of medium height and powerfully built, he had a commanding presence and a no-nonsense manner. Kelly was perfectly cast for the role of emergency chief, and his calm but decisive manner on TV reassured frightened New Yorkers. Although six people died in the initial explosion and a thousand sustained various injuries or

---

1. If the explosives had gone off an hour later, they would have destroyed a ballroom directly above, where a children's party would have been in progress.

smoke inhalation, over the course of the day and into the evening, police and fire crews got everyone out of the building without any additional loss of life.

In addition to directing the rescue operations, Kelly teamed with Jim Fox, head of the New York division of the FBI, to launch an immediate investigation. Cops and federal agents combed through the ruins, examining the twisted pieces of metal. In a truck, they found a vehicle identification number that was traced to a New Jersey car rental agency. The man who had rented it, a twenty-five-year-old Palestinian named Mohammed Salameh, showed up at the rental office claiming that his vehicle had been stolen and asking for his four-hundred-dollar deposit back. The employees notified the FBI, and he was arrested. Further investigation determined that a group of Islamic extremists in metropolitan New York had planned the attack. Eventually ten people were convicted for the World Trade Center blast.

The surprise on 9/11/01 was not the attack but the manner in which it was carried out and the casualties that resulted. Two hijacked airliners, flown by unqualified pilots, struck the twin towers of the World Trade Center twenty minutes apart, resulting in the death of nearly three thousand people.[2] The attack came as a huge shock to the American public, not only because of the large number of deaths but also because it illustrated that America was no longer safe from the sort of things that went on overseas.

Americans had never been as proficient at security policing as other world powers, because they did not need to be. For two centuries, Britain had a vast empire to defend. For three centuries, France and the German states confronted each other across a mutual border. The United States had no real empire and was protected by two vast oceans. In July 1916, German agents, seeking to disrupt the flow of munitions from the neutral United States to the Allies, carried out the largest act of sabotage in American history. They blew up an ammunition dump on Black Tom Island in New York Harbor. The Brooklyn Bridge swayed and the shock from the blast was felt as far south as Philadelphia. An even larger explosion followed a half an hour later. Although only six people were officially reported as killed, it is believed that a number of transients who slept near the island (which was actually a promontory off New Jersey) had died. No one ever stood trial for the offense, although three very likely suspects were known to intelligence agencies.

In 1920, a lone individual parked a horse-drawn wagon in the middle of the Wall Street district. After he left, it exploded, killing thirty-six people and

---

2. The first plane hit the north tower between the 92nd and 99th floors at 8:46 a.m. At 9:06 a.m., the second plane plowed into the 77th–85th floors of the south tower.

wounding hundreds. Again, though credible suspects were known, no one was ever charged with the crime.

In 1940, some person or persons set a bomb at the British pavilion of the New York World's Fair. During attempts to disarm it, two detectives were killed and two others severely wounded. In that instance, not even a credible suspect has ever been identified.

American security agencies faced problems that their counterparts in many countries did not. Police authority in the United States is fragmented because of the division between state and federal agencies. At the state and local levels, there are sixteen thousand separate police departments to compete with each other. At the federal level, there are interagency rivalries.

In the second half of the twentieth century, when ghettos and campuses exploded, the FBI had virtually no agents who could operate successfully in those places. While local police knew the ghettos, their officers were insufficiently trained to conduct counterintelligence work. In 1966, during an extensive racial disturbance, some Chicago police officers overheard black militants discussing revolutionary plans. The cops arrested the group and charged them with treason against the state of Illinois for conspiring to overthrow its government. In the history of the United States, there had been only two successful prosecutions for treason against a state.[3] The police were unaware that, in the 1950s, the United States Supreme Court had ruled that treason against a state was so intertwined with treason against the United States that only the federal government had jurisdiction in that area. In the Chicago case, the state's attorney declined to prosecute. No one at police headquarters was embarrassed by such a gaffe.

* * * *

In New York prior to 9/11, some steps were taken to deal with terrorist attacks, but more could have been done. In 1993 the response of the police and fire departments had been generally applauded. Commissioner Kelly provided the necessary leadership, and thousands of people in the towers were brought out safely. Police and FBI agents worked closely together, and the bombers were quickly apprehended. It was also reassuring that the plotters appeared to be bumbling incompetents rather than highly trained commandos. Instead of fleeing town or lying low, they tried to get a refund of the deposit on the truck they had used to haul the explosives. The greatest error they had

---

3. Thomas Dorr in 1842, for leading a rebellion against Rhode Island, and John Brown in Virginia, for carrying out the 1859 raid on Harpers Ferry Arsenal.

made was in their assumption that the blast would cause the north tower to topple into the south tower, causing it to fall. They did not know that it was constructed so that an uncontrolled explosion (as opposed to one set by engineering specialists contracted to demolish a site) would not cause the building to collapse. In fact, some experts were not so sure this was the case. They believed that if the terrorists had used more explosives, the north tower might have brought down its twin.[4] Even though Ray Kelly was no longer commissioner—at the end of 1993, mayor-elect Rudy Giuliani had not retained him[5]—it was natural for the public safety services to assume that "we did it before, we can do it again."

From 1994 to 2001, the city continued its counterterrorism efforts. Among possible methods of attack were chemical, biological or radiological devices, ranging from the release of gas in the subway, or some other closed space, to the detonation of a "dirty bomb" designed to contaminate an entire city district. A second possibility was armed groups attacking individuals or organizations. The most likely appeared to be bombs ranging from those in individual backpacks, through cars and trucks loaded with explosives, to missiles fired from a ship in the harbor. Countering a possible air raid was considered the responsibility of the military.[6]

Only seventeen NYPD officers were assigned full-time to counterterrorism duties, and they were part of an FBI joint terrorist task force. The Bureau provided the New York detectives with office facilities, cars, expense accounts and special credentials, but it was not a true joint venture. When the FBI obtained information on a possible threat, it was closely held, and the NYPD detectives on the task force were forbidden to disclose it to their department superiors.

The city's emergency command post was located on the eighth floor of police headquarters in Lower Manhattan. It was a relatively small and crowded facility, normally used for staff meetings like COMPSTAT sessions. Its most frequent emergency use was during snowstorms. In 1999, it was decided to open a larger, state-of-the-art center, leaving the one in police headquarters as an alternate. However, city officials made an elementary mistake. They located the new facility in a building that was part of the World Trade Center complex. It was not only a likely target but also just a few blocks from police head-

4. Which would have landed on top of my residence at the time.
5. In doing so, he was following standard practice in New York, where commissioners, though appointed to five-year terms, in reality serve at the pleasure of the mayor.
6. On 9/11, only four U.S. jet fighters were on alert in the Northeast air defense sector, which extended from the Canadian border to Virginia and Kentucky and from the East Coast into Kansas and Nebraska. The nearest fighters to New York City were stationed on Cape Cod in Massachusetts.

quarters. This created the possibility that one attack would knock out both command centers.

In 1993, some fire department radios had not worked in the towers. Afterward a new radio system was installed, but it continued to malfunction. The police and fire departments, traditional rivals, did not establish a unified command structure or conduct joint exercises.

The individuals who commanded the security forces in 2001 were not of the caliber of Ray Kelly. Neither the fire nor police commissioner had served as a top officer in his own or another fire or police department. Before his appointment, the fire commissioner, Thomas von Essen, had been head of the firefighters union. The highest post that the police commissioner, Bernard Kerik, had previously held in the NYPD was third-grade detective—the police equivalent of corporal. Under department regulations, his lack of a college degree would have barred him from promotion beyond the rank of sergeant. In the 1993 mayoral campaign, Kerik volunteered to chauffeur Giuliani. Afterward, the mayor named him to top jobs in the city jail system and in 2000 made him police commissioner. As happened many times in many places, a mayor's decision on a police chief would harm his reputation further down the line.

On 9/11, the new command center in the 7 World Trade Center building was too close to the towers to be used. It was struck by debris when the towers fell, and, later that day, it too collapsed. Police headquarters lost telephone service. The police and fire departments set up their own command posts at different locations and utilized separate radio systems.[7]

When the second plane hit, the command personnel realized they were not dealing with an accident but were under attack. Mayor Giuliani immediately contacted federal authorities to request air cover for the city. In general, Kerik remained at the side of the mayor rather than taking active control of police operations. The NYPD was largely directed by First Deputy Commissioner Joe Dunne, assisted by Chief of Department Joe Esposito. The fire department, too, was directed by its first deputy commissioner, William Feehan, and the chief of the department, Peter Ganci. All four were veteran cops or firefighters who had risen via the normal career ladder. It was immediately decided by commanders that, given the situation, the primary mission would be one of rescue rather than firefighting. Dunne was walking on crutches with his foot in a brace because of a recent operation. When the north tower started to fall, he

---

7. Some officials have maintained that separate command posts were necessary to mobilize the forces and provide observation of the conditions. However, there is a difference between a command post, an observation post and an assembly point. Command over an entire operation cannot be exercised from two separate locations.

was saved by a cop who flung him into an armored vehicle, where he landed among some police dogs awaiting assignment; the two top fire officials were killed. Because of the communications problem, police brass heard an erroneous report that Chief of Department Esposito had been killed, and they dispatched a counseling team to his home.

In the final analysis, the basic problem was that the collapse of the towers was totally unexpected. If it had not happened, most of the people below the floors where the planes had struck would have been saved. Police and firefighters began sustaining fatalities from the time they arrived on the scene. However, it was the crumbling of the buildings that contributed most to the four hundred three deaths among public safety officers (three hundred forty-three FDNY, thirty-seven New York and New Jersey Port Authority officers, including their superintendent, and twenty-three NYPD).

The first major response by Congress and the administration was predictable: throw money and bodies at the problem. Twenty-two disparate agencies were combined into a cabinet-level Department of Homeland Security, with a total of one hundred and eighty thousand employees. The DHS sought to be, as its title implies, the overall controller of U.S. domestic security. However, both the CIA and the FBI managed to avoid being included within it—wisely, as it turned out, because the DHS was troubled from the outset. Its ranks included such diverse groups as Secret Service agents who guarded the president, customs and immigration officers patrolling the borders and airport baggage screeners. To make such a hastily assembled force into an effective body, the DHS required chiefs with proven expertise in managing large-scale organizations and experience in handling emergencies. A good place to look for them would have been the military. Instead of Gen. Norman Schwarzkopf types, however, individuals whose essential qualification was their political standing filled many of the top posts in the department. In its early days the DHS was largely noted for its PR work. It issued color-coded alerts warning of the likelihood of attack: green for low, blue for guarded, yellow for elevated, orange for high and red for severe. It was like the children's game red light/green light, with everyone running around confused.

Police chiefs complained that the DHS and the FBI did not share information on terrorist threats with America's six hundred thousand—plus state and local police. Within the FBI, some agents charged that their superiors ignored pre-9/11 reports about such things as Middle Eastern men learning to fly (but not to land) jetliners. An investigating commission faulted the FBI and the CIA for not sharing information. A revamped intelligence structure was created under a director of national intelligence (DNI) who, in theory, outranked the CIA director. The grouping included a newly created National

Counterterrorism Center (NCTC), as well as such established entities as the National Security Agency (NSA), responsible for communications intelligence; the Defense Intelligence Agency (DIA), which collects intelligence for the military; the National Reconnaissance Office (NRO); and the National Geospatial-Intelligence Agency (NGIA). It was not clear that drawing boxes on an organization chart and ladling out a large helping of alphabet soup enhanced national security. For practical purposes, the DNI's office is just one more power center competing with the CIA, the FBI and the DHS. Since 2005 there have been four directors of the agency. The *New York Times* described the job as "a director who oversees sixteen agencies but does not run any of them."* Despite all the various entities, with their multibillion-dollar budgets searching for Osama bin Laden the world over, he was not found for nearly ten years. Then, instead of hiding in a cave, he was discovered to be living in an apartment complex near a military headquarters in Pakistan.

Perhaps the greatest personnel blunder occurred in 2005, when President Bush nominated Bernard Kerik to succeed Pennsylvania governor Tom Ridge as secretary of homeland security. If Kerik's appointment as police commissioner had been greeted with little enthusiasm by many NYC law enforcement experts, his appointment to head the DHS astounded them.

The Senate had not begun to consider his nomination when the president had to withdraw his name, allegedly because of Kerik's failure to pay taxes on the wages of a nanny (though she was never located). At the time of Kerik's nomination as homeland security secretary, a number of New Yorkers were aware of rumors about his extramarital rendezvous in an apartment made available to workers at the World Trade Center site, his associations with unsavory individuals and irregular financial dealings (which in 2006 required him to plead guilty to a New York State misdemeanor crime). But apparently none of the knowledgeable people were contacted by the White House. In 2007, federal prosecutors charged Kerik with evading taxes on gifts he had received and perjury, the latter for lying to investigators conducting a background check on his qualifications to head DHS. In 2010, after entering a plea of guilty, he was sentenced to four years' imprisonment. Kerik is the first former New York City police commissioner since the office was established in 1901 to go to prison.

The most effective counterterrorism forces in the United States at present are the NYPD and the FBI. In 2002, Mayor Giuliani was succeeded by Mike Bloomberg (then New York's richest person, with a net worth of twenty billion dollars), who named Ray Kelly police commissioner. Kelly, the first former commissioner in the history of the department to return to the post, has been given greater autonomy than any previous head of the NYPD. While the federal government floundered, Kelly moved to restore the safety and morale of New Yorkers, and he didn't care whose toes he stepped on. In addition to the normal responsibilities of his job, since 9/11 counterterrorism has become a responsibility of the police commissioner to an extent unimagined by his predecessors.

The task Kelly faced was unprecedented in American police history. He had to create a major police security capability from the ground up. The model for what he has had to do came from his own branch of the military service, the United States Marines. In 1915, the British navy, the mightiest sea power in the history of the world, attempted to land troops on the Gallipoli Peninsula as base for an attack on Constantinople, the capital of the Turkish Empire. At that time Turkey was, at best, a second-rate power. The concept for the invasion was essentially the brainchild of the forty-year-old first lord of the admiralty, Winston Churchill.

When the troops landed, they sustained overwhelming casualties. The Allies managed to establish small beachheads, where they were pinned down for the next eight months until they were finally evacuated. By that time, Churchill had been ousted from the government.

In the postwar military world, it was a given that ship-to-shore operations did not work. Nevertheless, in the 1920s, the United States Marines—a small elite force that the army constantly sought to absorb—began to develop plans for amphibious warfare. This required not only training but the development of new techniques and equipment, such as landing boats. In World War II, it was the ability to perform landings that led Marine divisions from island to island across the Pacific. At the end of the war, after the amphibious operations had been shown to be successful, the Marine Corps emerged as a major U.S. force and attempts to abolish it ceased.

Just as the Marines did in the interwar period, Kelly had to put the various pieces together. He also faced critics who claimed that the task was essentially beyond a local police department and should be left to the federal government. From the start, Kelly was not willing to accept the federal government's policy of refusing to share information with local police. He assigned a hundred detectives to the joint task force on terrorism and boldly demanded that the NYPD be put in command of it. The FBI agreed to a joint command.

Before 9/11 the NYPD intelligence division had largely been used as "coat holders"—the cops' name for detectives who escort dignitaries. Kelly wanted a true intelligence operation. To head it, he brought in as a deputy commissioner David Cohen, formerly the number-three official in the CIA. In an unprecedented move, Kelly and Cohen stationed detectives abroad in London, Tel Aviv, Singapore, and eight other cities to maintain liaison with the local police. When a terrorist incident occurs overseas, an NYPD detective quickly responds to the scene, gathers information and flashes it to New York. Working from an out-of-the-way facility in New York City, skilled linguists monitor the al Jazeera TV network and other Arab media, looking for clues to a future attack. Others listen to recorded conversations between terrorist suspects. As in the Pentagon, the National Security Agency (NSA) or CIA headquarters, highly educated specialists, working with streetwise operatives, prepare sophisticated studies analyzing various problems.

As deputy commissioner in charge of counterterrorism operations, Kelly appointed Frank Libutti, a recently retired Marine lieutenant general. When Libutti left, he was replaced by Mike Sheehan, a West Point-educated army colonel who had served as the U.S. ambassador-at-large on terrorism.

Under the leadership of the new deputy commissioners, NYPD security operations began to display a professional touch. Instead of seventeen officers assigned full time to counterterrorism duties as before 9/11, now at least a thousand are, and in periods of high alert, the number might be triple that figure. It has become a familiar sight for New Yorkers to see black vans suddenly pull up outside the United Nations complex, Rockefeller Center or similar places and disgorge teams of officers in helmets and flak jackets cradling automatic weapons. Sometimes these "Hercules teams" are sent out because of a possible threat, but mostly they are trying to keep potential terrorists off-balance. Additionally, on signal, each of the NYPD's seventy-six precincts can dispatch a patrol car on a "surge" to a designated location. Descents by the Hercules cops and surges, with squadrons of vehicles suddenly arriving at a location, are carried out with military precision. In 1977, a citywide blackout provided the opportunity for mobs to engage in widespread looting and arson. When a similar event occurred in 2003, instantly police sirens could be heard all over New York as the black Hercules vans and precinct squads raced to predetermined locations to secure the city. As a result, there were no serious disorders and the streets remained relatively calm.

In 2003 an al Qaeda operative, conducting a surveillance of the Brooklyn Bridge, was overheard in an intercepted phone conversation saying, "The weather is too hot." This meant there was too much of a law enforcement presence in the area for an attack to be contemplated.[8] In the same year, a New York cop, patrolling a Queens subway station after midnight, noticed some men filming trains. When he questioned them, they feigned an inability to speak English. In previous years, cops might have had to converse with them

---

8. The caller was a truck driver licensed to carry hazardous materials whom police suspected of plotting to bring down the bridge.

in pigeon English, which meant they would learn nothing. Now that the NYPD has officers fluent in sixty languages, that dodge no longer worked. In this instance, an officer of Middle Eastern background, fluent in Farsi, was summoned. The fact that he was able to converse with them in their own language flustered them to the point where their English rapidly improved, and they admitted they were security guards at the Iranian embassy. Detectives who investigated the incident suspected that they were intelligence officers, possibly planning a terrorist act. The NYPD reported the men to the U.S. State Department, which ordered them out of the country.

Though rarely discussed publicly, there are police officers, equipped with radiation detectors who quietly prowl the streets. Other officers carry detection devices on their belts. The NYPD takes seriously the possibility of a terrorist attempt to detonate a nuclear device or, more likely, a dirty bomb.

Following the bombings in the Madrid subway in 2004 and the London Underground in 2005, Commissioner Kelly flooded the New York subways with cops. The Madrid terrorists had planted explosives and fled. The London ones were suicide bombers who wore backpacks. Therefore the NYPD began spot-checking people carrying bags in the subway. Those who refused to allow the police to search their bags were not allowed on trains. Civil liberties lawyers filed suit, arguing that it was not only a violation of constitutional rights but a waste of time, since a bomber would simply go to another subway station until he was allowed to board a train. Anyone with an understanding of criminal psychology recognized that the police tactic was well conceived. Certain events attract copycats. Someone, hearing about bombings in Europe, might suddenly decide to plant a bomb in the New York subways to highlight his own grievances. However, were he to notice intensive police activity near a target area, he might rethink his options. Trained terrorist teams, observing the police activity, would likely regroup. In the meantime they could be infiltrated by an informer, their conversations might be intercepted, or their superiors might decide the risk of failure was too great and call the project off. A judge dismissed the suit.

On May 1, 2010, in the Broadway theater district, shortly before ticket holders began arriving to attend the evening performances, two street vendors noticed smoke coming from a Nissan Pathfinder. When police and firefighters examined the vehicle, they discovered a cache of explosives powerful enough to kill or injure hundreds of passersby. The device had been set by a U.S. citizen of Pakistani origin. Luckily, he had not armed it correctly. Police took him off an airliner bound for Dubai, and under interrogation he talked freely and expressed no regrets other than that he had failed in his mission. Apparently he had undertaken it for the Taliban. Brought to trial, he was sentenced to life imprisonment. Undoubtedly, other would-be terrorists have studied his technical mistakes to avoid repeating them.

The NYPD responds to possible disasters according to a tightly controlled procedure. If police receive a report of a suspected bomb at some location, they will send a relatively small force to the scene while other officers screen off the area so that any terrorist observing the target location cannot chart police procedures. Abroad it has been the practice of some groups, such as Hamas, to detonate hidden bombs at sites after rescuers arrive. This not only adds to the casualty list but strikes at the security forces themselves. In a major plot, it would be a means to weaken security units, making it easier for terrorists to launch a much larger attack at another location. The terrorist strike against Mumbai, India, began with an assault on the local police station. By maintaining strict control over its forces, the NYPD also lessens the possibility that terrorists could use stolen uniforms to infiltrate the police ranks. As in Central London, the Lower Manhattan financial district is surrounded by a "ring of steel": surveillance cameras that cover the entire area and can even identify the faces of known terrorists. License plate scanners are able to read the plates of vehicles entering Manhattan. Barriers block vehicle access to sensitive locations.

In September 2011, during an interview with *60 Minutes*, Commissioner Kelly mentioned that the NYPD had the capability of shooting down airplanes. This created a temporary sensation, because many people wondered if the department possessed anti-aircraft guns. What they have is very high-powered .50-caliber rifles which are plugged into police helicopters whose crews have been trained to use them. These would not be sufficient to shoot down a large plane but could knock out a crop duster trying to spray anthrax over the city. At the same time, it was revealed that federal agents in New York City had shoulder-launched Stinger missiles capable of bringing down a jetliner.

Not all people approve of the police operations. In August 2004, the Republican National Convention was held in New York City. For months before, various groups engaged in attempts to recruit people to come to New York and protest the Bush administration's Iraq policy. Many postings on the Internet spoke of creating disorder and engaging in violence at the time of the convention.

In Seattle in 1999, during a meeting of the World Trade Organization, an estimated fifty thousand to a hundred thousand protesters had engaged in acts of violence, destroyed property, set fires, overturned police and emergency vehicles, and looted local stores. For a time they paralyzed the city. In San Francisco in 2003, antiwar protesters shut down a large portion of the city. During the course of the disturbance, protesters fired bolts from slingshots at the police. That year in Miami, twenty thousand people engaged in protests against a free-trade meeting. Again there were violent clashes with police and fires set.

The New York demonstrators against the GOP meeting scheduled August 31 as a so-called "Day of Chaos." In response, the police channeled them away from the convention center and kept a close eye on individuals and groups suspected of planning acts of terrorism. One thousand two hundred people were arrested. Many of those arrested were held in a rented facility at Pier 57 along the Hudson River. The place had previously been used as a garage for city buses, so it was in no condition to receive guests. Many of the prisoners were processed through booking procedures that ran over 24 hours. Advocates of the protesters claimed it was designed to keep them out of action. Police countered that it was necessary to check identities through fingerprints because many of the protesters gave false names. Since 2004, there has been continuing litigation over the arrests, with the legal issues yet to be resolved.

In the fall of 2011, the police were confronted with the "Occupy Wall Street" movement, which camped out in a lower Manhattan private park which was also open to the public. After police temporarily cleared the area and removed tents and other camping equipment, the demonstrators staged protests all over Manhattan and portions of Brooklyn. The new phenomenon raises some of the same issues as in the 1960s and at the 2004 Republican convention.

Americans are not used to living in a state of constant high security. Even before the "Occupy Wall Street" demonstration, the area looked like a city under siege, with streets closed and truck barriers in many places. Those who walk through lower Manhattan know they are under surveillance by dozens of cameras. Entering buildings, individuals are often subjected to search by security guards, who obviously have not studied under Dale Carnegie or Emily Post. Airplane passengers, formerly pampered, are now treated like cattle. Once the prospect of a trip by air was exciting; now it is dreaded. In World War II, there was the danger of sabotage, but to the average person security did not seem as extensive or heavy-handed as today. In the middle of the war, German POWs hauling mailbags outside the Chicago main post office were a common sight. Despite the fact that they were enemy combatants, their only guard was one U.S. soldier with a shotgun. As a practical matter, if the prisoners escaped, there was no place for them to go without being spotted. A handful of Americans who gave aid and comfort to some escapees were given long prison terms and in some instances sentenced to death (although the latter sentences were never carried out). Perhaps there is something to be learned today from re-examining the World War II security procedures.

The agency that was hit the hardest by the 9/11 attack was the FBI. It followed over a decade of setbacks to the Bureau. In 1987, President Reagan appointed, as Judge Webster's successor, federal judge William Sessions of the District Court of West Texas. A decent man, he was not a commanding figure, nor was he wise in the ways of Washington. Sessions once told me that when he was appointed, his father (who had lived through the Great Depression) said to him, "Oh, Willie, what have you done? You gave up a lifetime job for a temporary appointment." It turned out that, as the popular 1950s TV show proclaimed, "Father Knows Best." It was later alleged that Mrs. Sessions sometimes attempted to play the role of co-director, and a woman who was Sessions' administrative assistant often came over as though she were deputy director of the Bureau. While petty in scale, this brought Sessions into disfavor with a lot of top FBI officials, and eventually he was brought down for billing unauthorized airplane trips and using government personnel and equipment to work on his residence. Sessions even flunked the FBI test in little things. He pinned his director's badge to his shirt, like a Western sheriff, rather than carrying it in a card case as the others had done. In 1993, he was compelled to resign.

In the 1990s, the FBI experienced two major disasters which brought much criticism on the Bureau. The first occurred at Ruby Ridge, Idaho, where Bureau agents besieged a white separatist named Randy Weaver. The affair began when four U.S. marshals went to Weaver's cabin to look for him after he had failed to appear in court on federal firearms charges. Shooting erupted, and when it was over, a U.S. marshal and Weaver's fourteen-year-old son were dead. When Weaver refused to surrender, an FBI hostage rescue team was dispatched to the scene. Because Weaver was deemed extremely dangerous, the team was authorized to shoot any adult they observed carrying arms. When an FBI helicopter began circling Weaver's cabin, he and two of his children came out with rifles. An FBI sniper, believing that they were going to shoot at the helicopter, fired his own weapon, wounding Weaver. As Weaver ran back into his cabin, the sniper fired at him again. This time the bullet missed and tore through the cabin's door, killing Mrs. Weaver and wounding her son. Weaver himself remained in the cabin for ten more days before he surrendered. A state prosecutor filed charges against the FBI sniper, but, as the law permitted, the case was moved to federal court, where it was dismissed. Eventually, Weaver was acquitted in federal court and received a $3.1 million settlement from a lawsuit he brought against the federal government. The affair was widely publicized by right-wing forces in the West as an example of government overreach.

The following year, agents of the Alcohol, Tobacco and Firearms (ATF) Bureau of the U.S. Treasury attempted to enter a compound outside Waco, Texas, occupied by a group known as the Branch Davidians. Four agents were killed and fifteen others were wounded or injured. The ATF had to retreat. Film of the operation, played every night on national television, looked like Custer at the Little Big Horn, with agents dropping like tenpins. The scalping that followed took place off camera in Washington, where some officials were forced out.

President Clinton ordered the FBI to take over the operation. After maintaining the siege for over a month, the Bureau decided to move in. Agents in tanks attempted to break into the compound. Shots were fired and the compound itself caught fire. Eighty Davidians, including twenty-five children, were killed in the fire.

In 1993, President Clinton selected Louis Freeh to be director of the Bureau. It was an appointment the president would bitterly regret. Freeh was a former "brick [street] agent" who became an assistant U.S. attorney, then a federal judge. A man of high moral character, he often manifested the views of the rank-and-file about management. It was an old story in law enforcement. The top brass sit in their offices while the field agents/street cops hunt criminals and face the prospect of catching a bullet, or flak from the citizenry, the press or their superiors. In some police departments, high-ranking officials deal with this problem by spending a lot of time on the street with their troops. The trouble is that when a deputy chief prefers to play detective sergeant, he leaves a great deal of work unattended or, more likely, taken over by one of his assistants. Thus, while the boss is out supervising one case, his office sergeant is supervising a hundred others going on at the same time. Because of the FBI's geographic size and the scope of the director's duties, it was almost impossible for Freeh to spend much time with the troops, though he tried.

He expanded the Bureau's role in intelligence work, opening a number of overseas offices. However, the typical FBI agent did not have as comprehensive a background in foreign affairs as CIA officers, who tended to spend their careers overseas, often spoke the language of the country and were familiar with its customs.

Freeh, too, experienced fallout from some cases. Espionage was an especially difficult area. One apparent fiasco was the arrest of Wen Ho Lee, a Taiwanese-born scientist at Los Alamos National Laboratory, who was suspected of passing intelligence secrets to China. Lee was held for nine months without bail in restrictive conditions. Even during his daily hour of exercise, he was required to wear leg shackles. In 2000 a federal judge freed the sixty-one-year-old Lee, noting that the case had "embarrassed our entire nation and each of us who is a citizen of it." During Freeh's tenure the FBI captured a major Russian mole operating inside the U.S. government. It turned out to be FBI agent Robert Hanssen, who, for fifteen years, had furnished information to his bosses in Moscow.

Another, more familiar type of problem occurred during the Olympics in Atlanta, Georgia, in July 1996. A pipe bomb exploded in a park, killing two and injuring one hundred eleven people. A security guard, Richard Jewell, had alerted police to a suspicious green backpack. Jewell was extensively interviewed by television, which hailed him as a hero. The FBI believed otherwise. It is not uncommon for someone to create a situation where he can attract attention. Building fires are sometimes set by the individual who reports them and then claims to have helped the occupants escape. Jewell was treated as a criminal suspect. It took three months to clear him, and after a five-year manhunt, the actual bomber, Eric Rudolph, was captured.

Although appointed by President Clinton, Freeh quickly became regarded as a White House enemy, particularly over his investigation of the Monica Lewinsky case, which led to the president's impeachment trial. So bitter were the relationships between the White House and Freeh that the FBI director postponed his resignation from the office until after Clinton had left the presidency, so he would not be able to appoint Freeh's successor.

On 9/11, Robert Mueller had just taken over as director of the FBI. At the time, the Bureau had approximately eleven thousand agents, two thousand of them assigned to counterterrorism investigations. Reports about possible terrorist plots were regularly funneled into Washington. It was agents in Arizona and Minnesota who provided warnings that Middle Eastern men were attending flight schools and in some instances behaving strangely, like only wanting to study airline security procedures or learning to fly a jetliner but not to land or take off.

In 2001, the Bureau was awash in restrictions designed to prevent ethnic profiling. It bent over backward to avoid offending people of Middle Eastern origin. The basic principle was to avoid breaching political correctness even where such a possibility was remote or far-fetched.

Director Mueller was an Ivy League graduate who had served as a Marine officer in Vietnam. After military service he became an attorney and took a job with a prestigious Boston firm. He decided he wanted more action, however, and he joined the Department of Justice. Eventually he served as the United States attorney in San Francisco and Boston. During his Justice Department service, he managed to become well acquainted with FBI operations. But his administrative style was not simply to preside over the agency but to sharply question Bureau managers. Those who were unprepared with answers felt his displeasure. In this respect, he resembled Judge Webster, whereas Clarence Kelley and Louis Freeh both relied on their background as agents to make management decisions.

Immediately after 9/11, Mueller shifted two thousand agents from criminal investigation to counterterrorism, making the total working in that area four thousand. As a result, many white-collar crime, political corruption or mob cases had to be put on the back burner. Eventually the Bureau was increased from eleven to thirteen thousand agents, and Mueller was able to restore the number assigned to criminal investigation work. Even before 9/11, the Bureau had begun to withdraw from many criminal investigations and leave them to local police. These included cases that were once the staple of the FBI, such as bank robberies. In Hoover's day, a star field agent was one who hunted violent criminals in the back alleys of a big city. Now he sat at a desk, combing through computer files looking for corporate fraud or trying to uncover terrorist networks. An outstanding arrest was no longer a stickup man but a hacker threatening America's computer infrastructure, or a potential bomber. When Police Commissioner Kelly organized his own counterterrorism operations, there were many in the Bureau who felt that this move was unnecessary. However, Mueller went in the opposite direction and ordered full cooperation with the NYPD.

Mueller's greatest contribution to the war on terror (a term that is now politically incorrect in some quarters) was to prevent the establishment of a separate U.S. security service modeled on Britain's MI5.[9] Mueller's Congressional testimony on the subject was so cogent that the proposal for an MI5-type agency faded away, although it is periodically revived.

One astute observer of the FBI suggested that in the infighting after 9/11, it was Mueller who preserved the Bureau in its traditional roles by impressing Congress, while Hollywood and TV saved it with the American people, who believed that the accounts they saw on their screens were the real FBI.[10**]

In the years following the 9/11 attack, New York was the center of counterterrorism operations. This was not surprising. The hijackers had struck at what were anticipated to be the most likely targets: New York City, the de-

---

9. MI5 is the United Kingdom's principal security agency. It does not have police authority, which is reserved to MI5's rival, the Special Branch of Scotland Yard. In America, after World War II, there were efforts made to create an MI5-type organization, but J. Edgar Hoover was able to retain for the FBI the primary role in conducting domestic intelligence operations. Perhaps because the United States had no MI5, despite legal restrictions, the CIA engaged in domestic security operations, therefore making it a rival to the FBI.

10. In my judgment, the screen version is not too far from reality. Many street cops love to denounce the Bureau, claiming it is totally uncooperative with local police. Within law enforcement there are jokes along those lines. One is that FBI stands for "famous but incompetent." Another is that the agency is so great that they name streets for it—"one way." My personal experience has been that if you play square with the Bureau, they will play square with you and, in some instances, go out of their way to be helpful.

facto capital of the United States and economic center of the world, and Washington, DC, the political and military nerve center of the nation and the world. It was not surprising that the specific buildings hit were the twin towers, which symbolized the financial district, and the Pentagon, headquarters of the U.S. Armed Forces.[11] Other cities lacked similar attractions, so while their security was increased, in most there was not the same urgency as in New York. It is entirely possible, though, that the terrorists will undertake an attack away from the usual targets in order to demonstrate that no area of the country is safe.

In a throwback to the Cold War, in 2010 it was revealed that the SVR (Russian intelligence) had established a ring of agents in the northeastern region of the United States. Though they were foreign nationals, they were able to pass as middle-class Americans. Once they even received a reprimand from Moscow, reminding them that they were not in the United States to have a good time but were supposed to be developing contacts in policymaking organizations up to the level of the president's inner circle. When ten of them were arrested, they were quickly exchanged with the Russians for some American agents being held in Russia.

In 2002, when Bill Bratton took over as Los Angeles chief, he sought to beef up that city's counterterrorism operations. However, with fewer than three cops per thousand population, compared to five per thousand in New York City (circa 2001), he lacked the resources to devote a thousand officers a day to counterterrorism. Instead, the Los Angeles authorities concentrated on building networks such as the Joint Regional Intelligence Center, which "provides collaboration between federal, state and local law enforcement agencies to integrate criminal and terrorism threat intelligence and provide intake, analysis, fusion, synthesis and dissemination of that information." The JRIC's basic job is to convert the information into operational intelligence to defend against various threats within the seven counties of the Los Angeles metropolitan area. In this respect, the LA area is entirely contained within one state, whereas the comparable New York area extends into New York, Connecticut and New Jersey. From an operational standpoint, it would make more sense for the NYPD jurisdiction on terrorism to range from New Haven, Connecticut, in the north, to Newark, New Jersey, in the south. However, such a move is politically impossible. So, while New York too has fusion (combined intelligence) centers and interagency intelligence networks, there is no central controlling force over the various units.

---

11. And if brave passengers had not brought one of the planes down, probably the White House would have been struck .

The basic weakness of American antiterrorism programs is that the security forces cannot fail even once, whereas the terrorists can attack repeatedly until they succeed. This conundrum explains why the U.S. carries out proactive operations, like the killing of Osama bin Laden, on a worldwide basis.

Chapter 12

Policing in the 21st Century: Old Problems, New Solutions

An American police chief who retired early in the twenty-first century, after forty years of service, did not leave the same occupation he joined in the early 1960s. Back then, policing was not vastly different from what it had been before World War II. If asked to assess the past forty years, some retired chiefs might respond negatively. A typical one might recall his rookie days as a time when cops were the bosses of their beat and hoodlums or corner boys who got out of line were summarily arrested. If someone complained, the police brass would back their officers all the way. A police captain in a big city was a powerful figure whose word was law, and a chief was God. Now it appeared that the police had become the whipping boys of a permissive society that rejected all the values cops had been taught to honor: family, religion, patriotism, law and order. In his own career, the chief had made it to the top by playing ball with people he did not respect. When he got there, he found that he didn't possess half the power the old-time chiefs did. One could quarrel with that assessment, but many veteran chiefs believed it.

A fellow chief of the same age, background and career path might feel more positive about the changes. He would recall that, when he started, police were subservient to sleazy politicians and, in some cases, organized crime figures. Police officers themselves were undereducated, and too many succumbed to corruption. Now the old cigar-chomping local boss, or the swaggering mafioso, if they existed at all, had no hold over the cops.

A relatively new element on the scene was the police unions, which neither type of chief liked—the former because they curtailed his autocratic power, the latter because he felt unions were often barriers to police achieving professional status.

A chief's assessment might also vary according to the part of the country he served in. If he was in the South, his world had changed completely. When he started as a rookie in the early '60s, some of his colleagues were either Klan members or at least sympathetic to racist thinking. "Bull" Conner was still riding high. Today, the mayor of his city might be African-American, as was the chief's predecessor. In his rookie days, a patrolman's salary was probably around three thousand dollars a year. By 2000, rookies were starting near forty thousand dollars annually—double, in constant dollars, the salary forty years earlier. A chief himself was getting more than one hundred thousand dollars; sums that went further in the South than they did in the North.

The old industrial cities of the Midwest and Northeast had declined considerably. In the short run, this benefited police departments. Back when their chiefs had come on the job, they made less than their friends in the steel mills. Now the mills were closed and even college-educated people sought police careers.

In the prosperous cities on the Northeast and West coasts, it is common for patrol officers, with their salary, overtime and other benefits, to make in excess of one hundred thousand dollars a year. In addition, many have a twenty-year retirement plan. Local chiefs realize that municipalities cannot afford such salaries and benefits and that someday there will be a reckoning. But, like Louis XV, their philosophy is "after me, the deluge."

Toward the end of the twentieth century, there was also a new look in the chiefs' offices. Some of the occupants were women. These included Penny Harrington of Portland, Oregon; Elizabeth Watson of Houston, Texas; and Beverly Harvard of Atlanta, Georgia.[1] Like most chiefs, they rose from the ranks and in office faced the same attacks from politicians, the media and police unions that their male colleagues did.

Community relations was a chief's primary job, and most had mastered it, at least to a certain extent. Their office walls were festooned with photos and plaques from every civic group in town, ranging from the NAACP to neighborhood block associations. When a chief was leaving, he often began to

---

1. Perhaps it was not a coincidence that all three were in areas where Lee Brown had been police chief (though in Portland his command was the county, not city, police).

feel nostalgic about the old days. One night, while having a chat in his office with an out-of-towner of his own age and background, a major city chief suddenly asked his visitor if he would like to see a picture. Half expecting what it was going to be, the visitor eagerly assented. It was a blown-up news photo of the chief back when he was a young detective. It showed him firing a machine gun to flush out a man who had just shot a police officer and taken refuge in a basement. Both men stared at it as if it were a priceless painting. Once, the photo would have had a prominent place on the chief's wall. Now, with machine guns out of fashion, and the fact that the man he fired at happened to be nonwhite, he felt that it was better to keep it hidden in a drawer. The brass were proud of such episodes because it meant they were not always bureaucrats but had soldiered on the front line—although, like Vietnam medal winners who never mention their war service, cops know they are more likely to be reviled than honored for their past.

There has also been a change in the work and status of detectives. No longer do some of them operate as a law unto themselves or, as writer Robert Daley described them, "Princes of the City."* Now they sat at computers doing paperwork. Thanks to the FBI, organized crime was no longer a power in its old strongholds. The remaining "mob bosses" were seventy going on thirty— i.e., seventy years or older and soon to be receiving thirty years or more in prison.

Is policing significantly better in the United States in the new millennium than it was forty or fifty years ago? Because law enforcement is so localized, a judgment would have to be yes, no and maybe. In Chicago, O. W. Wilson is a distantly remembered figure. When a new police training academy was opened, it was named for former commissioner Tim O'Connor an honorable man but not one who had ever been mentioned in the same breath as Wilson. As a consolation prize, Wilson's name was put on the academy library. It was as though the school of government at Harvard had been named for Calvin Coolidge and the library for John Kennedy.

In the 1980s, after the Greylord sting resulted in twenty judges, fifty-seven lawyers and sixteen policemen and deputy sheriffs being convicted of various crimes, Chicagoans shrugged. Two knowledgeable local reporters, in a book about Greylord, presented the old explanation of enduring corruption in the Windy City. "Most of the men [involved] were shaped to believe that if one did not grab some graft, while others all around were grabbing, one was a sucker."

In the '80s, Miami became the drug and murder capital of the United States—a fact that was not coincidental, since it was the drug dealers who sent the murder rates zooming upward. According to John Timoney, a former first deputy police commissioner of New York City who later served as chief in

Miami, the city also had the highest number of questionable police shootings.** In 2003, when Timoney arrived in town, thirteen of the department's twelve hundred cops were on trial for illegal shootings. In New York City, this rate of approximately one defendant per hundred officers would translate to four hundred cops on trial for illegal shootings. Police misconduct too was related to drugs. In the '80s, when crime began to rise rapidly, the Miami department hired a number of officers who were not qualified for the job. Not surprisingly, many them got into trouble. In New Orleans the police department virtually collapsed at the time of the 2005 Katrina disaster. An investigation disclosed that, during the chaos, some NOPD officers had wantonly shot people and criminal charges were leveled against them.

After Timoney put in new policies and training, Miami officers went twenty months without firing a single shot at any person. Conversely, about that time the Florida Legislature enacted a "stand your ground" law which reversed previous legal doctrines. Before 2005 all states required that a citizen who was in a situation where he felt himself in danger from another person was obliged to retreat if he could do so safely.[2] Florida chiefs like Timoney argued against passage of the law. Following its enactment the statute was used to justify killings ranging from drug dealers turf battles to road rage incidents.***

In 2012, Trayvon Martin, a seventeen-year-old black youngster was shot to death by a white citizen crime watch volunteer who had been following him allegedly because he thought Martin looked "suspicious." When the volunteer contacted police by phone he was instructed to cease following Martin that officers would be sent to the scene to investigate the matter. Apparently the volunteer chose not to follow this advice and went on to kill the unarmed teenager. The police department in Sanford, Florida, did not charge the volunteer for the shooting supposedly because they believed that his actions were covered by the "stand your ground" law. At present both state and federal authorities are investigating the matter. Thus while police shootings of citizens are down and those that do occur are subject to greater scrutiny, in some states laws are being enacted that make it legal for citizens to shoot other citizens in circumstances where it was heretofore illegal to do so.

Overall, most of the Southern police departments were better than they had been in the old days. In the Midwest, though, cities that had once fielded highly rated forces such as Cincinnati and St. Louis had ceased to do so. The

---

2. The idea was to prevent public altercations and to rely on the police, who were not required to retreat in the face of dangerous situations. The doctrine did not apply to citizens defending their homes or deny a person the right to defend his life if retreat was somehow foreclosed.

same was becoming true on the West Coast, where Los Angeles was no longer considered the best police department in the country.

Boston and New York were definitely better than they had been half a century earlier. It was no surprise that the two men regarded as America's greatest police chiefs, Bill Bratton and Ray Kelly, were products, respectively, of the Boston and New York police departments. Some of the most thoughtful scholars of policing came out of Harvard or were based at NYU, John Jay or Columbia in New York City. In contrast, the University of California-Berkeley's School of Criminology had never been restored. However, the country's greatest sociological writer on policing was still former Los Angeles detective sergeant Joseph Wambaugh. His novels, rather than being heroic yarns, changed the perception of cops from tight-jawed Dick Tracys to ordinary people struggling to carry out extraordinary tasks which took a heavy psychological toll on them. They were the police version of the protagonists of John le Carré spy novels, who were no longer James Bond types but troubled men or women in a morally ambiguous job.

* * * *

Despite some clear progress, there was much that had not been done in policing. The command structure in big cities had not been altered in one hundred years. Individuals who rise to high rank, including the chief's post, usually do so within their own department, not through a national competition. There is still no government-funded staff college to train future leaders and no mechanism that ensures they will be placed in the right jobs. As late as 2001 the NYPD, the most important police force in America, was headed by Bernard Kerik, who had never even made sergeant in the department and lacked a college degree.

In 1972, when J. Edgar Hoover died, it should have been possible to divest the FBI, basically a detective force, of the job of running an academy for police officials from largely patrol forces. Instead, the Bureau should have been training investigators and identifying potential detective commanders. The introduction of DNA revealed that a larger number of innocent people have been convicted and imprisoned than was previously suspected. Often this happened because of shoddy detective work.

With sixteen thousand separate police departments in the United States, eighty percent of them with fewer than fifty officers, the state chiefs' associations are often dominated by individuals who lead ten- or twenty-officer forces. In contrast, a chief with two thousand cops working under him may have no influence outside his own community. The reverse of this is that a small-town chief, no matter how competent, has virtually no chance to become a big-city police chief. [3]

Elinor Ostrom, a political scientist at Indiana University, won the Nobel Prize in 2009 for her study of common pool resources. As part of her research, she demonstrated that, contrary to popular belief, very small police departments were generally efficient.[+] Still, it is wasteful to have a chief for ten cops, along with a separate station and desk sergeants. There is no way a small police department can provide full services to its community. Solving major cases is usually beyond the capacity of its detectives, because an important component of investigative success is the level of experience of its officers, and in small communities major crimes like murder are rare. Small-town police cannot handle riots or similar large-scale events. They cannot provide the necessary administrative services like planning, training, personnel management, records and communications that a modern force requires. Invariably the small forces have to call on other departments for assistance. However, that raises problems of command and control.

More cops possess college degrees than in the past, but their occupation has not received professional status. Police officers still do not bother to study their field.[4] Thus, policing largely remains a craft learned by the apprenticeship method.

The police, as always, reflect the racial attitudes of the country. While those have changed a great deal in fifty years, blacks still point to the fact that arrest rates for members of their race are disproportionately higher than those for whites. Police officers counter that arrest rates are based on victimization rates, and these are even higher for nonwhites as a result of the prevalence of black-on-black crimes. Lawsuits have proven to the satisfaction of some courts that cops sometimes profile blacks and other minorities on the basis of their supposed propensity to commit crime. In a country where even Jesse Jackson once commented to the effect that he was more afraid of a black stranger on the street than a white one,[++] it is likely that some cops make decisions based on stereotypes. In the final analysis, it is difficult to maintain that in all cases black citizens are treated exactly the same by police as a white citizen would be. By the same token, blacks tend to excuse crime by citing long-range causes such as racism, poverty, etc., rather than supporting action (as opposed to

---

3. A notable exception was Robert DeGrazia, who went from patrolman to chief of a twenty-man force in Novato, California, then to chief of the four-hundred-officer St. Louis County Police Department and finally, in the 1970s, became commissioner of the twenty-five-hundred-officer Boston Police Department.

4. One time I was stunned when a high-ranking police official in charge of a major investigative bureau told me he had not heard of, much less read, James Q. Wilson's *The Investigators*. When I loaned him a copy, he never opened it. In contrast, military officers have been exposed to texts on Desert Storm and the Iraqi war as part of their staff college education.

words) against individuals who are shooting and pillaging in their own neighborhoods.

In instances involving race, a simple street stop can assume national significance. In 2009, a virtual White House summit conference was convened after a black Harvard professor, Henry Louis Gates, who did not have his house key, was mistaken by police for a burglar when he tried to break into his home. Some saw this as an example of police racism; others looked at it as an entitled individual abusing a cop for doing his job.

Basic media coverage of the police has not changed significantly in fifty years. A great deal is still sports reporting. Officer Jones scored the winning touchdown—that is, caught the murderer. There is also a tendency to exaggerate police misconduct. Some incidents deserve front-page exposure. In other cases, where the officer is exonerated by district attorneys or grand juries, the story drops back to page eighty-five.

A new phenomenon has developed in recent years involving big cases, where a detective looks to score a book deal, a prosecutor wants the movie rights and the judge is hoping to get his own TV show. The danger is that investigations, prosecutions and judicial decisions might be shaped by considerations of potential literary and film profits. This is part of a larger trend of the media and ordinary citizens alike to garner fame and fortune out of tragedy.

The worst distortions of American policing are found in the movies and television cop shows, where virtually every episode contains a shooting and/or car chase. Policing is often portrayed as analogous to the battle for Iwo Jima. On screen, individual cops seem able to do almost anything, regardless of laws or regulations. In real life, an officer like "Dirty Harry" would probably wind up in prison. Perhaps the worst aspect of the cop shows is that they portray a police career not as one of service but as an opportunity for an individual to fulfill his fantasies.

Beginning around 1960, more thoughtful articles on policing began to appear. However, ideology often overrode analysis. Most writers approached the subject from a liberal perspective, although the conservative side was presented more often than one would expect. Liberals condemn even lawful police practices like "stop and frisk" based on reasonable cause. Conservatives, who are easily worked up over government officials exceeding their authority, favor wide latitude for police discretion. They are sure that if they themselves are stopped they will receive kid-glove treatment.[5]

---

5. Some people love to possess police association cards or honorary badges. As one Eastern city police captain put it, "These only guarantee that the holder will be placed in a clean jail cell."

The Future

Predictions in so volatile a field as policing usually turn out to be wrong. Sometimes those whose job is to spot emerging problems miss them completely. In July 1830, the prefect of police of Paris, who headed an organization known for the spies and informers on its payroll, sent his evening intelligence report to the royal government.

> General Surveillance
> The most perfect tranquility continues to reign at all points of the capital. No event worthy of special attention has been recorded in any of the reports which have reached me.

The following day, a revolution broke out that drove the last Bourbon king from the throne of France.[+++]

A more successful seer was Supt. John McCarthy of Scotland Yard's Special Branch, a key component of British security. In 1908 he accompanied a member of the royal family on a state visit to Portugal. There McCarthy met a young Englishman named Harold Brust, who worked as a confidential messenger for the British ambassador. According to Brust, McCarthy tried to interest him in a career with the Special Branch, arguing that the next ten years were going to be critical for the world and Brust would be at the center of events. The following year Brust returned to England, joined the London Metropolitan Police and, after an apprenticeship on the beat, became a member of the Branch.

Over the twenty years that Brust served, he was engaged in combating German spies, Irish rebels, English and Scottish rioters, Communist agents and Indian nationalist assassins. When he entered the service, the British Empire was the most powerful political entity in the world. When Brust left, its very existence was threatened. On the European continent, kings and emperors whose families had ruled their domains for generations were no longer in power, and in many cases their countries had been carved up into successor states that competed with one another. Out of the morass emerged Hitler, Stalin and Mussolini.[^]

McCarthy had been right in his forecast. Of course, his spiel may just have been a recruiting sergeant's pitch to a likely recruit. On the other hand, those who believe the world is run by hidden forces might argue that McCarthy's secret work had revealed to him the shape of things to come.[6] Most likely he

---

6. The English writer John Buchan, author of *The 39 Steps* and later governor general of Canada, was one of those who adhered to the view that secret forces constantly threatened the British Empire. See, for example,

was reflecting the views of his occupational group, which always assumes its work is of paramount importance.

If Supt. McCarthy were around today, he might venture an opinion on whether the 9/11 attack opened a new era in law enforcement in which policing might be fundamentally changed. For example, the U.S. Department of Homeland Security might be assigned to police urban areas. At least twice in the twentieth century, it appeared that American policing was about to undergo a major restructuring. In the 1930s, when gangsters were running amok, holding up banks and shooting down policeman and citizens, it was frequently recommended that the job of pursuing crooks be given to the army or other military-type force. However, within a few years, the gangsters were defeated by a few hundred FBI agents. In the '60s riot era, experts suggested it would be necessary to form a constabulary-style police on the model of the French CRS, whose specially selected officers live in barracks and respond to disorder with a military-type approach. The riot era faded out after 1970.

Lacking the prescience of Supt. McCarthy, I can only point to a few emerging problems. While the drug gangs no longer rule the streets of most cities, youth gangs continue to be a problem. In New Jersey alone, police estimate there are seven hundred gangs with twenty thousand members. In 2006, gang members engaged in a five-day shooting spree in the capital city, Trenton, that left fifteen people wounded. According to the state police superintendent, the gangs imitate the famous Crips and Bloods gangs of Los Angeles. A study by the California Department of Justice estimated that they were over two hundred thirty-six thousand gang members in the state and more than twice that number nationwide.^^

Murders now occur over disputes that in the past would have been considered too trivial to lead to homicide. Killing sprees like the ones perpetrated by the Beltway Snipers and the massacre at Virginia Tech (as well as those at other educational institutions, including high schools such as Columbine) are taking place much more frequently than in the past and producing an ever higher number of victims. The phenomenon of workers suddenly going berserk and killing their fellow employees has led to the coining of a new phrase, "going postal," from the institution where it first manifested.

Certain problems arise out of new technology. One is hacking, a phenomenon that is a product of the digital world. It includes causing thousand-point drops in the stock market, or stealing vital secrets, and has the potential to shut down infrastructures, leaving cities without light or heat.

---

his semi-factual novel *Greenmantle* (1916).

A new gambit is the use of social networks to assemble so-called flash (as in quick) mobs of people at a particular location, Sometimes these are pranks (although those on the receiving end might regard them as criminal mischief) such as simultaneously dispatching five hundred people to a department store furniture section to buy an Oriental rug. In some cities, gangs using social networks have sent mobs roaming through the streets; when police respond, the gang leaders direct their members to move to another location and start up again. At Easter 2010, one such group rampaged through Manhattan looting and shooting. One woman was hit. Digital networks may be to twenty-first-century criminals what cars were to those of the twentieth.

Another possibility is that America will experience a new riot era, more serious than the one in the 1960s. Economic distress has fueled political riots in European cities. Lately, some of these are starting to occur in the United States, as witness such incidents as the occupation of Wall Street in the fall of 2011. This was an event facilitated by the use of social networks and the mobilization of organized cadres and financial supporters. So far they have not exceeded the level of the 1960s. It is possible, though, that the '60s is not the model for what is now happening; rather, it is the 1930s. Back then, street disorder in Germany helped bring down the Weimar Republic. In 1934, riots outside the French parliament came within a few inches of overthrowing the Third Republic. In America the 1934 dock strikes on the West Coast caused the attorney general to urge the president to use the army to break them. In 1937, the sitdown strikes and plant seizures practiced in Europe were employed in the Detroit automobile industry. In the 1960s, American police went through a long period of trial and error in handling disorders. If we are to see a repeat of the 1930s, the same thing would likely happen.[7]

The most probable lever of change will be the declining American economy. The United States cannot continue to spend at the current high levels. This is conceded by politicians and government officials. The present debate is whether to cut expenditures now or wait until a federal stimulus has jumpstarted the economy. In the law-and-order field, we may have already reached a point where municipalities can no longer maintain sizable police forces whose officers are paid six figures and whose retirement and other benefits exceed those of the private sector. The downsizing of police began

---

7. Those who would welcome a situation like the 1930s should be advised to study it more carefully. Had the New Deal failed to cope with the Depression, it would likely have led to the formation of a right-wing government. In the early 1930s, many wealthy and respected citizens called for a man on horseback. One likely candidate at the time was the dashing General Douglas MacArthur, who personally directed his soldiers from horseback when they crushed the Bonus Marchers' 1932 protest in Washington, DC.

even before the 2008 economic recession. New York City, for example, went from over forty thousand cops to thirty-five thousand in eight years.

Given current financial realities and forecasts for the future, it would probably make sense to significantly cut police strength. Unfortunately, one interest group will not cooperate in making the necessary adjustments. That is the criminals. Indeed, their lack of public spirit suggests that if a large number of cops disappear from the streets, the criminals will step up their activities. In addition, if disorder rises to the scale of the 1960s, much less the 1930s, more police will be needed.

At one time, scholars argued that the number of police had no permanent effect on the crime rate. The New York experience of the '90s demonstrated that additional police do make a difference if they adhere to certain caveats: (1) they must operate not simply in a reactive 911 response fashion but a proactive crime fighting one, and (2) community cooperation is important to police effectiveness. A police chief's job is to maintain an appropriate balance between the two. In practice, the efforts to achieve this balance are as difficult as economists trying to obtain the right balance between inflation and deflation.

In 1982, a group of New York state political and civic activists, working in conjunction with then gubernatorial candidate Mario Cuomo, attempted to solve the problem of how to obtain more police without bankrupting government. They designed an ROTC plan which was a variant on short-service officer schemes being considered in other areas of the country. It called for New York and other cities in the state to hire thousands of college graduates to serve for four years as police officers at salary rates below those of regular officers and to receive no pension benefits. In return, the state would pay off their college loans and provide them with the training in problem solving and other skills that would make them attractive to corporate management or elite graduate and professional schools. It was anticipated that some of those organizations would set aside a certain number of places each year for individuals who completed their service.

The plan was not adopted, and the attempts of Adam Walinsky, a former top aide to Senator Robert Kennedy, to sell it nationally met with little success. The principal opposition came from police themselves. Their unions thought it would lead to a general reduction in wages and an eventual total reliance on short-service officers. Police management was less open about its opposition, but many brass feared that a mass of college kids would not fully accept the basic tenets of police management, particularly the strict discipline. In fact, one of the goals of the program was to inject civilian input into policing and, in turn, to ultimately bring police experience into the corporate and professional worlds.

A few critics of the plan argued that ROTC recruits would not perform effectively because they would simply coast through their jobs for four years. The police ROTC program was in fact a description of the U.S. Armed Forces in the era from 1940 to 1975. Then, a mostly draftee army was led by officers and NCOs who were career regulars. Policing would have the advantage that there would be no draftees, since all candidates would be volunteers. Some minority leaders thought that bringing in so many rookies would exacerbate tensions. In actuality, the plan anticipated receiving many minority recruits.

In the long run, unions did not serve their members well by opposing the ROTC plan. Currently, most cops never rise above patrolman's rank. However, in a police force in which regulars constituted perhaps forty percent of the total force and volunteers the rest, virtually all of the former would eventually be promoted to at least a sergeant level or given some special assignment such as a detective's post. With fewer regulars, the department could be more selective about whom it appointed as career cops. Municipal governments could also use some of the cost savings from having many lower-paid short-service cops to increase the wages of the regular force. Ultimately, the greatest beneficiary of a police ROTC plan would probably be the regular cops.

If a police ROTC had been adopted, it might also have triggered other changes, such as a career path for command officers. In that scheme, a police captain who graduated from a national staff college would join a pool of personnel from his own and other departments who had been certified for top positions.

* * * *

A problem that has arisen since the 9/11/01 attack is how to structure police organizations for counterterrorism duties. A proposal that the United States create a security service modeled on Britain's MI5, which is not a law enforcement body, is attractive to many scholars and politicians. Indeed, one sometimes suspects that some proponents envision an exciting career for themselves as a spy master. A U.S. version of MI5 might have been a good idea after World War I or II. However, the public will not accept the idea of security officers who, as in Britain, are unarmed and do not stage raids, slap on the handcuffs, or conduct perp walks. American cops have always looked down on investigators who do not have arrest power or carry firearms. Thus, every conceivable group has sought such authority for its members. A U.S. MI5 would be no different. On the other hand, if it did not make raids and stage perp walks, Congress and the media would declare it a failure. At best, it would become a conventional police force rivaling others already in the field. At worst, it might constitute a secret police force of a type previously unknown to the United States. Better that federal-level security investigations be left to the FBI, whose agents have investigative experience, a grounding in law and are under the overall supervision of Department of Justice attorneys.

Then there is the question of what to do about DHS. If it is not meant to take over the CIA's duty of gathering foreign intelligence or replace the FBI as the main domestic intelligence agency, is its role to simply be a catchall for everything that's left? There have been suggestions that it be divested of some of its tasks and scaled down to performing certain core missions, such as safeguarding national transportation networks and protecting the border and entry points to the United States. As protector of the borders, the agency would be the principal cabinet department dealing with immigration issues.

The United States has never had a European-style ministry of the interior, with authority over the country's police, or maintained a national constabulary of the type found in some countries. However, if an agency like the DHS were headed by an ambitious empire builder, it might seek new missions, such as conducting field patrols in U.S. cities and even subsume an MI5 under its aegis. The current wave of violence perpetrated by Mexican drug cartels may cause some officials to suggest that DHS be used to supplement state and local police in the Southwest. The agency already controls the Border Patrol and customs agents, giving it a base on which to expand. If America is to go that route, it should not be done by simply inserting a paragraph in an omnibus law. Instead, there should be a vigorous national debate so the public will have a true appreciation of what they are getting into—a national security police force with both detective and patrol branches, like the old Soviet KGB.

A better answer may be to strike a balance between federal and state in domestic security. At the operating level, local agencies are the first line of defense. Despite the fact that the DHS has the lead role in airline security, all airports have detachments of state or local police on duty. On 9/11, after a plane crashed into the Pentagon, headquarters for the world's most powerful military machine, the resultant fire was extinguished by the Arlington County, Virginia, fire department. The NYPD, with over forty thousand employees, and departments like Los Angeles and Chicago are too large and important to be shut out of domestic security work. Unlike the feds, local police also have daily contact with ordinary citizens. If people trust their local police, they are very likely to give them information about such things as hidden terror cells.

Regionalization may provide a partial answer to coordination problems. In some states, governors have, or can be given, the authority to assume control of all major law enforcement agencies when serious problems arise. By utilizing interstate compacts, that authority could be extended beyond state boundaries.

An example of the problem of coordination was the series of shootings carried out by the so-called "Beltway Snipers" who in 2002 killed or wounded a number of people in several East Coast states and the District of Columbia. Coordination was left to the Montgomery County, Maryland, police chief rather than a state or federal agency. The result was confusion. A better arrangement would have been to utilize a previously selected individual with the authority to compel all agencies to cooperate and full powers to direct police in specific situations.

In the coming years, police problems are certain to be even more complex than they are today. In the face of terrorist plots, including attacks on our technological infrastructure, the possibility of a new riot era and changes in the nature of conventional crimes, a major overhaul is necessary in the structure of American policing. The Blue Parade will march on, but it will likely do so in different formations with different types of leaders.

APPENDICES

Appendix A

Crimes of the Century: The Top 10 Criminal Investigations Since 1945

Appendix B

Top Cops: The 10 Most Important Police Administrators Since 1945

Appendix C

Understanding Police Terminology

Appendix A

Crimes of the Century:
The Top 10 Criminal Investigations Since 1945

In selecting the crimes for analysis, I chose those that were of greatest significance, laying special emphasis on the detective work in each and what, if any, impact the case had on the public's impression of policing. For example, the Dahlia and the Zodiac killings lessened confidence in the efficiency of law enforcement.

Although most true crime books concentrate on murder cases, some of the most challenging investigations are those involving major property crimes. Unlike murderers, who are often seriously disturbed, property criminals are generally normal and many of them possess skills that, if applied to legitimate occupations, would allow them to make a very good living. However, they prefer criminal activity. Often solving major loss-property crimes is a better indicator of a detective bureau's competence than a high homicide clearance rate, in which ninety percent of the cases are "smoking gun" affairs, where the killer is standing over the victim holding the murder weapon when the cops arrive. In contrast, robbers and burglars do not wait at the scene for the police to show up. This is why the crime clearance rate is often eighty or more percent for homicide and only fifteen or twenty percent for burglary and robbery. Thieves also operate within a milieu of other thieves, which provides them both cover and established channels for disposing of stolen goods. Murderers (unless they are professional hitmen) are left to their own devices.[1]

The Top Ten

The Kennedy Assassination, Dallas, Texas, 1963

The Crime

On November 22, 1963, President John F. Kennedy, riding through the streets of Dallas, Texas, in the backseat of his open limousine, was shot and killed and Texas governor John Connally, who was sitting in front of him, was seriously wounded. A sixth-floor window in the nearby Texas Book Depository was pointed out as the place where the shots came from. Police recovered

---

1. Full disclosure: My view about the difficulty of property crime investigations is probably influenced by the time I spent as commander of the largest burglary investigation squad in the United States.

a rifle there and from workers received the name of a suspect, Lee Harvey Oswald. That afternoon Oswald was arrested for killing a Dallas police officer who had attempted to question him. Following an interrogation by detectives, he was charged with the murder of the president. On November 24th, two days after the shooting of President Kennedy, Oswald was murdered in police headquarters by Jack Ruby, while a national television audience watched.

The Investigation

Neither the Secret Service nor the FBI had jurisdiction because the murder of a president was not then a federal crime. The investigation was carried out by the Dallas Police Department. In the context of the events, this was a mistake. The investigation of a president's murder may well touch on state secrets that cannot be revealed to persons without proper clearance. After Oswald was killed, the Dallas police department itself fell under suspicion for allowing Jack Ruby free run of police headquarters and because Ruby ran a strip club that was frequented by many police officers.

The only possible remedy was for Congress to pass and the president to sign emergency legislation giving jurisdiction to federal authorities. The United States government should have then appointed a special prosecutor, preferably from outside the federal service, to lead the investigation, and granted him authority to draw on all resources of the U.S. government and to retain any necessary outside talent.

Instead, Ruby was handled by Dallas police and prosecutors and the broader investigation was turned over to a commission composed of Washington insiders, known by the name of its chairman, Chief Justice Earl Warren. At least two of its members, J. Edgar Hoover, the director of the FBI, and Allen Dulles, former director of the CIA, withheld information from the Commission that would have been embarrassing to their agencies.

The Aftermath

Although the Warren Commission found that Oswald acted alone, over the years doubts have been voiced about that conclusion, and today many people do not accept the findings. Questions have arisen about every aspect of the case. Even those who concede that Oswald was the shooter do not believe that he acted alone. Various organizations and individuals are alleged to have been behind the attack. For example, it was suspected that Ruby was a Mafia hitman.

To date the findings of the Warren Commission have not been disproven, while counter-theories have been found to contain many holes. For example, if the mob killed Kennedy, why is there no mention of it on any of the many bugs and wiretaps the FBI planted on various mafiosi both before and after November 22, 1963?

It is doubtful that the Kennedy assassination will ever be solved to general satisfaction. The lesson of the case for law enforcement is that an investigation of that magnitude has to be done with an eye to history. In 1963, from the Dallas Police Department through the FBI up to the Washington insiders on the Warren Commission and the president who appointed them, everyone had a possible conflict of interest. At the time, though, there was no mechanism to resolve this problem.

The Disappearance of Jimmy Hoffa, Detroit, Michigan, 1975

The Crime

On July 30, 1975, when sixty-two-year-old James Riddle Hoffa left his vacation home in Lake Orion, Michigan, he told his wife, Josephine, he was meeting someone at 2 p.m. at the Machus Red Fox Restaurant in Bloomfield, a suburb of Detroit. When he did not return home, a worried Mrs. Hoffa began phoning Jimmy's friends. The next morning she notified the Bloomfield Township Police Department, which quickly located Hoffa's green Pontiac in the restaurant's parking lot. An examination of Hoffa's office appointment book showed a listing on July 30: "2:30 p.m., Fox rest Tony G." Tony G. was assumed to be Anthony Giacalone, *aka* "Tony Jack," a Detroit mob capo long associated with Hoffa.

The Investigation

In the Hoffa case, acting under the provisions of the federal anti-kidnapping statute, the FBI took over the case. Suspicion immediately focused on the possibility that Hoffa had been murdered to silence him. In 1967, he had begun serving a thirteen year prison sentence. When he was paroled in 1971, one of the provisions of his release was that he not hold union office until 1980. At the time of his disappearance, Hoffa was fighting to void this restriction and was engaged in a war with his former friends, which included incidents such as a car bombing. By 1975 there were strong rumors that the courts would overturn the provision barring his return to office. If so, Hoffa could seek to regain the union presidency. Jimmy began warning his opponents that once he was back in power, he would reveal the corrupt dealings between the mob and union leaders that occurred while he was away.

Among the leading suspects in the case, besides Giacalone, was Tony Provenzano, a New Jersey mobster who had once been a close ally of Hoffa but by 1975 was his bitter enemy. At the time of Hoffa's disappearance, both Giacalone and Provenzano made sure they were in places where a number of people observed their presence so that they had an alibi. Some federal investigators believed that Hoffa was tricked into coming to the Red Fox on the promise that he would meet with Giacalone and other top figures. Instead, some of Provenzano's strong-arm men kidnapped Hoffa, killed him and disposed of his body, although there is no agreement on the exact details of when and where he was killed or who did it. However, government agents claim that the persons responsible for Hoffa's disappearance have been punished by being convicted of other crimes.

The Aftermath

Other than a few theorists who always argue that the real culprit in any political crime is the U.S. government, most people have accepted the notion that Hoffa was murdered by the Mafia to keep him from talking, although no one has yet been charged with abducting or murdering him. Had his body been found, a confession obtained from one or more of the perpetrators, followed by a conviction for murder, the case would be regarded as successfully resolved. However, because organized criminals were good at making bodies disappear and keeping their mouths shut, that did not happen. Thus, some writers and media outlets have put forth dubious accounts of how the murder was carried out, who committed it and where the body is buried. Over time all such claims have been rejected. If the case had occurred in the 1990s, when even Mafia bosses were blabbing secrets to the government, investigators might have been able to obtain a full resolution of the case.

The Disappearance of D. B. Cooper, Oregon, 1971

The Crime

The day before Thanksgiving in 1971, a man identifying himself as Dan Cooper boarded a Northwest Airline plane in Portland, Oregon. He appeared to be an ordinary passenger wearing a suit and tie. He gave the stewardess an order for a bourbon and soda. Then shortly after takeoff, he handed a note to the stewardess which said: "I have a bomb in my briefcase. You are being hijacked." He demanded two hundred thousand dollars in unmarked bills and two parachutes.

When the plane landed at Seattle-Tacoma Airport, Cooper exchanged the hostages on the plane for the money and parachutes and told the flight crew to take off for Mexico and fly low at minimum speed. Thirty minutes into the flight, Cooper lowered a backstair of the airplane, bailed out and was never seen again. In 1976 a Portland grand jury indicted John Doe, *aka* Dan Cooper, for air piracy, ensuring that the statute of limitations would not expire. Because of a misreading of his handwriting, Dan Cooper has come down to us as D. B. Cooper, the name under which he has acquired a modest degree of fame.

The Investigation

Searches of the area where Cooper parachuted produced nothing. The terrain is rugged, and of the type whereby, if he had been killed upon impact, his body might never be found. Despite a sketch of him released to the public, no credible information about his identity has ever turned up—although, from time to time, individuals, looking for their fifteen minutes of fame, or financial rewards, make claims in the case.

From an investigative standpoint, it is unlikely that Cooper was a skilled professional criminal. Even in 1971, two hundred thousand dollars was not so large an amount of money that pros would be willing to jump out of an airplane for it. The fact that he used a parachute suggests he may have been trained in the military and possibly knew the Pacific Northwest because he was once stationed there. However it is not likely that a veteran paratrooper would have jumped into the rain and high winds that prevailed at the time. In 1971, a comic book character known as Dan Cooper of the Royal Canadian Air Force, was popular in France. The hijacker did not speak with a foreign accent, but he may have become familiar with the Cooper character during service in Europe.

The Aftermath

The public attention paid to the Cooper case owes largely to his unusual method of escape. The puzzling feature is that the FBI has never received any solid information as to his identity or whereabouts. If he had been a professional criminal, it is likely that underworld sources, looking to cut a deal for themselves, would have informed on him. If he was an amateur, some friend or relative might have turned him in for the reward or for personal reasons. However, if he was a drifter, out of touch with family or friends, and was killed or escaped and went to some distant location, no one might miss him.

Conversely, he might have been a respected figure, like an officer of a small bank in trouble who no one suspected to be a criminal.

Despite the oft quoted statement that there is no such thing a perfect crime, only an imperfect investigation, the Cooper case may be one of those instances where, barring a lucky break, there will never be a solution.

The Brinks Holdup, Boston, Massachusetts, 1950

The Crime

The eleven Boston locals who attacked the Brinks headquarters in that city on the night of January 17, 1950, were professional criminals, though not top-drawer ones. They studied the Brinks headquarters, in Boston's North End, for eighteen months, yet their plan was amateurish. There were too many people involved, making it likely that when faced with pressure, one or more would be willing to cut a deal with law enforcement. Another was that things might go wrong if the guards put up a fight. As it turned out, the guards did not resist and the thieves made off with over two and a half million dollars in cash and checks—a sum that would be equivalent to ten times that amount today.

The Investigation

The Boston police and the FBI conducted the investigation. The two organizations were normally on bad terms, and during the six years during which the case dragged on, the relationship grew worse. Eventually investigators zeroed in on some of those who were involved. The gang had agreed not to spend the money until after the statute of limitations had run out and not to commit fresh crimes. However, rumors that those holding the money were siphoning it off led to conflict within the gang, and two of the robbers committed a burglary in Pennsylvania for which they were apprehended. The judge in the Pennsylvania court was made aware of the Boston situation, and he imposed a very stiff sentence to encourage the defendants' cooperation.

When one of the thieves showed signs of breaking with the others, a New York hitman was brought in to deal with him. He managed to wound Joseph "Specs" O'Keefe with a blast from a machine gun, but it did not kill him. O'Keefe then cut a deal with the feds for a four-year sentence and gave away his accomplices. All were convicted, given life sentences and served an average of fourteen years. Some of the proceeds of the robbery had been spent but the bulk of the money was never accounted for and only fifty thousand dollars was recovered. The best guess is that it was fenced at about twenty cents on the dollar and, therefore, with legal expenses, etc., the gang made nothing from the caper.

The Aftermath

The Brinks robbery might have been solved quickly if the FBI had been in sole charge of the case; but because the robbery was a state crime, the Boston cops could assert primary jurisdiction. In other locales, the local police might have been happy to play a subsidiary role to the FBI. In Boston, relations were so bad that would never happen. Thus there was virtually no cooperation between the two governmental law enforcement agencies. Another complicating factor was that some Boston police officers were thought to have had previous dealings with some of the robbers.

In the end, the authorities, particularly the FBI and its director, J. Edgar Hoover, could not allow criminals to get away with such a large robbery. So they were bound to utilize their full resources, spend nearly thirty million dollars and make whatever deal was necessary in order to crack the case. If the robbers had been more sophisticated, they would have realized this from the beginning.

Gardner Museum Robbery, Boston, Massachusetts, 1990

The Crime

The Isabella Stewart Gardner Museum, in Boston's Fenway area, was founded by its patron in 1903 as a repository for priceless European and American paintings as well as other artifacts. In the early morning hours of March 18, 1990 (following Boston's great St. Patrick's Day holiday), there were only two guards on duty at the museum. When two supposed Boston cops came to the security door, a guard broke the rules and let them in. One of the alleged policemen told the guard at the security desk that he recognized him as a man wanted on an arrest warrant and he should walk out from behind the desk to where the officer was. The guard should have pressed the alarm button to summon police and alert the other guard on duty in the building. Instead, he complied with the "policeman's" request and was taken prisoner. His captors then had him summon the other guard, and both men's hands, feet and heads were duct-taped to some pipes. They were not discovered until the next morning, when another guard arrived to relieve them.

An inventory of the losses included a number of priceless paintings by artists of renown such as Rembrandt and Degas. The total value of the stolen material has been placed as high as half a billion dollars. The museum has offered a five-million-dollar reward for information leading to its recovery.

The Investigation

The Boston police and the FBI specialized art recovery squad both conducted investigations. Forty years earlier, the police and FBI had feuded over the Brinks investigation. An even worse feud was going on at the time of the museum robbery. Local and state police believed that the FBI was shielding a notorious Boston criminal, James "Whitey" Bulger (whose brother was the powerful president of the Massachusetts senate). It was alleged that in previous investigations of Bulger the Bureau had misled detectives or stonewalled them.

In 1974 the Irish Republican Army (IRA) stole nineteen paintings from a gallery near Dublin, Ireland. Supposedly they were going to use the paintings to bargain for the release of some IRA members. In the '90s, two associates of Bulger claimed to have access to the paintings through ties with the IRA in gun-smuggling deals.

In 1995, Bulger fled Boston, as he was about to be indicted for murder. At the time, there were allegations that he had been tipped off by his friends in the FBI and that there would be no real attempt made to find him. Later, some agents were criminally charged in murder cases.

The Aftermath

Whitey Bulger was not located until 2010, when an informant, seeking the two-million-dollar reward, led the FBI to him. At the time, he was living with a girlfriend in California. During the investigation of the museum theft, Bulger was so powerful that he was likely to have at least known who was involved. Given Bulger's present age (eighty-two) and magnitude of the case against him, he may spend the rest of his life in prison. So there is no incentive for him to cut a deal by providing information on the museum robbery in return for leniency. Thus the most likely place to seek information on the crime is in the international art-theft world. If so, U.S. foreign intelligence agencies are probably in the best position to find a solution.

The Black Dahlia Case, Los Angeles, 1947

The Crime

In January 1947, the body of twenty-two-year-old Elizabeth Short was discovered in a vacant lot in Los Angeles. Short had been cut in two at the waist and her face had been slashed from ear to ear. A little over a week after the murder, someone (possibly the murderer) sent an editor of the *Los Angeles Examiner* some of Short's personal effects.

The crime has become an American legend. At first glance, it is not clear why. A number of young women, some of them horribly mutilated, are found every year in America. Why, then, does this case continue to fascinate writers, filmmakers and the public? The answer is Hollywood. If Short had been found in Sioux City, Iowa, she would have been quickly forgotten. A year before the killing, Paramount had released a murder mystery entitled *The Blue Dahlia,* starring Alan Ladd and Veronica Lake. Since 1947, the Black Dahlia has been a frequent subject or inspiration for Hollywood and TV movies.

The Investigation

On the surface the case should not have been difficult to solve. The killer was probably not a stranger. Investigation of Short's background disclosed that she had known various men. While there were rumors that she had been a prostitute, she was more likely what, in the wartime era, was called a "V (for victory) Girl," one looking for good times and willing to do anything for servicemen. There have been many theories and suspects in the case. Every time it is mentioned, someone either confesses to the crime or names the supposed offender. The famed Los Angeles detective John St. John, who worked on the case, remarked: "It is amazing how many people offer up a relative as the killer."

Some people have blamed the media for the failure to solve the case. A brief but brilliant portrait of how the Los Angeles press handled murder cases back then is contained in the Oscar-winning 1950 film *Sunset Boulevard.* At the scene of a murder, the real-life syndicated columnist Hedda Hopper takes over and begins barking commands to everybody, including the police. One reporter later claimed, "If the [Dahlia] murder was never solved, it was because of the reporters... they were all over, trampling evidence, withholding information..... [They] roamed freely through the department's offices, sat at officer's desks and answered their phones. Many tips from the public were not passed on to the police as the reporters who received them rushed out to get 'scoops.'"

The Aftermath

The failure to solve the case caused the public to criticize the LAPD and was a factor in bringing about a fundamental change in the department. Un-doubtedly the crime will be solved in the same way that the somewhat similar London Jack the Ripper case has been solved—between the covers of books. The problem is that every author names a different killer as the Ripper: a deranged doctor, a royal prince, Russian secret agents testing Scotland Yard, etc. Steve Hodel, a former LAPD detective, has written a book in which he has made a strong case that his physician father was the killer.

The Son of Sam Killings, New York City, 1976–77

The Crime

In New York City, between July 1976 and July 1977, a gunman killed six people and wounded seven more in eight separate incidents. The shooter prowled the streets of the city's outer boroughs at night, choosing young women as his targets. In some instances they were alone, in others with another girl or a male escort. The weapon he used was a .44-caliber "bulldog" revolver.

The first shooting took place in July 1976 in the Bronx. There one young woman was killed and another wounded. The second occurred in Queens in October, when the male escort was badly wounded. In November the killer wounded two women in Queens. In January 1977, he struck at an engaged couple in Queens, killing the woman. In March, he shot and killed a young woman on a Queens street.

The Investigation

Only after seven people had been shot did the NYPD begin to discern a pattern to the crimes. Two days after the March killing, the mayor and the police brass held a press conference, linking two of the cases through the use of the .44-caliber weapon. The next day they formed a special task force to carry out the investigation. In April 1977 the murderer returned to the Bronx, where he killed a man and a woman. By now the city was in panic mode. Hundreds of suspects were checked out. A theory that the gunman liked to shoot long-haired girls caused many women to cut or put up their hair.

While the hunt went on, the killer was sending letters to journalists and police officials claiming that he was instructed to carry out the shootings by a dog, acting at the direction of a man named Sam. In one letter he signed himself "Son of Sam." Because of the phrasing and certain literary allusions in several communications, some people suspected the shooter was an educated person, even some kind of artist.

By June there had not been a "Son of Sam" shooting for more than two months. Then, on the 26th, he shot at a young man and woman in Queens. Both were hit but their injuries were minor. On July 31, a year after he had begun, "Son of Sam," as he was now called, shot a man and a woman sitting in a parked car in Brooklyn. The woman died, and the man lost one eye and most of his vision in the other one. This time a number of people noticed a suspicious-looking man loitering in the vicinity. One woman reported seeing him remove a parking ticket from the windshield of a Ford Galaxy sedan parked near a fire hydrant. Police determined which officer had written the ticket and they traced the car license to David Berkowitz, who resided in the Westchester County suburb of Yonkers. Initially they assumed he might have witnessed the shooting. When the NYPD contacted the Yonkers police, they were shocked to learn that the local officers knew him as an oddball who was suspected of committing various strange acts.

NYPD detectives went to Yonkers and spotted the Ford Galaxy with a rifle in the back seat, waited until Berkowitz emerged from his house and seized him. His first words were reported to be "You got me. What took you so long?" Berkowitz was found to be acquainted with a man named Sam who had a dog whose barking apparently annoyed Berkowitz.

The Aftermath

To the disappointment of many people, Berkowitz was not an intellectual or an artist but a postal clerk. He was convicted and given multiple life sentences. Over the past thirty-plus years, the public has accepted that he is the killer, and because the case was solved, the criticism of the authorities has been limited. However, it is possible he might have been captured sooner if the police had been able to identify a pattern more quickly.

The Georgia Child Murders, Metropolitan Atlanta, 1979–1981

The Crime

Between July 1979 and March 1981, twenty-three African-American children went missing and were later found dead in the Atlanta, Georgia, metropolitan area. Not until a year after the case began did the television networks begin to pay any attention to it, and it never aroused anywhere near the public interest of the Son of Sam murders.

The Investigation

Some reporters pointed out flaws in the police investigation, alleging that a task force had failed to follow up on many leads provided by the public. The main agency in the case was the Atlanta police department, whose chief was Lee Brown, then in the early stages of his career. Although Brown was a competent police administrator, some people felt he was not forceful enough in directing the investigation.

Because physical evidence was being collected from the victims, investigators suspected that the killer would soon start depositing his victims in bodies of water. Police staked out a bridge over the Chattahoochee River between Atlanta, in Fulton County, and suburban Cobb County. On May 22, 1981, after an officer near the bridge heard a splash in the water below, he observed a white 1970 Chevrolet station wagon slowly driving away. An Atlanta patrol car and an unmarked vehicle containing federal agents followed and stopped the station wagon about half a mile from the bridge. The driver was twenty-three-year-old Wayne Bertram Williams, a freelance photographer. Williams claimed he was on his way to Cobb County to meet a woman on business. Police could never find any trace of her. Two days later the body of a twenty-seven-year-old man was found floating down the river a few miles from the bridge where Williams had stopped his car. The medical examiner determined the body had been in the river for no more than forty-eight hours. Police believe that Williams had killed the man and disposed of his body. Williams was identified by witnesses as having been seen with some of the other victims. There were also hairs from Williams' dog, found in his car, which matched similar hairs on some victims. In June 1981 a grand jury indicted Williams for first-degree murder in the deaths of two of the children killed. In 1982, after only eleven hours of deliberation, a jury found him guilty of two murders. He was sentenced to consecutive life terms in the Georgia State Prison.

The Aftermath

The fact that so many murders were committed in one metropolitan area over a relatively short period of time did not speak well for local detective operations. Even after Williams' conviction, many people were not certain that he had committed all of the murders, and a few believed he hadn't committed any. As late as 2005, the DeKalb County Georgia police chief ordered the reopening of the investigation of the murders of five boys who had been killed in his county. The chief announced that he thought Williams might have been innocent in those and other murders. The following year, the county police dropped the investigation.

In 2007 the State of Georgia agreed to allow DNA testing of the dog hair that was used to convict Williams. The tests failed to exonerate him. Prosecutors asserted that the results actually linked Williams to the killings. Defense lawyers called the results inconclusive. Thirty years after his original arrest, Williams remains in prison.

The Zodiac Killer, Northern California, 1968–69

The Crime

Between December 1968 and October 1969, an individual who called himself the Zodiac murdered two men and three women in Northern California. Generally he found his victims in secluded areas that might be described as "lovers' lanes." All were young (between sixteen and twenty-nine). During this time he sent letters to the newspapers identifying himself as Zodiac and providing details of the crimes not publicly known. On occasion, he included cryptograms which he claimed would reveal his identity, although when one was solved, it did not.

The first case occurred in December 1968, in Benicia, California, where the Zodiac supposedly shot and killed a teenage boy and a teenage girl. On July 4, 1969, in Vallejo, California, he killed a girl and wounded her male escort. In August, newspapers received letters from Zodiac claiming that the motive for his killings was to make the victims slaves in his afterlife. In September 1969, there was another shooting, at a lake in Napa County. Again the girl died but the man survived. After this attack, an unknown man phoned the police and described the two earlier attacks and claimed credit for the recent one.

The Investigation

The investigation went into high gear after the Zodiac extended his area of operations to the city of San Francisco. In October 1969, a passenger, believed to be the Zodiac, shot and killed the driver of a cab. Two blocks from the scene, police officers noticed a white man walking. Because the police dispatcher broadcast an incorrect description that the suspect was nonwhite, they did not stop him. Next the supposed Zodiac spoke to prominent lawyer Marvin Belli by phone on a TV show. The two men agreed to meet, but Zodiac did not show up.

The Aftermath

The murders have never been solved. One suspect who was investigated by the Vallejo police was actually served with search warrants for his residence, although no arrest followed. He died in 1992. DNA tests later tended to rule him out as a suspect. Though never confirmed, Zodiac has been a suspect in other murders and assaults.

A number of persons have named members of their family as the Zodiac. In one case a woman said that her father was the killer, but she also claimed that she was the illegitimate daughter of President Kennedy. The police detective who identified his own father as the Dahlia murderer also claimed that he was probably the Zodiac killer. It is unlikely the case will be solved because over forty years has passed since the last killing.

JonBenét Ramsey, Boulder Colorado, 1996

The Crime

Although the murder of 23 children in Atlanta did not receive overwhelming attention, one child's murder in Colorado got plenty.[2] On December 26, 1996, Patricia "Patsy" Ramsey, the wife of a successful businessman in the upscale resort town of Boulder, allegedly found a note on the staircase of her home. It purported to come from a foreign group and claimed that they had kidnapped Mrs. Ramsey's six-year-old daughter, JonBenét. They demanded a one-hundred eighteen-thousand-dollar ransom for her release. That was the exact amount of the bonus check that Mr. Ramsey had received earlier in the year. Despite instructions to the contrary in the note, Mrs. Ramsey notified the police. In a search of the Ramsey house, the body of six-year-old JonBenét was found. She had a cord around her neck and her wrists were tied. An autopsy determined that she had been strangled and her head had been badly injured.

The Investigation

It was alleged later that in the initial investigation, police made several mistakes. For example, they did not secure the crime scene and allowed family and friends free access to the house. Mr. Ramsey and two friends were told to search the house, and in doing so they discovered JonBenét's body in a wine cellar in the basement. It was also alleged that the investigating officers did not perform requisite forensic tests. Instead, early on, they formed the opinion that Mr. or Mrs. Ramsey or their nine-year-old son had killed JonBenét. Supporting this hypothesis was the fact that no signs of forcible entry were found and the Ramseys did not seem eager to cooperate with the investigation.

An item that gripped the American public was that Patsy Ramsey, a former beauty contest winner, had entered JonBenét in many beauty pageants (including some that the mother was affiliated with) and made the girl up like a sexy Miss America rather than a six-year-old child. The fact that the family moved to Atlanta, not long after the murder, also cast them in a bad light. Some investigators believed that the author of the ransom note was Patricia Ramsey herself, but they could not prove it. In 1999, the governor of Colorado

---

2. Which is not to argue that the Colorado murder did not deserve attention, but the ones in Georgia also should have become well known nationally.

declared that the parents of JonBenét should "quit hiding behind their attorneys, quit hiding behind their PR firm."

The Aftermath

Despite mainstream investigative opinion, some of those who worked on the case did not believe that Mrs. Ramsey had killed her daughter. They leaned toward the notion that the murder was committed by an intruder. A confession was received from one such individual, but when it was checked out, it did not hold up.

Gradually opinion swung away from the police suspicions to the notion that the Ramseys were innocent. In 2009, the district attorney of Boulder County issued a formal statement exonerating the family in the case. In 2006, Patsy Ramsey died at the age of forty-nine. She is buried in a Georgia cemetery alongside her daughter. To date, no murder charges have been filed in the case.

The case is recent enough that someone may come forward with information leading to the killer.

Summary

Based on the top ten cases, some generalizations might be offered about major criminal investigations. Only three of the ten examined—the Brinks robbery, the Hoffa disappearance[3] and the Son of Sam—have been solved to the satisfaction of the public, and those took an inordinate amount of time to break.

The delay in the Brinks case should not have occurred. If the police and the FBI had worked together instead of being bitter rivals, the investigation might have gone more smoothly. Instead the break came nearly six years later after one of the gang fell out with his partners and they tried to have him killed.

In Son of Sam, the size of the area over which he operated and the decentralized nature of the NYPD may have been the reason police were slow to recognize a pattern. A smaller police force, with a central homicide squad, might have picked up the pattern earlier. Although the police were beginning to focus on David Berkowitz as the killer, the case was solved by the lucky break of a woman witnessing him removing the parking ticket.

---

3. Although *solved* it was not *cleared* by arrest.

In the Hoffa disappearance, the fact that the body was probably disposed of immediately, and the discipline of the Mafia in those times, accounts for the failure to charge someone with the crime.

Some cases have been officially solved, but much of the public does not accept the finding. In the murder of President Kennedy, too many important leaders and institutions protected state secrets and/or their own hides. Later, when this was revealed, it caused many people to doubt the findings of the report. This was in part due to the fact that it is hard to accept that an obscure sociopath could kill the most powerful man in the world. It is easier to believe that a powerful international group like the Mafia was able to do the job. Half a century later, no real evidence has been found to refute the Warren Commission's findings.

In the D. B. Cooper extortion, the problem was probably that he was either a loner whom few people knew anything about or of such status that no one would suspect him to be a criminal.

In the JonBenét Ramsey investigation, the local police department was too small to be able to handle a case of that importance and complexity.[4] In the initial stages, investigators focused so strongly on Patsy Ramsey they probably felt they were within inches of breaking it. When the case appeared to be at a standstill, the locals were still reluctant to step aside.

The Black Dahlia case was investigated by a police department just emerging from second-rate status. It allowed journalists to virtually take over the proceedings. Many of them may have alerted the killer by their own inquiries or withheld vital information from the police.

The Gardner Museum case in Boston was probably directed from abroad. It might have been expected, though, that there would have been rumbles in the Boston underworld. At the time Whitey Bulger was riding high, and this may have dried up the flow of information.

The Zodiac case was spread across several jurisdictions, complicating the police efforts. No strong hand directed the total investigation.

The investigation of the Atlanta child murders also involved a number of jurisdictions, and it was generally thought that the police investigation was deficient. Even after there had been an arrest, some law enforcement officers did not believe that Williams was guilty of the crimes—although, in thirty years, nothing has turned up to exonerate him.

---

4. According to one writer on the Ramsey case, the Boulder PD had only sixteen detectives to handle all criminal investigations and the unit commander had never before directed a homicide probe. In New York or Chicago a case of that magnitude might have had fifty detectives assigned to it and the commander, as well some of his detectives, would probably have handled at least a score of murders each.

Two major problems emerge from the foregoing cases.

Investigative

The organization of the investigative effort may be flawed, or a particular agency may have problems such as conflict of interest or lack of resources. In multi-jurisdiction cases such as the Zodiac killings and the Atlanta child murders, it was to be expected that the various agencies involved would not work as a single entity. In the Brinks and Gardner Museum robberies, relations between the FBI and police meant that they would not work well together. In the Kennedy assassination, the FBI kept secret its own problems with Oswald. This suggests that in such instances a single individual should be placed in complete charge of the case. At the state level, this might be an assistant attorney general (as was done in Massachusetts during the hunt for the Boston strangler) or, at the federal level, an assistant United States attorney.

Given the traditions of American policing, however, there is reluctance for agencies to yield to rivals or outsiders. Often when a task force is formed, all parties simply agree to keep out of each other's way, which is quite different from cooperating. The best way to handle a task force situation is not to form one after a crime has occurred but to have a permanent body in existence that takes charge in certain cases. In most metropolitan areas, there are sufficient multi-jurisdiction crimes to justify the permanent existence of such a body.

Media Coverage

Heavy media coverage is a two-edged sword. It can help or hurt an investigation. In the Black Dahlia murder, the media overpowered the police investigation. Conversely, in the Cooper airline heist, heavy national publicity might have provided some useful tips. Under the First Amendment, journalists cannot be denied the right to gather news. The best way to deal with them is to establish good working relationships beforehand. In the Son of Sam case, several reporters withheld stories at the request of the NYPD. The quid pro quo was that when an arrest was about to be made they would receive advance notice and their stories would be out first. In dealing with the media, it is always useful have an astute police public relations official who has built up a high level of trust and confidence with journalists.

Appendix B

Top Cops:
The 10 Most Important Police Administrators Since 1945

The following list does not purport to name the ten best American police chiefs in the postwar era. There is no way I could know that. The best police administrator in America might have been a small-town chief in the 1950s, but no one outside his own community ever heard of him. Our criterion here is who the most important chiefs were from a national standpoint. That leaves out the locally powerful Frank Rizzo of Philadelphia, because his influence did not extend beyond his own metropolitan area. Two chiefs I never met, but often heard spoken of as outstanding, were Robert Igleburger of Dayton, Ohio, and Pete Ronstadt (brother of singer Linda Ronstadt) of Tucson, Arizona. Neither was a national figure. On the other hand, William Webster was not a professional police officer, but the nine years he spent as director of the FBI resolved many of the post-Hoover and Watergate troubles of the Bureau and restored some of the standing of America's most important law enforcement agency.

Undoubtedly many people will disagree with my choices. Some may even be angry because their names were left off the list. I recall once, when I was meeting with two high-ranking NYPD chiefs, I casually asked them, "Who was the best police commissioner in your time?" After a lot of conversation, the answer each gave was, in essence, that he was, but he never got the job.

The careers of all ten have been described in the previous chapters. In the brief profiles that follow, I try to sketch their careers and management styles, and evaluate their national importance.

J. Edgar Hoover, Director of the FBI, 1924–1972

Career

By 1945, J. Edgar Hoover had already served twenty-eight years in the United States Department of Justice, twenty-one of them as head of the FBI. Before 1933, he was largely unknown to the public. Afterward he became a living legend. His acclaim was based on two accomplishments. In the 1930s, his G-men shot or captured the high-profile killers and bank robbers spawned by the end of Prohibition and the onset of the Depression. In the 1940s, the FBI took the lead in arresting Nazi spies and saboteurs. Behind the scenes, Hoover forged a close alliance with President Roosevelt.

Management Style

Hoover's greatest strength was his administrative ability. It was not easy to maintain tight control over an organization with several thousand employees engaged in sensitive investigations. The potential for scandal or failure was always very great. In Hoover's case, it was multiplied by the fact that his agency's operations stretched from Latin America to Alaska. His style was to rule by fear. Every member of the Bureau either adhered to the rules, formal or informal, of "Mr. Hoover" or was fired.

During his tenure, Hoover actually had two jobs. He was the chief national criminal detective and also head of domestic security policing. The tasks differ and in most countries are not administered by a single person. Wearing both hats was in some ways an advantage for Hoover. He was able to use information gathered in criminal investigations to enhance his agency's security work, and vice versa. The mere existence of his confidential files ensured that many officials and private citizens would bow to his demands.

Evaluation

Hoover's greatest mistake was that he stayed too long at the dance. In the 1950s, he dragged his feet at pursuing the bosses of organized crime because he feared that their political friends would retaliate against the Bureau. In the '60s, his handling of civil rights investigations and his reaction to the social changes of the time were largely influenced by his distaste for ideas that he could never accept. It is ironic that a man who so valued his own image ended up engaging in actions that would tarnish it in the future. Had he retired in 1960 (or, better yet, 1945), his reputation would be much higher than it is today.

William H. Parker,
Chief, Los Angeles Police Department, 1950–1966

Career

Given Parker's honesty and rigid moral code, his willingness to serve in the corrupt Los Angeles Police Department in the 1920s and '30s is difficult to explain. Probably he realized that one day there would be a change and he would rise to the top. However, he went along with the system to the extent of working as an aide to a corrupt police chief. Finally, when the reformers took control of the city at the end of the 1930s, Parker began to move up rapidly, becoming an inspector and deputy chief. By 1950 it was obvious that, among eligible candidates, he was the man best qualified to remake the LAPD.

Management Style

When Parker took over the LAPD, it was still a second-rate operation. He turned it into the best police department in the United States. It recruited on a merit basis, trained its officers better than other forces and policed its territory effectively with a proportionally smaller complement than comparable cities. Atty. Gen. Robert Kennedy was among many observers who thought Parker might make a very good successor to J. Edgar Hoover. Parker certainly had some of the Hooverian qualities, such as extreme protectiveness of his turf, a propensity to spiteful behavior when challenged, the maintenance of private files on VIPs and an autocratic management style. Parker's problem was that, on his watch, Los Angeles changed from a town of migrant Midwestern farmers and conservative local businessmen to an increasingly minority city with a liberal elite.

Parker feuded with the press, the courts and other law enforcement agencies. His cops often employed hard-line tactics in making arrests and field stops. In 1965, the Watts riot revealed that the country's leading police force could not handle large-scale civil disorder, whereas, the previous year, both New York and Philadelphia had managed to do so. At the time, suffering from the heart trouble that would kill him the following year, Parker remained in his office issuing confusing orders while the Watts riot raged.

Evaluation

Like Hoover, Parker had stayed at the dance too long. He should have left around 1960. Instead, he remained in office but failed to comprehend, much less come to grips with, the new trends in American society, and his attempt to maintain the status quo placed the LAPD on the wrong side of history.

O. W. Wilson, Chicago Police Superintendent, 1960–1967

Career

Wilson's rise came about because he was a protégé of Chief August Vollmer, who for many years was leader of the police reform movement. Wilson started out as a Berkeley cop in the early 1920s. After receiving his degree in police studies from the local university, he began to carry on Vollmer's work of promoting police professionalism. From 1928 to 1939, he headed the Wichita, Kansas, police department. From 1950 to 1960, as dean of the school of criminology at the University of California, Berkeley, and author of the leading textbook on police administration, Wilson was the generally acknowledged intellectual leader in the field. He had no desire to leave the college, but a new university administration believed that Wilson and his school were doing insufficient scholarly work. In 1960, realizing that his days at Berkeley were numbered, he jumped at the offer to head the Chicago Police Department, which was then reeling from a massive scandal.

Management Style

The heart of Wilson's system of professional police administration was centralized control; but unlike Hoover or Parker, Wilson was not a martinet nor would he stoop to blackmail to gain his way. Although machine-ruled Chicago seemed like a strange place for a police reformer, he started out well. When he arrived, the police department was still operating as it had in the 1930s. Wilson was able to increase the number of police officers, provide better working conditions and higher salaries, and introduce the latest management techniques. However, because he had never been a member of a big-city police force, he did not really understand how one worked. He could not see behind the masks worn by some of his subordinates or grasp the complex "arrangements" that were woven around his organization.

The poor performance of the police at the 1968 Democratic Convention, the year after Wilson retired, and the scandals that continued to occur demonstrated that Wilson's reforms were more superficial than fundamental. On the other hand, if he had not come along, the civil disorders of the '60s and the crime wave of the '80s might have overwhelmed the antiquated force.

Evaluation

In the final analysis, Wilson could not change the ethos of a police department where most people believed that one either went along with the system or got out of the way and kept his mouth shut. Unlike Hoover and Parker, Wilson did not stay too long at the dance; he arrived about ten years too late. A decade earlier, businessman Martin Kennelly was the mayor, young war vets constituted the bulk of the field force and the political machine was at a low ebb. In those circumstances, Wilson might have been able to improve the police department on a more permanent basis.

Stanley Schrotel, Chief of Police, Cincinnati, Ohio, 1950–1966

Career

Schrotel is probably the name on the list that the fewest people will recognize. In his day, however, he was as highly thought of in the police field as Parker or Wilson—perhaps more so, because he did not have Parker's off-putting manner and, unlike Wilson, was experienced in big-city policing. Like Parker, Schrotel possessed a law degree and moved up rapidly in his department. He made chief at thirty-six, whereas Parker did not reach the top until he was forty-eight.

Management Style

Schrotel's force employed the same kind of field tactics as in Los Angeles, but the Ohio officers seemed much more relaxed than their California counterparts. They came from the local area and had ties to its people, whereas in Los Angeles, both police officer and citizen were often from other places, and many times they did not understand one another. Joe Wambaugh would have been hard put to find, in staid Cincinnati, material for the kind of successful police novels that he wrote in Los Angeles. Schrotel, like Parker, was frequently mentioned as a possible replacement for J. Edgar Hoover.

Only in the '60s did Cincinnati begin to change along with the rest of the country. This is probably why Schrotel, at the comparatively young age of fifty-two, retired and went on to become a corporate executive.

Evaluation

Because Cincinnati was only a regional center compared to a great world metropolis like New York, Los Angeles or Chicago, its doings did not get regular national attention; thus, Schrotel failed to receive as much publicity as he deserved. In 1972, he was still young enough to be a good replacement for Hoover after the latter died. However, the Nixon administration wanted a "yes man," not a seasoned professional. Schrotel's most important contribution to law enforcement was that he demonstrated professional-style policing could be carried on in a more restrained fashion and in a more typical city than Los Angeles.

Herbert Jenkins, Chief of Police, Atlanta, Georgia, 1947–1970

Career

When Herb Jenkins was appointed to the Atlanta Police Department, in 1931, he was just another urban Southerner seeking a job in the midst of the Depression though in his case one that carried with it at least pro forma membership in the KKK. However Jenkins never subscribed to Klan values His rise in the department was based on his intelligence, affable personality and ability to achieve the changes that progressive mayors of the city wished to have made. In 1947, at age thirty-eight, he was the obvious man to be appointed chief of police.

Management Style

Unlike Hoover, Parker and Schrotel, Jenkins did not create a model police department, nor was he a leading spokesman for professionalism. His challenge was much broader. In the Jenkins era, Atlanta was part of the Old South. White supremacy was the law and class privilege, the tradition. Yet, in a time when politics revolved around race baiting, Jenkins was able to carry out more moderate policies, such as hiring African-American policemen.

In making changes, Jenkins sometimes had to deal with the disapproval of "his own folks" while being criticized by civil rights advocates for upholding segregation. Too often the latter found it convenient to pretend that all Southern police chiefs were clones of the old-line politician "Bull" Connor or Governor Wallace's highway patrol chief, Al Lingo. Throughout his career, Jenkins was the voice of reason in Southern policing. His personal manner enabled him to deal with a hard-line segregationist like Georgia Governor Lester Maddox and even persuade him to withdraw some of his harsher orders. Jenkins always retained the respect of his fellow Southern chiefs.

Evaluation

The fact that during turbulent times Jenkins was able to remain chief for twenty-three years until he voluntarily retired, at the age of sixty-one (and was then called back for two years to fill the specially created post of police commissioner), indicates how well he was able to solidify his position. When integration was established in the South, Jenkins' department served as the model for other police forces on how to deal with the changes. Thus, his importance in policing was not just what he did in Atlanta but also the influence he had over the entire Southern region.

William Webster,
Director of the Federal Bureau of Investigation, 1978–1987

Career

Webster, an American patrician, had been United States attorney in St. Louis and, at the time of his appointment, was a judge of the U.S. Court of Appeals. He fit the profile of the type of person appointed to the U.S. Supreme Court. Webster was not a professional policeman when he took the FBI job, nor did he ever become one. He was selected to head the Bureau because the future of the agency was in doubt. Director Hoover had died in 1972. In the next six years, his job was held by several individuals of varying capacity. It was the time of reaction to Watergate, and Congressional committees were washing the Bureau's dirty linen in public. The Carter administration needed a director who was strong enough to ensure that the FBI survived in the Washington jungle.

Management Style

Webster had the experience and intellect not to be fooled by Bureau dog and pony shows and was of sufficient personal status that he could resist pressure from politicians. Under Webster, undercover operations and stings became part of the Bureau's standard operating procedure, and women agents were no longer regarded as a novelty. He also moved the priorities of the FBI away from chasing public enemies toward investigating fraud and corruption. By pushing the ABSCAM investigation that netted seven members of Congress, Webster demonstrated that the Bureau was still a force to be reckoned with.

Evaluation

Webster won the respect of the Washington elite, his troops and the public. He was so well thought of that he was made director of the CIA. Had he not succeeded at the Bureau, it is likely that the FBI, which had been the premier U.S. law enforcement agency for over forty years, would have been reduced to another Washington alphabet outfit. Webster saved the Bureau and restored a large measure of its former prestige.

Daryl Gates, Chief of Police, Los Angeles, 1978–1993

Career

Daryl Gates had a ringside seat at the founding of the Parker LAPD, when, shortly after joining the force in 1949, he was appointed chauffeur/bodyguard for the great man himself. As a result of the Parker connection, Gates' rise in the LAPD was rapid. Parker would sometimes point him out as a future chief. However, when Parker died in 1966, Gates did not have sufficient service to jump ahead of men like Tom Reddin or Ed Davis. So twelve years went by before he became the chief.

At the time of Chief Davis's departure in 1978, many city officials doubted whether Gates would make an adequate replacement. One person who had little weight in the selection was Los Angeles' African-American mayor, Tom

Bradley. The chief's job was covered by civil service, and the appointment was actually made by a board of five civilian commissioners. The board could pick any of the top three, and after some hesitation, they chose Gates. He turned out to be the wrong man for the time.

Management Style

Under Gates, the LAPD was still regarded as the nation's outstanding police department, and what it did influenced the profession. Like Parker, Gates was a vigorous defender of traditional police practices, and made it clear he had no intention of modifying LA's hard-nosed policing. In retrospect, the right course of action would have been to make certain changes while preserving the many good features of the department.

The fall of Gates was triggered by the arrest of Rodney King, when cops were caught on tape beating him. The final nail in his coffin was the riots that followed the acquittal of three of the officers who were tried for the King beating. In 1965, the LAPD could argue that in the Watts riot they were taken by surprise. In 1992, everybody knew there was a possibility that there might be serious disturbances after the court decision. The judge even agreed to hold off announcing the verdict until the police could be properly positioned. As it turned out, the LAPD was unprepared for the widespread homicidal violence that broke out and Gates's handling of the department during that time was severely criticized.

Evaluation

Gates, a protégé of Parker, sought to carry on the master's work. For a long time, most people still believed that the LAPD was the best police force in the United States. But it was gradually undone by a number of incidents, the final one being the Rodney King riot. The public asked, "How could the police fail? Was the LAPD simply a public-relations operation with nothing behind it?" Gates's answers were unsatisfactory. If William Webster saved the traditional FBI, Gates lost the Parker-style LAPD.

Patrick Murphy, New York City Police Commissioner, 1970–1973, President of the Police Foundation, 1973–1985

Career

A New York City cop for twenty years, Murphy also served as police chief of Syracuse, New York, director of public safety in Washington, DC, police commissioner of Detroit and a few other posts. Until 1967, when he became safety director of Washington, DC, Murphy was not well known. Then he began to emerge as America's liberal police chief, the antithesis of Frank Rizzo or William Parker. In 1970, when the Knapp Commission scandal broke in New York, liberal Mayor Lindsay cast about for a new police commissioner and was advised to choose Murphy.

Management Style

As a veteran of the NYPD, Murphy was well aware of the failings of the organization. In office, he was able to break the historic system of payoffs known as "the pad" and impose the doctrine of command accountability on the department. Many of the brass whose careers he ended were longtime colleagues. However, Murphy did not lead his officers but drove them. A native New Yorker and career cop from a police family, he often came over as an outside critic who did not particularly like cops. It was not an accurate perception, but he did little to dispel it. He became so identified with Mayor Lindsay's brand of liberalism that he alienated the rank-and-file. The breaking point was reached when police brass released from custody men suspected of murdering a police officer.

Evaluation

In reaction to the excesses of the 1960s, by the 1970s, with Richard Nixon as president, the country was swinging back toward more conservative policies. Murphy had hoped to be considered for director of the FBI, but there was no chance of that happening in the Nixon and Ford era. He was also passed over by Jimmy Carter.

Murphy became head of the Police Foundation, a Ford Foundation-funded liberal think tank. In that post he helped institute police reform programs across the country. Murphy was not content to occupy a sinecure, and sought other chief jobs without success. After he left the force at the age of fifty-three, he never again held a police administrative post. By his death in 2011, Murphy, who was once thought to be the most significant figure in postwar American policing, was largely forgotten.

William Bratton, Police Commissioner of New York City, 1994–1996, Chief of Police, Los Angeles, 2002–2009

Career

Bill Bratton became a cop at twenty-three, and by thirty-three he had reached the number-two post in the Boston Police Department. It looked as though he would soon be police commissioner. Unfortunately, he sought the job too avidly and had to leave the department. He later headed two smaller police forces in Massachusetts, but did not get the top job when several state law enforcement agencies were merged.

In 1990, he took over the New York Metropolitan Transit Authority Police, previously a little-known and low-prestige force. He quickly improved the organization and began putting it on the map. In 1993, Bratton was chosen by incoming New York mayor Rudy Giuliani to be his police commissioner.

Management Style

Bratton was different from most other police administrators in that he was not afraid to engage in conflict and to address larger questions of American society. He quickly became a national and international figure. He also threw down a bold challenge to the academic belief that cops could do nothing about crime. He demonstrated that he could do a great deal to reduce both crime and disorder. In doing so, he caused many criminologists to rethink the previous wisdom. Using the COMPSTAT system, Bratton promulgated strategies that reduced crime by more than fifty percent. According to Franklin Zimring of the University of California, the New York decreases have been the greatest to occur in any city in American history and in large part were attributable to policing operations.

While successful on the professional front, Bratton was less so in his relationship with Giuliani, and in 1996 he was pushed out by the mayor. After a period in the private sector, he was appointed chief in Los Angeles, where he replicated his crime-fighting successes but did not achieve the level of local popularity that he had enjoyed in New York. In 2008, despite having made commercials for the election of Barack Obama, he was not offered a top federal law enforcement post.

Evaluation

In 2009 Bratton returned to New York, possibly in the expectation that, when Mayor Bloomberg's term ended, the commissioner's job would be open and he might be picked. However, Bloomberg managed to get mayoral term limits extended and was re-elected. As a result, Ray Kelly remained as commissioner and is likely to do so until the end of 2013. In 2011, British prime minister David Cameron floated the idea of appointing Bratton police commissioner at Scotland Yard. The proposal did not fly with the British police establishment or Cameron's cabinet.

Bratton, whose career has had so many sudden changes, is likely to surface as head of a major police department or federal agency before too much time has gone by. If so, it is certain that he will continue to play a significant role both within the police profession and on larger national issues.

Ray Kelly, Commissioner, NYPD, 1992–1994, 2002–?

Career

Ray Kelly is a New York native who worked his way up from patrolman to commissioner. In 1963, Kelly was sworn in to the NYPD at the same time he was commissioned a Marine lieutenant, so he was able to take the sergeants exam before leaving for Vietnam. When he came back, he began his NYPD career in that rank. When Lee Brown resigned in 1992, Kelly, who was then first deputy commissioner, replaced him. However, the defeat of David Dinkins in the 1993 mayoral election spelled the end of Kelly's commissioner-ship because incoming mayor Giuliani did not retain him. In 2002, when Michael Bloomberg became mayor, Kelly returned as police commissioner. He is the only man to serve two separate periods as commissioner in the one-hundred-eleven year history of the office.

Management Style

Kelly is a born leader, with the style of a Marine colonel that he once was. His greatest accomplishment to date has been creating, from the ground up, America's first major police counterterrorism system. Among its elements is the assignment of a thousand cops daily to security duties, the creation of an intelligence division modeled on organizations like the CIA and the stationing of detectives abroad to gather information. While accomplishing all this, Kelly has managed to keep the crime rate going down, by refining COMPSTAT methods, even though, by 2012, he had six thousand fewer officers than when he returned to the NYPD.

Evaluation

Like Bratton, Kelly is now an international figure. Because of his work in counterterrorism, he has positioned the NYPD at the center of national security forces and has already assured himself a place in American law enforcement history. If Bloomberg had not managed to overcome the two-term limit, there was speculation that Kelly would have run for mayor. Prior to

Kelly, the average NYPD commissioner served two and a half years in office. Kelly has now served ten and a half years. Once almost universally praised, he now receives criticism from many sources. Mayor Bloomberg continues to strongly back Kelly. But the term-limited mayor is also under siege. Still, Kelly retains considerable support. For example, his name has been suggested for FBI director by such powerful people as New York senator Charles Schumer. It is likely that the commissioner job will not be Kelly's last career stop.

The Top 10 in Retrospect

In many instances, the success or failure of the top ten police administrators was related to the tenor of their times and the environment in which they functioned. Hoover, Parker and Wilson were raised in the pre-1920s era, when traditional Victorian values still remained strong. None of the three were street cops. Hoover and Parker were strict disciplinarians with an autocratic personal style. Wilson (at least, when I worked for him) played the "dear old dean." The three all got their biggest job with a mandate to clean up a law enforcement agency in the aftermath of scandals such as Teapot Dome, Brenda Allen or the Summerdale burglars. Hoover and Parker entrenched themselves in their jobs, where they remained until their deaths. Wilson could never have done so in Chicago. In the end, all three were frustrated when the world changed in the 1960s. What had worked in the past was wrong for that time.

Herbert Jenkins, Stanley Schrotel and Pat Murphy all joined the police during the Great Depression or, in Murphy's case, immediately after returning from World War II. In a different economy, Jenkins and Schrotel might have done well in the private sector. Pat Murphy was the son whose parents wanted him to be a priest, but the war intervened and the need to support his family sent him into the NYPD. Jenkins integrated the Atlanta police force at a time when that was a monumental task. Schrotel moved the Cincinnati police department into the front rank of American law enforcement. Murphy ended the hundred-year-old "pad" system of payoffs in New York. Jenkins had no ambitions beyond Atlanta but was content to be the outstanding chief in the South. Schrotel and Murphy would like to have been named FBI director. While Schrotel made a successful transition to the private sector, Murphy continued to pursue top police jobs, without success.

William Webster is the odd man out among the ten. He would never have considered being a police officer. Still, his experience as U.S. attorney and a federal judge gave him a good understanding of the way the FBI worked. Because of his skill and high personal status, he was able to not only survive but thrive in the Washington jungle. The Beltway crowd gave him the ultimate compliment by making him the director of the CIA and later tapping him for other important positions.

Gates, Kelly, and Bratton came of age in postwar America. In the 1960s, Gates was already securely ensconced as a command officer in the LAPD. Bratton and Kelly were off fighting in Vietnam. None of the three spent much time as a field cop. From the beginning, they all thought like bosses. Gates was commonly seen as Parker's protégé. With Kelly's Marine background, his advanced college degrees and overall competence, promotions came to him regularly. Early on, he was recognized as a man who would reach the highest posts. Bratton was not marked for success in his first few years, but he quickly demonstrated that he was an exceptional, if somewhat unorthodox, individual. He particularly excelled at grasping new ideas and being able to turn them into workable police operations. Eventually, he rose more quickly than either Gates or Kelly did.

Gates essentially failed as a chief because he could not adapt to the times. Bratton, on the other hand, embraced change with both hands and used his knowledge to achieve unprecedented crime reductions in New York. Kelly has proven to be a master organizer/administrator. He is the only American police chief who has ever managed to gain a seat at the first table of American policymakers.

Mayors and other officials might take note that in the selection of a police head, besides the obvious requirements of intelligence, integrity and experience, they should determine whether the candidate is in tune with the spirit of the times. They should also keep in mind that the choice of a chief may determine their own place in history. Had Mayor Daley not chosen Jim Conlisk, Mayor Lindsay, Howard Leary and Mayor Giuliani, Bernie Kerik, they would have been spared much grief.

Appendix C

Understanding Police Terminology

Jargon

Writers on policing often seek to demonstrate their inside knowledge by explaining what a certain phrase means "in cop lingo". They neglect to mention that it only means that in the time and place about which they are writing, and would not be understood by police officers in other eras or jurisdictions. What is called a good "collar" (arrest) in New York would be described as a good "pinch" in Chicago. When a Los Angeles cop wrote in a report that he had stopped a motorist and "shook him down," it meant that he frisked the violator. In Chicago, such an expression never appeared in a report because it had an entirely different meaning.

A recent international news article talked about the "billy clubs" Chicago cops carried at the 1968 Democratic convention. Police stationed there had clubs or batons, but I never heard them described as billy clubs. Sometimes writers mention the term "paddy wagon" as deriving from the fact that many of the prisoners they hauled were Irishmen, known derisively as "Paddys." In Chicago, a city with a large Irish contingent on the police force, it was understood that the term was a corruption of "patrol wagon."

Police patrol cars have had many different names in various cities. In Chicago they were squad cars. In some other cities they were called scout cars. In New York they were RMPs (radio motor patrols).

Detectives in Chicago were known as "dicks." It was a somewhat awkward term to use in mixed company, though it did not relate to an anatomical part. I do not know where it came from. In some times and places, detectives were known as "bulls." A two-detective team was called "harness bulls." In Chicago the "bull dick" was a patrolman or sergeant who gave orders to all the other detectives in the local district station. Such a position was never officially recognized; indeed, it was forbidden. Nevertheless, it existed, and they were mighty men in their day. No lieutenant ever got in their way. In some districts the "bull" came with the station—put there by the local ward boss—so even the captain looked to him for direction. In New York, precinct detective squads were headed by a lieutenant known as "The Loo."

A New York cop on the midnight shift might spend a few hours in the "coop." A Chicago cop went into the "hole." Sometimes these were as simple as the backseat of a patrol car parked in a secluded area; other times, they were in a building where the custodian allowed the cops to hang out.

An off-duty cop in San Francisco might identify himself to an on-duty one by saying, "I'm in the business." In New York or Chicago, the equivalent phrase was "I'm on the job." A Chicago cop who was assigned to duty in plain-clothes would say he was in "soft." A New York cop said he was working in "clothes."

In Boston, a "special" was an officer assigned to a special detail. In the FBI, a "special" was an operation run out of headquarters by a top Bureau boss, and its reports went directly to Hoover. In other cities, a "special officer" was a civilian rent-a-cop who had been granted limited police authority such as the right to carry a club.

Police Ranks

There is considerable difference in rank structure among various police departments. In many cities, there are three basic civil service ranks above patrolman: sergeant, lieutenant and captain. But sometimes individuals, par-ticularly in detective commands, have been given higher acting ranks. In Los Angeles, until 1938, out of three hundred eighty-one detective lieutenants two hundred seventy-two held "brevet" rank. So did about half of the eighty detec-tive captains. In Chicago, ranks above captain were occasionally filled by civil service lieutenants, even sergeants. In recent years, the city has removed the captain rank from the civil service, and it too is now appointive.

Across the country, the title of inspector was a source of great confusion. In San Francisco and a few other places, it was bestowed on detectives who were civil service patrolmen or sergeants. In New York and Los Angeles, it was the command rank above captain. The popular 1950s television show *San Fran-cisco Beat* featured Tom Tully as an inspector and Warner Anderson as a lieu-tenant. Many cops who watched were puzzled by the way the inspector seemed to defer to the lieutenant, not realizing that the latter actually held a higher rank.

Bibliography

Books

Behn, Noel. *Big Stick-Up at Brink's*. New York: C. P. Putnam and Sons, 1977.

Blair, Clay. *The Forgotten War: America in Korea*. New York: Times Books, 1987.

Blakey, G. Robert, and Richard N. Billings. *The Plot to Kill the President*. New York: Times Books, 1981.

Bopp, William J. *"O. W.": O. W. Wilson and the Search for a Police Profession*. Port Washington, New York: Kennikat Press, 1977.

Boser, Ulrich. *The Gardner Heist: The True Story of the World's Largest Unsolved Art Theft*. HarperCollins Publishers, 2008.

Bouza, Anthony V. *Bronx Beat: Reflections of a Police Commander*. Chicago: Office of International Criminal Justice, 1990.

———. *The Police Mystique: An Insider's Look at Cops, Crime and the Criminal Justice System*. New York: Plenum Press, 1980.

Braga, Anthony and David Weisburg. *Policing Problem Places: Hotspots and Effective Prevention*. New York: Oxford University Press, 2010.

Branch, Taylor. *Parting the Waters, America in the King Years, 1954–63*. New York: Simon & Schuster, 1988.

Bratton, William, with Peter Knobler. *Turnaround: How America's Top Cop Reversed the Crime Epidemic*. New York: Random House, 1998.

Breo, Dennis L. and William J. Martin. *The Crime of the Century: Richard Speck and the Murder of Eight Student Nurses*. New York: Bantam Books, 1993.

Brust, Harold. *In Plain Clothes: Further Memoirs of a Political Police Officer*. London: Stanley Paul, 1937.

Bugliosi, Vincent. *Outrage: The Five Reasons Why O. J. Simpson Got Away with Murder*. New York: W. W. Norton & Co., 1996.

Citizens' Police Committee. *Chicago Police Problems*. Chicago: U. of Chicago Press, 1931 (The Bruce Smith Study).

Coakley, Leo J. *Jersey Troopers*. New Brunswick, N.J.: Rutgers University Press, 1971.

Conti, Philip M. *The Pennsylvania State Police*. Harrisburg, PA: Stackpole Books, 1977.

Cooley, Robert with Hillel Levin. *When Corruption was King, How I Helped the Mob Run Chicago*. New York: Carroll and Graf, 2004.

Daley, Robert. *Target Blue*. New York: Delacorte, 1973.

———. *Prince of the City*. New York: Houghton Mifflin, 1978.

Daughen, Joseph R. and Peter Binzen. *The Cop Who Would Be King: The Honorable Frank Rizzo*. Boston: Little Brown and Company, 1977.

Dickey, Christopher. *Securing The City: Inside America's Best Counterterrorism Force—The NYPD*. New York: Simon & Schuster, 2009.

Domanick, Joe. *To Protect and Serve: the LAPD's Century of War in the City of Dreams*. New York: Pocket Books, 1994.

Ehrlich, J. W. *A Life in My Hands*. New York: Crown, 1954.

Epstein, Edward Jay. *Agency of Fear: Opiates and Political Power in America*, rev. ed. London: Verso, 1990.

Esposito, Richard and Ted Gerstein. *Bomb Squad: A Year Inside The Nation's Most Exclusive Police Unit*. New York: Hyperion, 2007.

Fogelson, Robert M. *Big-City Police*. Cambridge, Mass.: Harvard University Press, 1977.

Fox, Stephen R. *Blood and Power: Organized Crime in Twentieth Century America*. New York: W. Morrow, 1989.

Fracchia, Charles A. *City by the Bay: A History of Modern San Francisco, 1945–Present*. Encinitas, CA: Heritage Media Corporation, 1997.

Freeh, Louis J. with Howard Means. *My FBI: Bringing Down the Mafia, Investigating Bill Clinton, and Fighting the War on Terror*. New York: St. Martin's Press, 2005.

Gans, Herbert J. *The Urban Villagers*. New York: The Free Press 1962.

Gates, Daryl F. with Diane K Shah. *Chief: My Life in the LAPD*. New York: Bantam Books, 1992.

Gelb, Barbara. *Varnished Brass: The Decade After Serpico*. New York: G. P. Putnam's Sons, 1983.

Graysmith, Robert. *Zodiac Unmasked: The Identity of America's Most Elusive Serial Killer Revealed*. New York: Berkley, 2002.

Giuliani, Rudolph W. with Ken Kurson. *Leadership*. New York: Hyperion, 2002.

Heidenry, John. *Zero at the Bone*. New York: St. Martin's Press, 2009.

Hodel, Steve. *Black Dahlia Avenger: The True Story*. New York: Arcade Publishing, 2003.

Jacobs, James B. with Christopher Panarella and James Worthington. *Busting the Mob: U.S. vs Cosa Nostra*. New York: New York University Press, 1994.

Jacobs, Jane. *The Death and Life of Great American Cities*. New York: Vintage, 1961.

Jenkins, Herbert T. *40 Years on the Force: 1932–1972*. Atlanta: Emory University, Center for Research and Social Change, 1973.

Jurgensen Randy and Robert Cea. *Circle of Six: The True Story of New York's Most Notorious Cop Killer and the Cop Who Risked Everything to Catch Him*. New York: The Disinformation Company Ltd. 2007.

Kantor, MacKinlay. *Signal Thirty-Two*. New York: Random House, 1950.

Keating, William J. and Richard Carter. *The Man Who Rocked the Boat*. New York: Random House, 1956.

Kelling, George L. and Catherine M. Coles. *Fixing Broken Windows: Restoring Order and Reducing Crime in Our Communities*. New York: The Free Press, 1998.

Kerik, Bernard B. *The Lost Son: A Life in Pursuit of Justice*. New York: HarperCollins Publishers, 2001.

Kessler, Ronald. *The FBI: Inside the World's Most Powerful Law Enforcement Agency*. New York: Pocket Books, 1993.

——. *The Secrets of the FBI*. New York: Crown Publishers, 2011.

Kirtzman, Andrew. *Rudy Giuliani: Emperor of the City*. New York: W. Morrow, 2000.

Lait, Jack and Lee Mortimer. *Washington Confidential*. New York: Crown Publishers, 1951.

Lardner, James and Thomas Reppetto. *NYPD: A City and its Police*. New York: Henry Holt, 2000.

Lardner, James. *Crusader: The Hell-Raising Police Career of Detective David Durk*. New York: Random House, 1996.

Lehr, Dick, and Gerard O'Neill. *Black Mass: The True Story of the Unholy Alliance Between The FBI and the Irish Mob*. New York: HarperCollins, 2000.

Levitt, Leonard. *NYPD Confidential: Power and Corruption in the Country's Greatest Police Force*. New York: St. Martin's Press, 2009.

Litt, Edgar. *The Political Culture of Massachusetts*. Cambridge, MA: MIT Press, 1962.

Maas, Peter. *Serpico*. New York: Viking Press, 1973.

Maple, Jack, with Chris Mitchell. *The Crimefighter: Putting the Bad Guys Out of Business.* New York: Doubleday, 1999.

Martinez, Al. *Jigsaw John.* New York: Avon Books, 1975.

Marx, Gary T. *Undercover: Police Surveillance in America.* Berkeley: University of California Press, 1988.

McAlary, Mike. *Cop Shot.* New York: Jove, 1992.

Mullen, Kevin J. *The Toughest Gang in Town: Police Stories From Old San Francisco.* Novato, CA: Noir Publications, 2005.

Murphy, Patrick, with Thomas Plate. *Commissioner: A View From the Top of American Law Enforcement.* New York: Simon & Shuster, 1977.

Nickel, Stephen. *Torso! Eliot Ness and the Hunt for the Mad Butcher of Willow Run.* New York: Avon Press 1990.

Nunnelley, William A. *Bull Connor.* Tuscaloosa, AL: University of Alabama Press, 1991.

Paolantonio, S. A. *Frank Rizzo: The Last Big Man in Big-City America.* Philadelphia: Camino Books, 1993.

Peterson, Virgil. *Barbarians in Our Midst: A History of Chicago Crime and Politics.* Boston: Little, Brown, 1952.

Powers, Richard G. *Broken: The Troubled Past and Uncertain Future of the FBI.* New York: Free Press, 2007.

———. *Secrecy and Power: The Life of J. Edgar Hoover.* New York: Free Press, 1987.

Reppetto, Thomas A. *American Mafia: A History of Its Rise to Power.* New York: Henry Holt, 2004.

———. *American Police: The Blue Parade, 1845–1945.* New York: Enigma Books, 2010.

———. *Battleground New York City: Countering Spies, Saboteurs and Terrorists Since 1861.* Washington, D.C.: Potomac Books, 2012.

———. *Bringing Down The Mob: The War Against the American Mafia.* New York: Henry Holt, 2006.

Reynolds, Quentin. *Headquarters.* New York: Harper, 1955.

Roemer, William F., Jr. *Accardo: The Genuine Godfather.* New York: D. I. Fine, 1995.

Royko, Mike. *Boss: Richard J. Daley of Chicago.* New York: Signet Books, 1971.

Sayre, Wallace, and Herbert Kaufman. *Governing New York City.* New York: Russell Sage Foundation, 1960.

Schiller, Lawrence. *Perfect Murder, Perfect Town.* New York: HarperCollins Publishers, 1999.

Sheehan, Michael A. *Crush The Cell: How to Defeat Terrorism Without Terrorizing Ourselves.* New York: Crown Publishers, 2008.

Silberman, Charles. *Criminal Violence, Criminal Justice.* New York: Random House, 1978.

Silverman, Eli. *NYPD Battles Crime: Innovative Strategies in Policing.* Boston: Northeastern University Press, 1999.

Skogan, Wesley G. *Disorder and Decline: Crime and the Spiral of Decay in American Neighborhoods.* New York: Free Press, 1990.

Skolnick, Jerome H. *Justice Without Trial.* New York: John Wiley, 1967.

Sloan, Arthur D. *Hoffa.* Cambridge, MA: MIT Press, 1991.

Smith, Bruce, Jr. *Police Systems in the United States.* 2nd rev. ed. New York: Harper, 1960.

Smith, Gene. *The Life and Death of Serge Rubinstein.* Garden City, New York: Doubleday, 1962.

Stead, Philip John. *The Police of France.* New York: Macmillan, 1983.

Straetz, Ralph A. *PR Politics in Cincinnati.* New York: New York University Press, 1958.

Sullivan, William C., with Bill Brown. *The Bureau: My Thirty Years in Hoover's FBI.* New York: W. W. Norton, 1984.

Timoney, John F. *Beat Cop to Top Cop: A Tale of Three Cities.* Philadelphia: University of Pennsylvania Press, 2010.

Tuohy, James and Robert Warden. *Greylord: Justice Chicago Style.* New York: G. P. Putnam's Sons, 1989.

Walker, Samuel. *A Critical History of Police Reform: The Emergence of Professionalism.* Lexington, MA: D. C. Heath, 1977.

Webb, Jack. *The Badge: The Inside Story of One of America's Great Police Forces.* Upper Saddle River, N.J.: Prentice-Hall, 1958.

Weiner, Tim. *Enemies: A History of the FBI.* New York: Random House, 2012.

Welch, Neil J., with David W. Marston. *Inside Hoover's FBI: The Top Field Chief Reports.* Garden City, N.Y.: Doubleday & Co., 1984.

Westley, William A. *Violence and the Police: A Sociological Study of Law, Custom, and Morality.* Cambridge, MA: MIT Press, 1970.

White, Theodore H. *The Making of the President, 1960.* New York: Atheneum Publishers, 1961.

Whitehead, Don. *The FBI Story.* New York: Random House, 1956.

Wilson, James Q. *Varieties of Police Behavior: The Management of Law and Order in Eight Communities.* Cambridge, MA: Harvard University Press, 1968.

——. *The Investigators: Managing FBI and Narcotics Agents.* New York: Basic Books, 1978.

Wilson, Orlando W., and Roy Clinton McLaren. *Police Administration.* 3rd. ed. New York: McGraw-Hill, 1972. (Original 1950).

Woods, Joseph G. *The Progressives and the Police: Urban Reform and the Professionalization of the Los Angeles Police.* Los Angeles: UCLA, 1973.

Zimring, Franklin E. *The City That Became Safe: New York's Lessons for Urban Crime and Its Control.* New York: Oxford University Press, 2011.

——. *The Great American Crime Decline.* New York: Oxford University Press, 2007.

Articles

——. "10 Agents Freed In Illinois Raids." *New York Times,* April 3, 1974.

——. "Hall Is Believed Abduction Slayer; FBI Presses Search for Second Man." *New York Times,* October 9, 1953.

——. "John J. 'Johnny' Klevenhagen, 1912–1958." Texas Ranger Hall of Fame and Museum.

——. "Bailing Out the Sheriff." *Time,* May 18, 1970.

——. "Police Chief Quits Pennsylvania Post." *New York Times,* April 10, 1966.

——. "Ratterman New Kentucky Sheriff." *New York Times,* November 8, 1961.

——. "Sheriff in Florida Is Ousted After Months of Dispute." *New York Times,* May 27, 1979.

——. "Thomas Reddin, 88, former LAPD chief is dead." *AP,* December 6, 2004.

——. "Weathermen March on Washington," *New York Times,* November 16, 1969.

——. "Woman Is Accused In Kidnapping Tip." *New York Times,* October 26, 1953.

Baker, Al. "Britain Turns to Former New York and Los Angeles Police Official for Help." *New York Times,* August 13, 2011.

Brean, Herbert. "A Really Good Police Force." *Life,* September 16, 1957.

Burns, John F. "Britain Debates a Plan to Turn to U.S. 'Supercop.'" *New York Times,* August 15, 2011.

Doherty, James. "History of the Chicago Crime Commission." *Police Digest* (December 1960).

Frankel, Max. "Militants Stir Clashes Later." *New York Times*, November 16, 1969.

Goldberg, Jeffrey. "The Color of Suspicion." *New York Times*, June 20, 1999.

Goldstein, Richard. "Howard Unruh, 88, Dies; Killed 13 of His Neighbors in Camden in 1949." *New York Times*, October 20, 2009.

Hessler, William H. "Cincinnati: The City That Licked Corruption." *Harpers*, November, 1953.

Kifner, John. "Tear Gas Repels Radicals' Attack." *New York Times,* November 16, 1969.

Mazzetti, Mark. "Nominee Promises Action as U.S. Intelligence Chief." *New York Times*, July 21, 2010.

Mustain, Gene. "Fever: The Crack Scourge." in J. Maeder (ed.), *Big Town, Big Time. Daily News,* 1999, p. 183.

Nolte, Carl. "San Francisco/The Dark Side of V-J Day." *San Francisco Chronicle*, August 15, 2005.

Oliver, Myrna. "Tom Reddin, 88; Ex-LAPD Chief Introduced Community Policing." *Los Angeles Times*, December 5, 2004.

Reppetto, Thomas A. "The Influence of Police Organizational Style on Crime Control Effectiveness." *Journal of Police Science and Administration*, volume 3, number 3, September, 1975.

Schmidt, Dana Adams. "Nixon Plans Unit on Drug Addicts." *New York Times*, June 1, 1971.

Shaplen, Robert. "Profiles: Not Like Taking the Waters." (Bruce Smith) *The New Yorker* 30 (27 February 1954).

Sherman, Lawrence, Patrick Gartin, and Michael Buerger. "Hotspots of Predatory Crime: Routine Activities and the Criminology of Place." in *Criminology.* 27:27–55 (1989).

Tett, Gillian. "'I Don't Have a Lot of Close Friends.'" (William Bratton) *Financial Times*, September 3, 2011.

Timoney, John F. "Florida's Disastrous Self-Defense Law." *New York Times*, March 24, 2012.

Trussell, C.P. "FBI Chief Says Reds Incite Youth." *New York Times*, July 18, 1966.

Turner, Ralph F. "Hans Gross: The Model of the Detective." in *Pioneers In Policing*, edited by Philip John Stead, Montclair N.J.: Patterson Smith, 1977.

Uchitelle, Louis. "Two Americans are Awarded Nobel in Economics." *New York Times*, October 13, 2009.

Wilson, James Q., and George Kelling. "Broken Windows: The Police and Neighborhood Safety." *Atlantic Monthly*, March 1982, 29–38.

Wollan, Malia. "Gang Injunction: Names Names and Suit Follows." *New York Times*, May 15, 2010.

Reports

A City in Crisis: A Report by the Special Advisor to the Board of Police Commissioners on Civil Disorders in Los Angeles (Webster Commission). Los Angeles: The Institute for Government and Public Affairs, UCLA: 1992.

Final Report of the National Commission on the Causes of and Prevention of Violence (Eisenhower Commission). *To Establish Justice, To Ensure Domestic Tranquility.* Washington, DC: GPO, 1969.

Mayor's Committee On Management. *The New York City Police Survey (Bruce Smith Report).* New York: Institute of Public Administration, 1952.

New York City Police Department. *Policing New York City in the 1990s: The Strategy For Community Policing.* January 1991.

Pate, Anthony, M. A. Wycoff, Wesley Skogan and Lawrence Sherman. *Reducing Fear of Crime in Houston and Newark: A Summary Report.* Washington, D.C.: The Police Foundation, 1986.

Report of the Commission to Investigate Allegations of Police Corruption and the City's Anti-Corruption Procedures (Knapp Commission), New York, 1974.

Report of the Commission to Investigate Allegations of Police Corruption and the Anti-Corruption Procedures of the Police Department (Mollen Commission). New York, 1994.

Report of the Independent Commission on the LAPD (Christopher Commission), 1971.

The 9/11 Commission Report: Final Report of the National Commission on Terrorist Attacks Upon the United States. New York: Norton, 2004.

The President's Commission on Law Enforcement and the Administration of Justice. *The Challenge of Crime in a Free Society.* Washington, DC: GPO, 1967.

———. *Task Force Report: The Police.* Washington, DC: GPO, 1967.

U.S. Senate. Special Committee to Investigate Organized Crime in Interstate Commerce (Kefauver Committee). *Hearings,* 1951.

Cases

Mapp v. Ohio, 367 U. S. 643 (1961)

Miles v. Weston, 60 Ill. 361 (1871).

Monroe v. Pape, 365 U.S. 167 (1961).

United States v. Holovachka, 314 F2nd 345 (1963).

United States v. Weeks, 232 U. S. 383 (1914).

References

Introduction: A Lifetime of Crime

1. Policing at the Crossroads

The state of policing in the postwar era in the three cities profiled is contained in <u>New York City</u> Kantor, *Signal Thirty-Two, Mayor's Management Report, Police Survey (Bruce Smith report)* and Sayre and Kaufman, *Governing New York City.* <u>Chicago</u> Peterson (head of the Chicago Crime Commission), *Barbarians in Our Midst.* <u>Los Angeles,</u> Domanick, *To Protect and Serve* and Woods, *The Progressives and the Police.*

Accounts of the VJ Day riots in San Francisco are contained in Fracchia, *City by the Bay,* Mullen, *The Toughest Gang in Town* and Nolte, "The Dark Side of V-J Day."

Citations

* Citizens' Police Committee, *Chicago Police Problems,* p. 8.
** 300 Houses of prostitution, Ehrlich, *A Life in My Hands,* p. 97.
*** On Gross case and Mayor O. Dwyer, Lardner and Reppetto, *NYPD,* pp. 261–65.
\+ Shaplen, "Profile (Bruce Smith)," *New Yorker,* February 1954, p. 51.
\+\+ See *Weeks v. US* (1914) and *Mapp v. Ohio* (1961).
\+\+\+ Unruh case, Goldstein, "Howard Unruh, 88, Dies," *New York Times,* October 20, 2009.
^ Deputy Chief on the San Francisco police having no coherent plan, Nolte, "The Dark Side of V-J Day."

2. Professional Policing Emerges: Parker in Los Angeles and Schrotel in Cincinnati

On Parker's LAPD see Domanick, *To Protect and Serve;* Woods, *The Progressives and The Police;* Gates, *Chief;* Webb, *The Badge.* The Domanick book is a journalistic account, Woods a scholarly dissertation, Gates the memoir of Parkers protégé who was later police chief himself and the *The Badge* is "Joe Friday's" (Webb) glorification of the LAPD along the lines of his TV show *Dragnet.* However, it contains some useful information.

On Donald Leonard see File Michigan Historical Collections, Bentley, Historical Library, University of Michigan. Michigan State police career (boxes 14 to 20) his Detroit police career (boxes 20 and 21).

Career of O. W. Wilson, Bopp, *"O. W."*

On Cincinnati and Schrotel, Brean, "A Really Good Police Force," *Life,* September 16, 1957. Straetz, *Politics in Cincinnati.* Hessler, "Cincinnati: The City that Licked Corruption," *Harpers,* November, 1953. Also Reppetto, "The Influence of Police Organizational Style on Crime Control Effectiveness," *Journal of Police Science and Administration,* September, 1975.

On Boston see Reppetto, *ibid.,* and Litt, *The Political Culture of Massachusetts.*

On models of police organization, Wilson, *Varieties of Police Behavior* and Skolnick, *Justice Without Trial.*

On Washington D. C., Lait and Mortimer, *Washington Confidential.*

On Gary, Indiana, Westley, *Violence and the Police.*
On state police, Conti, *The Pennsylvania State Police* and Coakley, *Jersey Troopers.*

Citations

* White, *The Making of the President 1960*, p. 235.
** Shaplen, "Profile (Bruce Smith)," p. 51.
*** On the 1953 Gary scandal see *United States v. Holovachka.*

3.   Detectives, Hoover, the Mob and Youth Gangs

On the Greenlease case see Heidenry, *Zero at the Bone,* "Hall is Believed Abduction
   Slayer." *New York Times,* October 9, 1953, and "Woman is Accused in Kidnapping
   Tip." *New York Times,* October 26, 1953.
On the Rubenstein murder see Smith, *The Life and Death of Serge Rubinstein.*
On Keating and the Crime Commission see Keating and Carter, *The Man Who Rocked
   the Boat.*
J. Edgar Hoover bios are numerous but are often mostly polemics. One that manages
   to avoid that is Powers, *Secrecy and Power: The Life of J. Edgar Hoover.*
On the murder of eight nurses by Richard Speck, see Breo and Martin, *The Crime of the
   Century.*
On individual detectives see "John J. 'Johnny' Klevenhagen, 1912–1958." Texas
   Ranger Hall of Fame and Museum website and on Kern "Bailing Out the Sheriff."
   Time, May 18, 1970. On John St. John, Martinez, *Jigsaw John.*
On Gross see Turner, "Hans Gross: The Model of The Detective," *Pioneers in Policing.*

Citations

* On Fiaschetti, Reppetto, *American Mafia,* chapter 5 and on Cordes, Joel Sayre,
   "Profile," *The New Yorker,* September 5 & 12, 1953.
** Nickel, *Torso! Eliot Ness and The Hunt For The Mad Butcher of Willow Run.*
*** Marshall on Hoover, Anthony Cave Brown, *Wild Bill: The Last Hero,* p. 159.
\+ Mafia in New Jersey, Reppetto, *Bringing Down the Mob,* p. 127.
\+\+ *Monroe v. Pape.*

4. Reading the Riot Act: Jenkins in Atlanta, the Bull in Birmingham

On Chief Jenkins see his autobiography, *40 Years on the Force: 1932–1972* and Fogelson,
   Big-City Police.
There are many accounts of Dr. King's journey from Montgomery to Memphis.
   Among the most helpful in the present work was *Parting the Waters,* volume 1 of
   Taylor Branch's trilogy *America in the King Years.*
On the riots following the King assassination see Wikipedia, the Assassination of
   Martin Luther King Jr.
On "Bull" Connor see Nunnelley, *Bull Connor.*
On Harlem riot of 1964 see Lardner and Reppetto, *NYPD,* pp. 253–56.
The Philadelphia Riot of 1964 is described in Paolantonio, *Frank Rizzo,* pp. 74–76.
On the Watts riot see Gates, *Chief,* chapter 7.

Citations

* Trussell, "FBI Chief Says Reds Incite Youth," *New York Times*, July 18, 1960.
** "I have a dream" speech,www.stanford.edu/group/kingspeeches.

5. Far from the Ivory Tower: O. W. Wilson in Chicago

On O. W. Wilson in Chicago see Bopp, *"O. W.",* Royko, *Boss.* The first book is objective whereas the second is hostile.

Citations

* Mrs. Wilson's description of Conlisk is from Bopp, *"O. W.,"* p. *128..*
** FBI List of corrupt cops, Roemer, *Accardo,* pp. 229–233.
*** On Michaelis see Blair. *The Forgotten War,* pp. 145–46, 693, 866.

6. Nixon's Schemes Fail, Webster Saves the FBI

For general background see The President's Commission on Law Enforcement and the Administration of Justice. *The Challenge of Crime in a Free Society.*

An account of the Nixon administration's scheme to set up a national police force based on narcotic enforcement is contained in Epstein, *Agency of Fear* and Schmidt, "Nixon Plans Unit on Drug Addiction." *New York Times,* June 1, 1971.

Voluminous works on the JFK assassination are in print but many of them stray a long way from the facts. The report of a Congressional investigating committee is contained in Blakey and Billings, *The Plot to Kill the President.*

On Chicago Mob's attempt to infiltrate Dallas in the 1940s see Fox, *Blood and Power,* pp. 285-86.

Citations

* FPA doggerel, Allen, *Only Yesterday,* pp. 257–58
** "The Battle at the DOJ," Kifner, "Gas Routes Radicals," and Frankel, "Militants Start Clashes Later," *New York Times,* November 15, 1969.
*** On Greylord, see Reppetto, *Bringing Down the Mob,* pp. 263–266 and Tuohy and Warden, *Greylord.*
+ On Gambat, Reppetto, *ibid.* 216-17 and Cooley and Levin, *When Corruption was King*
++ On New York organized crime prosecutions, Jacobs, *Busting the Mob.*

7. Contrasting Command Styles: Murphy of New York, Rizzo of Philadelphia

On Pat Murphy see Murphy and Plate, *Commissioner* and Daley, *Target Blue.*

On Rizzo see Paolantonio, *Frank Rizzo,* Daughen and Binzen, *The Cop Who Would Be King.*

On Serpico, Maas, *Serpico.*

On Durk, Lardner, *Crusader.*

For a discussion of the mosque shooting and alleged police cover-up see Jurgensen and Cea, *Circle of Six.*

Citations

* On the Move confrontation, Paolantonio, *Frank Rizzo,* pp. 224–27.

** On Reddin, Oliver, "Tom Reddin, 88," *Los Angeles Times,* December 5, 2004; and Domanick, *To Protect and Serve,* pp. 203–207.

*** On Purdy, "Sheriff in Florida Is Ousted." *New York Times,* May 27, 1979.

 + On Ingersoll see "Profile," deamuseum.org.

++ On Bouza see his *Bronx Beat* and *The Police Mystique.*

8. Chaos: Cops Lose the Streets

On street disorder and vagrancy generally see Kelling and Coles, *Fixing Broken Windows* and Skogan, *Disorder and Decline.*

Citations

* Forecast about urban crime see *To Establish Justice, To Ensure Domestic Tranquility* (Eisenhower Commission), pages 46–47.

** On the Torres killing spree in upper Manhattan see Mustain, "Fever, The Crack Scourge" in *Big Town, Big Time,* 1999.

*** On Arjune and Officer Byrne, McAlary, *Cop Shot.*

+ On LAPD tactics see Domanick, *To Protect and Serve* and Gates, *Chief.*

++ See *Miles v. Weston.*

+++ See Wilson and Kelling, "Broken Windows," *Atlantic Monthly,* March 1982.

^ On Larry Hogue, see Lardner and Reppetto, *NYPD,* pages 310–11.

^^ *San Francisco Chronicle* article quoted in Kelling and Coles, p. 212.

^^^ Henry George, *Social Problems,* p. 12.

9. New York Community Policing and Gates' LAPD Style Both Fail

On community policing see NYPD, *Policing New York City in the 1990s.* Gates views presented in Gates, *Chief.*

On Newark and Houston see Pate, *et al., Reducing Fear of Crime in Houston and Newark: A Summary Report* and Skogan, *Disorder and Decline,* pp. 93–124

On the Crown Heights and Washington Heights riots see Lardner and Reppetto, *NYPD,* pp. 306–309.

On the Rodney King riot in Los Angeles see *The City in Crisis: A Report by the Special Advisory Commission to the Board of Police Commissioners on the Civil Disorder in Los Angeles.* Institute for Government and Public Affairs, UCLA, Los Angeles, CA, 1992.

Citations

* On Lee Brown, Lardner and Reppetto, *NYPD,* pp. 296–307

** Herbert Gans, *Urban Villagers.*

*** Jane Jacobs, *The Death And Life Of Great American Cities.*

+ "He won it for *that?*" Lardner and Reppetto, *NYPD,* p. 300.

++ "East cupcake," *ibid.,* p. 312.

+++ Skogan, *Disorder and Decline,* pp. 14–15.

10. Fighting Crime by the Numbers: Bratton Defies the Experts

On Bratton and Maple see Bratton, *Turnaround* and Maple, *The Crimefighter.*
On Giuliani, see his *Leadership* and Kirtzman, *Emperor of the City.*
CompStat is evaluated in Zimring, *The City That Became Safe.*

On hotspots see Braga and Weisburg, *Policing Problem Places* Sherman, *et al.* "'Hot Spots of Predatory Crime."

Citations

* Thomas Byrnes, *Professional Criminals of America.*
** Silberman, *Criminal Violence, Criminal Justice* p. 33.
*** Quotation from Zimring, *The Great American Crime Decline*, p. 74.
+ Did not once mention crime, Timoney, *Beat Cop to Top Cop*, pp. 207–8.
++ Giuliani on loyalty, *Leadership*, p. 16.
+++ See Timoney, *Beat Cop to Top Cop*, pp. 168 and 220.

11. Terrorism: Kelly in Command

On terrorism see Reppetto, *Battleground New York City*, Wright, *The Looming Tower* and *Final Report of the National Commission on Terrorist Attacks Upon the United States.*
On Sessions at the FBI see Kessler, *The FBI.*
Louis Freeh's recounting of his directorship of the FBI is contained in Freeh, *My FBI.*
On Los Angeles area counterterrorism programs see website joint regional intelligence Center, Norwalk, California, http://jric.org

Citations

* Mazzetti, "Nominee Promises Action as U.S. Intelligence Chief," *New York Times*, July 21, 2010.
** Powers, *Broken: The Troubled Past and Uncertain Future of the FBI.*

12. Policing the 21st Century: Old Problems, New Solutions

Citations

* Robert Daley, *Prince of the City.*
** Miami police shootings see Timoney, *Beat Cop To Top Cop*, p. 276.
*** Timoney, "Florida's disastrous self-defense law," *New York Times*, March 24, 2012.
+ On Ostrom see Uchitelle, "Two Americans Share Nobel in Economics." *New York Times*, October 13, 2009.
++ Jackson comment, Goldberg, "The Color of Suspicion," *New York Times*, June 20, 1999.
+++ Stead, *The Police of France*. pp. 56-57.
^ Brust, *In Plain Clothes.*
^^ Level of violence in California, Wollan, "Gang Injunction Names Names," *New York Times*, May 15, 2010.

Appendix A

On the JFK investigation see Blakey and Billings. *The Plot to Kill the President.*
On Hoffa, Sloane, *Hoffa.*
On DB Cooper, "In Search of D. B. Cooper" and "New Developments in the Unsolved Case" FBI website, March 17, 2009.
On Brinks, Behn, *Big Stick Up at Brink's.*
On the Gardner case see Boser, *The Gardner Heist.*

On the Black Dahlia case see Hodel, *Black Dahlia Avenger.*
On the Son of Sam case, see Wikipedia, "David Berkowitz."
On the Georgia child murders, see Wikipedia, "Atlanta murders 1979–81."
On the zodiac killer see Graysmith, *Zodiac Unmasked.*
On JonBenét Ramsey see Schiller, *Perfect Murder, Perfect Town.*

Acknowledgments

I would like to thank the following organizations that were helpful to me in gathering material for this book. The FBI, NYPD, Atlanta History Center, the Pace University Law School Library, San Francisco Public Library, Texas Ranger Hall of Fame, The Lloyd Sealy Library of John Jay College of Criminal Justice, and the Westchester County Library system.

Among individuals I wish to thank are Deputy Commissioners Paul Browne and Mike Farrell of the NYPD, Christa Carnegie, James Curran, Frank Hickey, John Jemilo, Martin Mitchell, Martha Reppetto, Taryn Rucinski, Robert Schnell and Larry Sullivan.

At Enigma I was guided by my editor, Robert Miller, and my copyeditor, Jay Wynshaw.

In a work like this my greatest debt is to literally hundreds of individuals I have learned from over several decades. Alas, many are no longer alive, but their spirits live on. Two who were great mentors to me must be singled out. First is my old boss, the late Captain/Director Michael Delaney of the Chicago Police Department. Second, is my academic mentor, the late Prof. James Q. Wilson of Harvard University, to whom this book is dedicated.

Index